John A. Overman

Economies of the World

EDITED BY
NITA WATTS

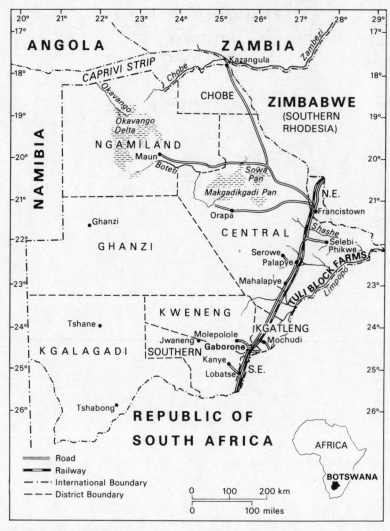

The Republic of Botswana *Map based on original supplied by courtesy of Director of Surveys and Lands, Government of Botswana*

The Political Economy of Botswana

A STUDY OF GROWTH AND DISTRIBUTION

BY

CHRISTOPHER COLCLOUGH

and

STEPHEN McCARTHY

OXFORD UNIVERSITY PRESS

1980

Oxford University Press, Walton Street, Oxford OX2 6DP

OXFORD LONDON GLASGOW
NEW YORK TORONTO MELBOURNE WELLINGTON
KUALA LUMPUR SINGAPORE JAKARTA HONG KONG TOKYO
DELHI BOMBAY CALCUTTA MADRAS KARACHI
NAIROBI DAR ES SALAAM CAPE TOWN

Published in the United States by
Oxford University Press, New York.

British Library Cataloguing in Publication Data

Colclough, Christopher
    The political economy of Botswana.–(Economies
    of the world).
    1. Botswana–Economic conditions
    2. Botswana–Politics and government
    I. Title II. Series
    330.9'68'1   HC517.B6   79-42919

ISBN 0-19-877136-3

Set by Hope Services, Abingdon
and Printed in Great Britain by
Richard Clay & Co Ltd., Bungay

ACKNOWLEDGEMENTS

The writing of this book would not have been possible without the co-operation of the Botswana Government in providing free access to records, ministry libraries, and the National Archives. Even though parts of it may be considered controversial, we hope that its publication will repay that trust by contributing to a greater general understanding of development in Botswana. On a more personal level, many government officials—former colleagues and friends—as well as staff of the parastatal corporations and mining companies readily and generously gave their time in answering our questions and in searching for half-remembered reports in the recesses of their offices. They are too numerous to acknowledge by name, and it would be unfair on many to mention but a few. We should nevertheless like to record our gratitude to them all.

We have received material support from three sources. An initial grant from the Ford Foundation financed the necessary research in Botswana itself, and this gave us encouragement that the project was worthwhile. The Institute of Development Studies at the University of Sussex has also provided generous financial and institutional support, together with a suitable environment in which to undertake most of the writing, which, as usual, took longer than originally anticipated. Finally, Carol McCarthy has contributed beyond the usual duties of sympathy and encouragement required of an author's wife by turning family bread-winner during the early stages of the work. Later, she willingly put up with evenings, holidays, and weekends being turned over to work on the book.

Paul Bennell, Andrew Bird, Robert Chambers, Ray Crotty, Ron Dore, John Gerhart, Richard Jolly, Martin Marriott, Carol McCarthy, Hugh Murray-Hudson, Ray Purcell, Chris Ronald, Rod Ryman, Percy Selwyn, and Martin Taylor provided useful and very welcome comments on various parts of the early drafts. But we owe a particular debt of gratitude to Charles Harvey, Quill Hermans, Peter Landell-Mills, Michael Lipton, Jack Parson, and Diane Wilderspin, who read and commented on all, or most of, the manuscript. Each was able to offer a different perspective which has enabled the final version to be a better, more accurate, and more balanced discussion of the problems facing contemporary Botswana than it would otherwise have been. It has not always been possible to agree with all these readers' comments or incorporate them in the pages which follow, if only because they frequently argued with each other in the margins! So the authors must take full responsibility for the published work and, in particular, for the defects which remain. Finally we offer our sincere thanks to Fiona Pearson, who cheerfully typed her way through successive drafts, which initially were considerably longer than the book now is.

CONTENTS

LIST OF ABBREVIATIONS

AAC	Anglo American Corporation
ADB	African Development Bank
ADF	African Development Fund
ANC	African National Congress
ARDP	Accelerated Rural Development Programme
BAMB	Botswana Agricultural Marketing Board
BCL	Bamangwato Concessions Limited
BDC	Botswana Development Corporation
BDP	Botswana Democratic Party
BEDU	Botswana Enterprises Development Unit
BHC	Botswana Housing Corporation
BIP	Botswana Independence Party
BLS	Botswana, Lesotho and Swaziland
BMC	Botswana Meat Commission
BNF	Botswana National Front
BPC	Botswana Power Corporation
BPP	Botswana People's Party
BRST	Botswana Roan Selection Trust
CAP	Common Agricultural Policy
CCM	Chama Cha Mapinduzi
CDC	Commonwealth Development Corporation
CIDA	Canadian International Development Agency
DANIDA	Danish International Development Agency
DC	District Commissioner
DCF	Discounted Cash Flow
DDC	District Development Committee
DDF	District Development Fund
EPU	Economic Planning Unit
GDP	Gross Domestic Product
GNP	Gross National Product
IBRD	International Bank for Reconstruction and Development (World Bank)
IDA	International Development Association
ILO	International Labour Organization
MFDP	Ministry of Finance and Development Planning
MLO	Mine Labour Organization
NEMIC	National Employment Manpower and Incomes Council
NDB	National Development Bank
NORAD	Norwegian Agency for International Development

ODM	Ministry of Overseas Development
OPEC	Organization of Petroleum Exporting Countries
OSAS	Overseas Service Aid Scheme
PAC	Pan Africanist Congress
PDL	Poverty Datum Line
PDSF	Public Debt Service Fund
RIDS	Rural Incomes Distribution Survey
RSF	Revenue Stabilization Fund
RST	Roan Selection Trust
SACUA	Southern African Customs Union Agreement
SIDA	Swedish International Development Agency
TANU	Tanganyika African National Union
UBLS	University of Botswana, Lesotho and Swaziland
UBS	University of Botswana and Swaziland
UDI	Unilateral Declaration of Independence
USAID	United States Agency for International Development
WNLA	Witwatersrand Native Labour Association
WUC	Water Utilities Corporation

General note

Citizens of Botswana are Batswana, and an individual citizen is a Motswana. Whenever the Tswana group of tribes or members of them are referred to in the text, rather than citizens of the country as a whole, no prefix is used. The same convention is used when reference is made to other tribes.

Prior to August 1976 when the Pula was introduced, Botswana used the South African Rand. Initially the Pula was introduced with the same value as the Rand, so for simplicity of presentation all monetary figures in this book are expressed as Pula, even when they refer to years before 1976. Towards the end of 1978, 1 Pula = $1.15.

Readers who are more interested in general development issues than in the detail of Botswana itself should concentrate particularly upon Chapters 3–7 together with the introduction and conclusions.

Throughout the book we use the convention of referring to Southern Rhodesia for the whole period of history up to the present day. For the future we refer to Zimbabwe.

INTRODUCTION

The problem of how to alleviate the extreme poverty presently faced by over half the world's population has been seen, until recently, mainly in terms of how to increase the national incomes of the countries in which these people live. Planning in the newly independent countries which emerged in the 1950s and 1960s was conceived almost entirely in terms of enhancing aggregate national income. However, although many poor countries have experienced healthy economic growth over the last two decades, the benefits of this have been very unequally distributed, not only between different countries, but also among various groups of citizens within them. In some parts of the world this growth of aggregate income even appears to have been accompanied by a further impoverishment of the poorest population groups. In consequence serious and concerned students of the process of development now have less confidence in national income per capita as an effective index of economic and social welfare, especially in the absence of information on how national income is distributed. National economic growth is now seen as a necessary but far from sufficient condition for a reduction of the incidence of poverty in the Third World.[1] The exploration of this general theme in the particular context of Botswana is the principal purpose of this book.

The advocacy of development strategies which include measures to create or strengthen the means of eliminating poverty and securing a redistribution of income has had both theoretical and practical dimensions. The theoretical debate has been concerned with the extent to which adjustments and manipulations of the pricing mechanism can be used to this end. Planning frameworks have been proposed which assign different weights to income increments, depending on the social and economic groups to which they accrue (Seers, 1972; Chenery *et al.*, 1974). In these terms, strategies which seek to maximize the growth of the national product are little more than special cases in which the value weights assigned to the growth of income of each section of the community are equal to the proportion that each currently controls. A concern to reduce poverty itself implies that these weights should change.

The practical debate has focused upon the specific policy changes which seem to be required at the national and sectoral levels. In a series of case studies—most notably that for Kenya (ILO, 1972)—the International Labour Organization has systematically analysed government policies in a range of countries from this perspective. Although obviously the circumstances of individual countries differ, the analyses showed the need for intervention and adjustment in a range of different areas if the needs of the poor are to be addressed. The most important of these are: the prices and distribution of ownership of capital and land; incomes and employment policies; education health and the provision of other public services; the regulation of commodity markets and technological transfer and change. The balance of market forces at both the national and international levels, it was suggested, could be significantly and constructively modified by adjustments to government policy in each of these areas, and, under such circumstances, it would be possible to accelerate the improvement in the welfare of the poorest population groups.

The most important contribution of these theoretical and practical studies is not merely the increased prominence that they have given to the need for poverty-focused planning, although most would agree that this itself is a major advance. Rather, that they have also shown that rapid economic growth and significant redistribution of income are not incompatible goals: there *are* cases of countries where the poorer groups have increased their incomes faster than other groups in society over periods of time when healthy rates of growth of total output have been maintained. At a theoretical level it is argued that there is no reason why this pattern should not be universalized.

There is considerable disagreement, however, over whether or not a more widespread adoption of redistributive strategies can in fact occur without major political change in most poor countries. Radical analysts have tended to dismiss strategies of 'redistribution with growth' as naïve reformism. They find fault not so much with the conclusion that such strategies would benefit the poor, but with the assumption that the rich and (generally) politically powerful groups could ever see it as being in their own interests to pursue such objectives. Proponents of redistributive strategies however—not all of whom advocate the Platonic notion of philosopher kings—stress the longer term benefits to all of investments in and for the poor and the diversity of sectional and economic interests which make up most governing classes, which thereby hold out the possibility of either gradualist or radical reforms.[2]

This debate has informed many of the questions posed in this book. Whilst we do not pretend to provide final answers, the recent history of Botswana provides a case-study illustration of the complexity of some of the problems involved.

Botswana itself is a vast land-locked tableland occupying a central position in southern Africa. Except for a tiny border with Zambia, it is completely surrounded by South Africa, Namibia, and Zimbabwe. Each of these have been minority-ruled countries—rich, powerful, and potentially hostile to Botswana. Much of the country, which is more than 700 kilometres in length and breadth, is relatively featureless —its sandy terrain and limited rainfall supporting no more than a bush savannah type of vegetation. At the same time, it is a place of great ecological contrasts. Whilst the semi-arid Kgalagadi Desert covers about two-thirds of the land area, in the north-west the Okavango river flows in from Angola which—as a result of the tail-end of the great fault which runs down most of the eastern side of Africa—fans out into a large inland delta, covering about 16,000 square kilometres, about 3 per cent of the land area of the country. This region, therefore, with its stunningly beautiful swamps, lush grassland, and perennial water stands in major contrast to the aridity of much of the rest of the country. The only other perennial surface water is the Chobe river, which drains into the Zambezi and forms part of the northern border with Namibia, and the Limpopo river which, in the south-east, divides Botswana from South Africa.

The availability of water, and the fertility of the soils have been the dominant influences on the pattern of human settlement. More than 80 per cent of the population, which currently comprises some three-quarters of a million people, live in the catchment area of the Limpopo, along the eastern side of the country. Here, there are reasonably fertile soils, unlike those in the Okavango Delta, and in most years the rainfall is sufficient to produce good pasture for cattle and to permit arable agriculture to be pursued. Less than one tenth of the land area enjoys these relatively favourable circumstances, and even here the variability of rainfall, combined with high evapo-transpiration rates, bring a considerable risk of crop failure. The main crop is sorghum, but maize, millet, and beans are also grown, especially in the south.

Until 1966, Botswana was a British protectorate—it was called Bechuanaland in those days—and the population had been almost entirely dependent upon cattle rearing, the subsistence production of the crops mentioned above, and upon remittances from migrant labourers in South Africa. Only two 'modern' towns existed—each with a population of less than 10,000 people—and the administrative headquarters of the protectorate had been at Mafeking in the Republic of South Africa. Since then, not only has the country become independent, but mineral discoveries have led to considerable investments being made in Botswana, and the construction of a new capital together with two other mining towns has led to some shift in patterns of settlement and of economic activity. By 1978, some 15 per cent of the population were living in the urban centres, and this proportion was increasing rapidly. Although these changes are very significant, the rural sector continues to provide the main livelihood for the majority of people.

The object of this book is to provide a politico-economic history of Botswana. The emphasis is on the post-colonial period, which began in 1966, after a long and debilitating drought. Independence inaugurated a period of seven or eight years of good rains. Agricultural recovery and minerals development combined to produce an exceptionally high and sustained growth of total output, albeit starting from a low base, over the following decade. A major concern of the book is to explain how this growth occurred, and to analyse its impact upon the incomes and productive capacity of the population. Our research shows that whilst most people have benefited in some way from this growth, this is mainly a result of the sustained run of good weather, which could easily be reversed, and the fundamental productive capacity of the rural population has remained basically unchanged. Meanwhile, income distribution has become worse, and unless policies are changed these trends will continue in the future.

The diagnosis of why this has happened, however, is not a simple one. It is not only the result of the emergence of a new élite which, having replaced the colonial administration, now promotes its own class interests in opposition to those of the majority—although this is undoubtedly part of the story. There has also emerged a new conflict between external forces—nourished by the increasing internationalization of production in Botswana—and domestic interests, particularly as regards policies towards incomes, employment, and taxation. This is not to say that the international pressures have always won out, but that they have forced compromises in domestic policies which have often worked against the interests of the poorest groups.

Many of the problems in this area are encapsulated in the notion of 'dependence'. As with the issue of distribution, this concept is of considerable significance. It refers to the degree to which a country's incorporation into the international economy—particularly in terms of exports, imports, and investment—conditions and constrains internal economic and political developments. There can be little doubt that the development patterns of many countries have been dominated by external influences during the colonial and post-colonial periods. Botswana, however, is an unusually dependent economy in a number of ways.

First of all, although the country is large in terms of area and mineral resources, it has a small and poor population. Thus the size of the local market is very limited, and, particularly for production processes where economies of scale are to be gained, the establishment of industries based upon supplying the domestic market is extremely difficult. At least using conventional technologies, Botswana's market is not large enough to support the economic production of a very wide range of manufactured or semi-manufactured goods. As a result, the economy has a very strong external orientation, based upon the import of manufactures and the export of primary products to pay for them. Historically, the main export commodity has been beef, and fluctuations in prices, or in the number of carcasses exported, have been the major determinants of the level of domestic economic activity and incomes. More recently the diversification into minerals production for export has had the effect of spreading some of the risks. But the country remains critically dependent upon the levels of international demand for its products, and upon their prices, being maintained.

Second, Botswana's land-locked position in southern Africa—surrounded by powerful, minority-ruled countries—has caused particular concern about some aspects of its dependence. The region as a whole is dominated by South Africa, and Botswana has been linked explicitly to that country through a customs union, through trade and transport arrangements, and through its use of the rand currency until 1976. In addition, the flow of workers from Botswana to South Africa has brought a dependence for many families upon remittances from migrant workers in that country. Throughout the colonial period, Botswana had client status in most aspects of economic policy with regard to her wealthy neighbour. The relationship since independence has been an uneasy one. Although the political paths of Botswana and South Africa are divergent—now, more clearly than ever before—Botswana's economic dependence upon South Africa has continued in a major way. This has influenced the Government's economic policies and has significantly affected its stance on international political issues—particularly with regard to Botswana's role in the independence struggles of Zimbabwe and Namibia.

There have been other circumstances too which, for more technical reasons, have tended to increase Botswana's dependent status—at least in the short term. The country's extreme poverty and narrow production base implied that taxable capacity was very limited. The number of skilled and experienced Batswana able to undertake professional or managerial roles were very few. At the same time the task of providing for the basic needs of Batswana—in terms of their schooling, health, transport, water, electricity, and other services—has always been much more formidable, and costly on a per capita basis, than in countries with a larger population living closer together. In practice this has increased the Government's reliance upon foreign aid, and upon private foreign investment, as sources of project finance and as supplements to government revenues. The number of expatriate workers has also continued to increase. As a result, new patterns of foreign influence within the country have become entrenched.

In the following chapters we shall be analysing, and in many places criticizing, the policies followed by the Government. The analysis will show how past policies have increased or changed the choices for the future, and will point to ways in which government actions could be modified or maintained, when viewed particularly from the perspective of the poorest groups in the population. Nevertheless, the smallness, poverty, and geographical position of Botswana impose severe limits upon the possible range for public policy, and the fact that these initial circumstances have heavily constrained the room for manœuvre should never be far from the reader's mind.

CHAPTER 1

HISTORICAL BACKGROUND: FOUNDATIONS OF THE INDEPENDENT STATE

PEOPLE, SETTLEMENT, AND PRE-COLONIAL ECONOMY

The Tswana form one of the three major divisions of the Sotho group of Bantu peoples, and are thought to have come to southern Africa at the time of the Bantu migrations from the north several centuries ago. Most of the tribes which form the great majority of the population of Botswana come from this common stock, although they arrived in the territory at different times in the eighteenth and nineteenth centuries, having moved north and west from their original areas of settlement in the Transvaal. There are eight principal tribal groups, seven of which— the Ngwato, Kwena, Ngwaketse, Tawana, Kgatla, Tlokwa, and Rolong— are direct descendents of the original Sotho migrants. The first of these is by far the largest, and its leaders have been the most influential throughout the history of the territory. The eighth group are the Lete, who are not Tswana, but Ndebele, although they have completely assimilated Tswana custom and language. Historically, these tribes were concentrated in their own separate areas which came to be called 'reserves' by the colonial administration. At the end of the nineteenth century these comprised about 40 per cent of the land area of Botswana, the remainder being mostly unoccupied and undeveloped, except for a small area, representing about 3 per cent of the total, which had been granted to European farmers.

In addition to these eight major tribes, a large number of smaller, related, or subjected tribes have lived amongst them in the reserves and under the authority of the Tswana chiefs. Some of these like the Kaa and the Kgalagadi are of Tswana origin. But a range of others, including the Kalanga, Koba, Mbukush, and Herero came from different stock, some as refugees from colonial wars in South West Africa and Angola. Included in this group also are the Sarwa, or Bushmen, who are the oldest race in Botswana, and who are regarded as the original inhabitants of most of southern Africa. This group were driven into the Kgalagadi desert by the early Tswana immigrants, and they have always been amongst the poorest and most oppressed sections of the population. Some of them were taken into serfdom by their Kgalagadi and Ngwato conquerors, with no recognized legal rights and no property except for occasional gifts of cattle from their masters. The remainder lived a precarious existence based upon hunting and gathering outside the tribal areas, and many of them remain dependent upon these activities even today.

The pre-colonial Tswana economy was relatively self-sufficient. Families depended upon the land to satisfy their wants. Their diet was a healthy one of sorghum porridge, milk, the meat of wild and domestic animals, vegetable dishes made from crops and wild plants, and beer. Clothing was made mainly from animal skins and was decorated with bead-work, and iron, copper, or bone ornaments. Household implements were home made, and included baskets, clay pots, iron-bladed hoes, spears, axes and knives, skin bags, mats, wooden bowls and pails, spoons, cups, scoops, and bottles. 'All these goods were required in the first instance for maintaining the household itself. But every man owed certain forms of gifts and tribute to his kinsmen, neighbours and chief, so that he worked to satisfy not only his own domestic needs, but also his obligations to others' (Schapera, 1971: 105).

The tribal territory and all its resources were administered by the chiefs, through the headmen of villages and wards (village subdivisions). The chief's responsibilities included allocating land, free of charge, to members of the tribe for purposes of building their homes, cultivation, and grazing cattle. Under this system everyone had common rights to land, the allocation of which varied only according to family size. No-one had private rights to game or other natural resources, and each person could hunt, gather wood, grass, water, and plants from wherever they found them. Their personal accumulation of cattle and other goods was unrestricted.

Unlike the tradition of most African tribes, the Tswana have from the time of their earliest settlement lived in large villages—in part for reasons of defence and also because dependable sources of surface water in the area are few and far between.[1] Each tribal capital, being the home of the chief, was the centre of political and social life of the tribe, and was the place where all important gatherings and meetings were held. Although many members of the tribe kept their main household in this central village, many also maintained an additional dwelling at the place where they grew their crops (traditionally called 'lands'), which were often many miles away. As the summer approached, the chief would decide the moment that ploughing should begin. At that time most people would move to their lands, leaving the villages populated mainly by children and elderly people. In addition, for frequent, and sometimes long, periods during the year, the men and older boys would be absent at their cattle post—often even further away than the lands—where larger cattle owners would often maintain a third dwelling. Thus, the livelihood of most families depended upon the men and women of working age being away from the village, often at different places, for large parts of the year. This high degree of mobility and of economic interdependence remain features of rural life in Botswana even today.

EARLY EXTERNAL INFLUENCES

European penetration and the introduction of colonial economic structures brought profound changes to the traditional economy. The changes were complex, and differed in certain important respects from those which took place in other parts of Africa. Foreign interest and involvement in the area which is now Botswana stemmed not so much from its attraction in terms of resources, but rather from its proximity to South Africa. Events in that country, and particularly the competition throughout the nineteenth century between the British and the Boers, had a critical effect upon the fortunes and political destiny of the Tswana.

Cape Town was occupied for a second time by the British in 1806. They introduced a more humanitarian form of government to South Africa, which restored civil liberties for blacks and abolished slavery. These changes threatened the way of life of the Boers, who had established the Cape settlement 150 years earlier. Rather than submit to the authority of the Cape Government many of them migrated northwards, to settle land which was then occupied by the Matabele. The Great Trek of the Boers, as it has subsequently been called, led to the settlement of about 14,000 whites in the western Transvaal, and by 1837 the Boers had established themselves in the Magaliesburg Hills, close to the borders of modern Botswana (Sillery, 1974: 26). Meanwhile, further to the west, small numbers of British missionaries and traders were making their first expeditions into Tswana territory from the Cape. In 1820 Robert Moffat had established his mission station at Kuruman (see Fig. 1.1) just south of the area that is now Botswana. With the arrival of David Livingstone in South Africa in 1841 the London Missionary Society decided to extend its activities further north. After settling first at Mabotsa amongst the Kgatla, Livingstone in 1847 attached himself to the Kwena led by Chief Setshele, and built a mission on the Kolobeng river, about fifteen miles west of Gaborone which is now the capital of Botswana.

British policy at this time was opposed to the expansion of white settlement in southern Africa. Whilst the missionaries' initiatives in the north were welcomed, support for British involvement did not extend to providing any organized military assistance to the northern tribes to help defend them against territorial intrusions by the Boers. In 1852, for example, a Boer commando raid against Setshele—which resulted in the capture of a large number of women and children prisoners by the

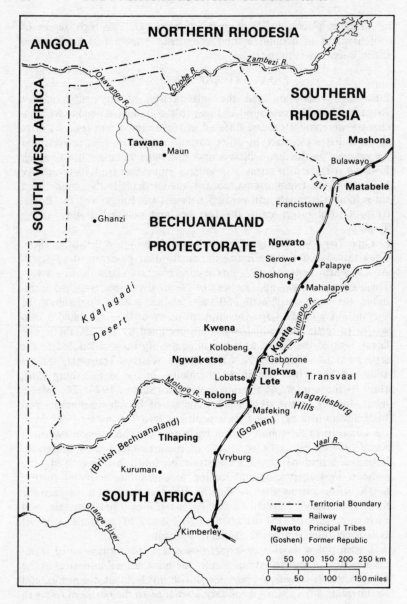

FIG. 1.1   The Bechuanaland Protectorate in the early twentieth century

Boers, and the associated sacking of Livingstone's mission[2] —was met with no more than mild remonstrances from the British authorities. Furthermore, over the following two years both the Boer Republics of the Transvaal and the Orange Free State were granted independence from the Cape Colony.

The next few years were marked by persistent attempts by the Boers to extend westwards and to annex land occupied by the Tswana tribes. There were three main motives behind these initiatives. First, the main direct route to the north ran through Tswana territory from Kuruman to Shoshong, and whoever controlled this would also be able to regulate access to the interior; the Boers correctly believed that the increasing British influence in the area would act as a barrier to their own expansion. Second, the appetites of the Transvaal farmers for more and more land appeared to be limitless. The well-watered lands around the Molopo and Limpopo rivers were attractive areas for large-scale ranching and the Transvaal Government supported the successive encroachments of tribal land which were being made by recognizing the ownership rights of all farmers who staked their claim—irrespective, in many cases, of whether the land in question was already settled and worked by an African population. And third, the discovery of gold in the Tati area in 1867, and subsequently of diamonds near to the Vaal river, increased the territorial ambitions of the Boers.

As a result of these developments the threat to the Tswana lands became more obvious. In 1867, Chief Matsheng of the Ngwato, acting on the advice of the able British missionary, John Mackenzie, applied to the High Commissioner to request British protection of the Tati area. Matsheng's fears were vindicated, when, shortly afterwards the Transvaal Government issued a proclamation annexing much of northern Bechuanaland. This claim was dropped following protests from the British, and the prospect of more formal protection at that time was not pursued. But there were a number of other areas where the British and the Boers were competing for territory and this led eventually to the First Anglo-Boer War in 1880. The British were quickly defeated, and in the following year the Pretoria Convention formally delineated the boundaries of the Transvaal and excluded the trade route north through Botswana. This agreement was reiterated in the London Convention three years later, but the ambitions of the Boers remained untamed, and it was to be many years before the fears of the Tswana concerning the compulsory annexation of their territory—first by the Boer Republics and later by the Union of South Africa—were to be allayed.

It soon became clear that these agreements were worthless when, a few months after the signing of the London Convention, a renewed incursion was made by the Boers into Ngwaketse territory north of the Molopo, resulting in many casualties among the Rolong, and the annexation of Goshen by the Transvaal. Accordingly, a strong force of troops under the command of Sir Charles Warren was dispatched from London in 1885 to reassert order in the area, and to declare British protection over Bechuanaland south of the Molopo, that is, up to the southern border of what is now Botswana. As it happens, opposition melted away in the face of such a show of strength, and Warren's mission was accomplished without fighting. Meanwhile, the British Government became increasingly concerned that the Germans in South West Africa and the Portuguese on the east coast would between them annex the central part of southern Africa and thereby close off to the British the route between the Cape Colony and Central Africa. Awaiting Warren at Mafeking, was a telegram instructing him to pursue his journey further, and to inform the chiefs of northern Bechuanaland that British protection was to be extended to their territory south of latitude 22°S. The three principal chiefs—Khama of the Ngwato, Setshele of the Kwena, and Bathoen of the Ngwaketse—for whom the idea of British protection was nothing new,[3] welcomed the proposal. On 30 September 1885 the British Government declared that the part of what is now Botswana south of latitude 22° was henceforth a British protectorate, whilst the area south of the Molopo and north of Cape Colony was proclaimed to be a British colony under the name of British Bechuanaland.

The Bechuanaland Protectorate was thus established by the British, after much hesitation and reluctance, in order to guarantee the route to the north. It was not a territory that the British wanted on account of its economic resources or for purposes of British settlement. Rather the extension of British authority to the area was viewed as a necessary cost if other settler interests in the region were to be kept at bay. As a result of this attitude the British aimed to keep the financial costs of their involvement to a bare minimum. The High Commissioner, who was also Governor of Cape Colony and of British Bechuanaland, stated in 1885 that the British Government would do 'as little in the way of administration or settlement as possible'.[4]

This attitude is perhaps best exemplified by the history of relations between the British Government and the British South Africa Company which was established by Cecil Rhodes. In addition to his growing commercial interests in the north, Rhodes, a prominent politician in the Cape, had already had a strong influence over political affairs in Bechuanaland. Accordingly when Rhodes established an amalgamated company in 1889 for the purpose of pursuing mining concessions obtained from Lobengula, chief of the Matabele—a Central African tribe—he was rewarded by a royal charter which gave substantial authority to his operations. The British South Africa Company, as it was named, was authorized not merely to pursue its commercial interests throughout what are now Botswana and Zimbabwe, but also to exercise whatever powers were necessary for the purposes of government and the preservation of public order. The British Government saw the company as a means of protecting its colonial interests in the region at no cost to the public purse, and for some years its intention was to hand over responsibility for the governance of the Bechuanaland Protectorate to this commercial concern.

Between 1894 and 1897, the railway between Mafeking and Bulawayo, undertaken to enable the settlement of Matabeleland by Europeans, was completed by the British South Africa Company. Meanwhile, however, the Tswana were becoming increasingly uneasy about the role that the company was likely to have in their country. Following the confirmation by the British Colonial Secretary that it was intended to transfer the administration of the protectorate to the company, chiefs Khama, Sebele, and Bathoen journeyed to England in 1895 to protest in person. After a series of public meetings and receptions for the chiefs, organized by the London Missionary Society in various parts of the country, public opinion became sympathetic to the chiefs' cause, and an initial rebuttal of their case by the Colonial Office was reversed. The chiefs, it seems, got all they asked for, including a resident representative from Britain and the preservation of their own tribal boundaries. Only the territory outside the tribal reserves, but including also a narrow strip for the railway, would be administered by the company. In the event, however, Rhodes lost the opportunity of exercising even this more limited administrative role in the protectorate when the Jameson raid on Johannesburg, which provided the spark for the Second Anglo-Boer War, failed. As this had been executed with his support, and launched from the Bechuanaland Protectorate, his credibility with the British Government was undermined. In spite of the costs of imperial involvement, the risks of placing exclusive faith in Rhodes's diplomatic and political skills were now seen to be too great, and all question of the future transfer of the protectorate to the British South Africa company was dropped.

These were the main external forces which influenced the early political history of Botswana. By the turn of the century the structure and geographical boundaries of the protectorate administration's responsibilities had basically been settled. British Bechuanaland was incorporated in the Cape Colony in 1895, and the administrative headquarters for the protectorate was moved from Vryburg to Mafeking, where it remained until 1966. In 1890 the northern limit of British jurisdiction has been extended from latitude 22° up to the Zambezi. Two years later the Tati Concession, which had been granted by Lobengula in 1880 and had thereby been recognized as part of Matabeleland, was proclaimed part of the Bechuanaland Protectorate. The other areas of European settlement that remained as authorized concessions, following the recommendations of a Concessions Commission in 1893, were a number of small, but important, farming blocks in the Ghanzi, Gaborone, Lobatse, and Tuli areas. The five major tribal reserves for the Ngwato, Kwena, Ngwaketse, Tawana, and Kgatla were demarcated by proclamation in 1899. The rest of the country, excluding the concessions and the Rolong farms, which had been held on an individual tenure basis since 1885 as a means of protecting the tribal land from seizure by Europeans, were soon to become crown lands. Only the two small reserves for the Lete and Tlokwa remained to be demarcated, in 1909 and 1933 respectively.

ECONOMIC AND POLITICAL RELATIONS WITH SOUTH AFRICA

Between 1899 and 1902 the British fought the Boers in southern Africa for the second time. In 1910 the two defeated Boer republics (Transvaal and the Orange Free State) were joined with the two former British colonies of Natal and the Cape to form the Union of South Africa. The South Africa Act, which established the Union, and was prepared by a National Convention of the four colonies, included provisions relating to the future of Basutoland (now Lesotho), Bechuanaland, and Swaziland. The view of both the British and the South African Governments was that the destiny of the three protectorates lay in their incorporation with the Union, and South African policy towards the territories was to be strongly influenced by the wish to secure this goal. However, because no agreement was reached over the issue of franchise rights for Africans in the negotiations leading to the creation of the Union, the immediate transfer of the territories was unacceptable to the British. The South Africa Act accordingly specified conditions under which the three territories would be governed in the event of any future transfer, which included provisions to guarantee the inalienability of tribal lands and the protection of existing civil rights. In addition, when the South Africa Bill was before the British Parliament, pledges were given that both Parliament and the inhabitants of the three territories would be consulted before any transfer took place. Although it was never said that the consent of any of these parties would be necessary, British policy over the following half-century consistently showed that this was to be a major implicit condition for securing a transfer.[5]

Although the Bechuanaland Protectorate, along with Basutoland and

Swaziland, had participated in customs-union arrangements with the British colonies and Boer republics in South Africa since the 1890s, the most significant of such agreements—which was to determine the main terms of their economic relationships with South Africa for over half a century—was signed soon after the Act of Union, in 1910. The terms of this agreement were simple: the High Commission Territories were to receive a share of the total import duties collected by South Africa equal to the share of total imports to the area consumed by each territory over the three years immediately prior to the signing of the agreement. The level of tariffs chargeable on all imported goods was to be determined by South Africa. Sales duties were also brought within the terms of the formula in 1913.[6] Since the South African Government collected and apportioned all duties on behalf of the other partners, the High Commission Territories received revenue benefits from the agreement without incurring administrative costs. On the other hand, these smaller partners had no control over the rates chargeable and therefore were unable to take revenue initiatives by varying their own levels of excise or import duty. At the time, this was viewed as of little importance, since it was expected that these territories would be incorporated with the Union before very long.[7]

One important benefit of the agreement was seen as being the provision for 'free interchange of products and manufactures' of each of the parties. This was obviously of benefit to South Africa in that the manufactures of the Union, with the exception of alcoholic beverages, would thereby circulate freely in the High Commission Territories and be protected against external competition. This provision was also important to the other partners since South Africa was the main market for their exports. However, South Africa soon took measures which restricted the import of cattle, the major export of Bechuanaland and the main source of income for the majority of its inhabitants. As a result, the potential benefits to the protectorate of the 1910 agreement were scarcely realized. In part, this move against the cattle exports of Bechuanaland reflected an unwillingness on the part of South Africa to allow competition from products of the High Commission Territories in cases where this threatened South African producers. The introduction of these measures, however, was also not unconnected with the issue of transfer.

South Africa had begun to press the British Government for incorporation of the High Commission Territories soon after the formation of the Union. At the end of the First World War Prime Minister Botha suggested the immediate transfer of Swaziland, to 'enable the Union Government to spend money on the development of the territory which is very badly wanted, both in its own interest and in that of the

Union'. He specifically suggested the construction of a railway and the promotion of coal mining in the territory. In 1924, the lack of response to this offer prompted the new Prime Minister, General Hertzog, to take a tougher line. South Africa had already been facing a growing surplus of cattle from her domestic producers: beef prices fell by 40 per cent in real terms between 1918 and 1926,[8] and the need for imports from other countries was much reduced. Accordingly, in 1924 the South African Government introduced minimum-weight restrictions for cattle imported from the High Commission Territories.[9] In 1926 these were intensified: henceforth only oxen with a live weight at Johannesburg of at least 1000 lb., and cows of at least 750 lb. could be imported.[10] These measures were against both the spirit and letter of the 1910 Customs Agreement, and were introduced, in part, to demonstrate the costs to the territories of remaining outside the Union.[11]

These restrictions hit the cattle industry in Bechuanaland hard—particularly in the case of African producers who, as the South Africans undoubtedly realized, were more vulnerable to minimum-weight restrictions than the more efficient European farmers. Total exports of cattle from the protectorate declined from a peak of 34,000 head in 1925 to 25,000 in 1932, most of the loss being shouldered by African exporters. (UK, 1933: 161). The losses would have been even greater if alternative markets had not been found. Prior to 1920 South Africa accounted for almost all the exports of cattle from the protectorate. But by the 1930s the South African share was down to about one-third of the total, with roughly equal shares going to the Northern Rhodesian and overseas markets. The overseas trade in chilled beef, however, was much less profitable than the local market. The unit value of all cattle exported from Bechuanaland declined by over 20 per cent between 1928 and 1931 and, in consequence, the decline in sales revenues following the introduction of weight restrictions was much greater than the decline in numbers sold. The costs to the protectorate of the trade restrictions imposed by South Africa were therefore very considerable. They were a recurring theme of correspondence between the British and South African Governments during the years 1924 to 1938, and, since the restrictions would no longer apply to the territories after their incorporation with the Union, Hertzog frequently attempted to use this as an inducement to speed the decision on transfer. When, in 1934, this strategy seemed not to be having much effect, he made scarcely veiled threats to prohibit the immigration of labour from the territories for work on the mines and in other sectors, and to impose additional import controls.

All of these pressures continued to be resisted by the British. There seemed no prospect of moving towards an African franchise in the

Union, and the British Government was unwilling to surrender the future of the territories to an increasingly racialist regime. Moreover, the Statute of Westminster of 1931 and the subsequent South Africa Statute Act gave South Africa effective independence and rendered the safeguards of the 1909 Act, in the event of transfer, worthless. For these reasons also, as well as a strong suspicion of the motives of South Africans, which were based upon their experience of them since the middle of the nineteenth century, the Batswana (as well as the Swazis and Basothos) strongly resisted any idea of incorporation with their southern neighbour. The most the British would agree to during a visit to London by Hertzog in May 1935 was closer co-operation between the Union Government and the High Commission Territories. Essentially it was proposed that South Africa should provide aid for development projects, which might lead the inhabitants of the territories to interpret the overtures from the Union as being in good faith. But when in 1936 Hertzog suggested in the House of Assembly that the transfer of Swaziland might be achieved within two years it caused a strong reaction from the chiefs in the three protectorates, and the proposal to introduce financial assistance from the Union was dropped on the advice of the British Secretary of State for Dominion Affairs.

Equally, by the end of the 1930s South Africa's ability to exert leverage on Britain by refusing imports from the High Commission Territories was becoming less powerful. Beef prices in the Union began rising again from about 1935 onwards, and in 1941 the shortage of domestic beef prompted the Union Government to suspend the weight restrictions on imports. The effect on Bechuanaland's sales was dramatic —the number of cattle exported to the Union increased from less than 20,000 head in 1940 to about 35,000 by the end of the Second World War. In the post-war years, however, the South African market became less important—initially owing to increased sales further north in Africa, and later because access was secured to European markets. This new trade in beef carcasses was made possible by the opening of an abattoir in Bechuanaland, at Lobatse, in 1954. The development of other markets continued, and South African sales dropped to little more than one-quarter of total beef exports during the 1960s. The opening of the Lobatse abattoir was the single most important step in reducing the territory's dependence upon the Union market for beef.

Although the tactics of the Union Government changed, the wish to secure the incorporation of the High Commission Territories remained. The question of transfer had again been raised after the Second World War, when Dr Malan came to power at the head of a Nationalist Government, but the subsequent introduction of 'apartheid' and the movement towards more repressive social policies in South Africa made the possibility of transfer less and less likely. Accelerated political developments in the territories and moves towards independence during the 1950s confirmed this trend, and it was finally settled when South Africa became an independent republic and was expelled from the Commonwealth in 1961.

South Africa's interest in securing control over the three protectorates was initially based upon the wish to acquire more land for white farmers. Equally, however, the rather different 'native policy' pursued by the British administrations to that in South Africa was a source of growing embarrassment to the Union Government.[12] Comparisons were often made between the different approaches: the absence of pass laws, the more relaxed liquor controls, and the less discriminatory legislation in the High Commission Territories could only lead to growing tension among South African blacks. By the mid-1950s, however, an additional reason for securing transfer appeared. This arose from the new Bantustan policy which, it was thought, would only be viable if the three protectorates were included within the grand design. It was intended that they would form the nucleus for three of the eight units that were to be created, and this would result in the total land area that was to be 'given' to the Africans increasing from a mere 14 per cent to over 40 per cent of the area of South Africa. This, of course, was mainly due to the vast area of Botswana in comparison with the other territories. The incorporation of the protectorates within the Union therefore appeared critical to securing any international respectability for this strategy.

The resistance of the British Government was mainly based upon disapproval of the racial policies of the Union Government, and upon the fact that African opinion in the territories was strongly opposed to transfer. On the other hand Britain did agree with the South African argument that incorporation within the Union seemed to be the most sensible course from an administrative point of view. The British therefore remained hopeful, and at times optimistic, that social policy in South Africa would take a more liberal turn. In part as a reflection of this attitude, the affairs of the High Commission Territories were handled by the Dominions Office, and its successor, the Commonwealth Relations Office, which also had responsibilities for South Africa together with Britain's other self-governing dominions. These administrative arrangements help to explain why the British remained uncommitted on the question of transfer for so long—opposition to transfer by that office would have meant openly criticizing South Africa's racial policies, thereby endangering diplomatic relationships which were viewed to be important. They also partly explain why the three protectorates at independence were even less advanced than other colonial territories. Not only was there reluctance to spend much money on territories that were to be handed over to another Government, but also the Commonwealth Relations Office was less well equipped to initiate economic development in the territories for which it was responsible than was the Colonial Office.

DOMESTIC ECONOMIC AND POLITICAL DEVELOPMENT, 1900–1966

Colonial taxation and its effects

In common with other colonial territories, the Bechuanaland Protectorate was governed according to the system known as 'indirect rule'. Under this approach to colonial government the administration aimed to preserve earlier patterns of tribal authority, and traditional rulers were subject to restrictions only where, in the view of the colonists, it was necessary for the purposes of 'good' government. Bechuanaland was an extreme example of this approach: the British did not intend to establish a central administration within the territory, and the assurance given to chiefs Khama, Sebele, and Bathoen by the Colonial Secretary in 1895 was that they would 'rule the people much as at present'. Accordingly the Resident Commissioner for Bechuanaland remained in Mafeking; he was formally responsible to the High Commissioner for the three protectorate territories, who was also, after 1910, Governor-General of the Union of South Africa.

Although Britain's administrative role was to be limited, it was made clear to the Tswana from the outset that the costs involved in extending protection to their country would have to be paid for by themselves. The chiefs agreed to collect a hut tax from their people, and from 1899 onwards, they were made responsible for the appointment of collectors and the upkeep of tax registers. In return for these duties the British authorities paid them a commission of 10 per cent of the revenues they collected.[13] The costs of administering the protectorate, however, turned out to be higher than the British initially expected. Expenditures on the police force alone were running at about £40,000 per year and an annual subsidy to the British South Africa Company in return for free transportation of official goods accounted for another £20,000. By contrast, domestic revenues never exceeded £30,000 until 1908, two thirds of which came from hut tax and customs revenues with the remainder from postal and other charges. Accordingly, direct budgetary grants from Britain were needed to meet recurrent expenditures. Prior to 1903 the annual grant was about £70,000, but it declined to about £40,000 in 1909. In that year the administration doubled the rate of hut tax to one pound per year, which resulted in a considerable increase in tax revenues. Since the subsidy to the railway was terminated at the same time, by 1911 the administration was able to balance its budget. No further financial assistance from Britain was received until the 1930s.

In 1919 an additional tax, called the Native Tax, was levied on the African population. This was in the form of a surcharge of three shillings on each pound of Hut Tax collected. The proceeds were paid into a 'Native Fund' which was to be used for financing African education, medical development, the eradication of cattle diseases, and any other measures which would be of benefit to Africans. In 1932 the Native Tax, now at the rate of five shillings per year, was amalgamated with the Hut Tax, and became payable by every African male of the apparent age of eighteen years or more. This new African Tax was collected by Tribal Treasuries from 1938 onwards. The Treasuries continued to receive a portion of the tax collected for use on local projects.

Throughout the whole period 1899-1965 these were the main taxes paid by Africans in Bechuanaland. Since they were essentially poll taxes—although they were called different names at different times— their effect was regressive, and their burden was particularly heavy on the poorer families.[14] Although an additional graded tax was introduced for Africans in 1949 which was slightly progressive, it affected only a few people, and never contributed more than 2 per cent of the amount raised from African Tax between 1949 and 1965. These poll taxes on the African population made a large contribution to the general revenues of the administration. In some years prior to the Second World War, as much as 60 per cent of revenues came from this source, and the average contribution over the first thirty years of this century was 40 per cent (Hermans, 1974: 97). Thus, although in the post-war years a growing proportion of revenues from the African Tax was credited to the Tribal Treasuries, and its importance to general revenues thereby declined,[15] over the whole period a very significant proportion of the expenditures made by the colonial administration was financed by taxes on the African population.

The introduction of taxation had profound implications for the evolution of socio-economic structures and relationships in Botswana. It helped to form some characteristic features of the distribution of income and wealth which still remain, and which are themes of subsequent chapters of this book. The effects of taxation upon two institutions, or phenomena, are important in this context: the first is the system of migrant labour; the second is the distribution of cattle ownership.

In other colonies in southern Africa which introduced taxation at about the same time as Bechuanaland, a primary motive for so doing was the wish to create a black labour force which could be utilized in the expanding industrial sector of those economies.[16] In Bechuanaland, the motivation was less subtle—it was inspired by a simple need to raise revenue (Massey, 1977). Unlike the situation in the Cape or the Transvaal, both the settler community and the administration itself in Bechuanaland were too small to be troubled by a shortage of labour. The British were, however, extremely anxious to avoid a commitment to continue budgetary subventions to Bechuanaland indefinitely, and the taxes were introduced for that reason. Nevertheless, although the reasons for their introduction were different, their effects were the same as elsewhere: the Batswana had few sources of cash, and those without cattle were forced to seek paid employment. Since domestic wage employment was almost non-existent this meant that most had to look for work abroad—on the farms and, increasingly, the mines of South Africa.

Whilst it is clear that the colonial administration did not introduce taxes for the purpose of creating a labour supply, there was a certain confluence of interest between the Bechuanaland authorities and the mining employers in South Africa. Perhaps the clearest case of collusion between those parties occurred in the 1930s. Until that time, recruitment for the mines had been confined to southern Botswana, owing to an apparently high death rate amongst Africans recruited for mine work from more tropical areas. In 1934, however, the mines—which then were suffering from a severe labour shortage—proposed a trial period of recruitment from the north in order to examine whether there was indeed a significant difference in the mortality rate of such workers. The administration collaborated fully with this initiative, and officials in the north—together with the chiefs in the area—actively encouraged Batswana to sign up for mine work, despite the fact that the mine recruits themselves were unaware of the nature of this rather cold-blooded experiment. The Resident Commissioner of the time justified his position as follows: 'it will help the natives to get a little money which they badly need, and will enable the Adminstration to get in a certain amount of additional hut tax, which they need no less badly'.[17] There are examples, then, of men being encouraged, and sometimes coerced, by both colonial and tribal authorities, to seek work on the mines in order to pay the Hut Tax. With or without official encouragement and with or without taxation, it is probably true, of course, that the system of migrant labour would have become established in Bechuanaland in any case. But the numbers involved would probably have been less, or the wages offered would have had to be more. Protection of 'African interests' had its practical limits! Labour flows from Botswana to South Africa increased from a few hundred at the turn of the century to over 50,000 by the 1960s,[18] representing a very significant increase in the dependence of Botswana upon South Africa over the period and posing considerable difficulties for future policy.[19]

The introduction of taxation by the colonial authorities also had a significant, if largely unintended, effect upon the distribution of cattle ownership. Although there are hardly any reliable data on the historical pattern, two things appear to be fairly clear: first, the distribution of ownership has been getting more unequal for a very long time; second, the ways in which taxes were levied during the colonial period tended to exacerbate this trend.

The size of the national cattle herd has increased substantially since the end of the nineteenth century. The number of cattle owned by the Tswana at that time is not known, but in 1895 there was a virulent outbreak of rinderpest, which is said to have killed over 90 per cent of the nation's cattle. It seems that less than 50,000 head remained alive when the epidemic was finally controlled at the end of 1896, and the initial cattle population was therefore unnaturally low. From then on the available statistics suggest a regular increase in the size of the herd— to over 300,000 in 1911, 420,000 in 1921, almost 800,000 in 1932, one million in 1950, two million in 1970, and about 3 million head by 1978.[20] These data by their very nature are imprecise and cannot be taken to indicate more than rough orders of magnitude. Nevertheless the general picture of a roughly tenfold increase in the size of the national herd since the beginning of the century is probably correct.

It is also known that the distribution of the ownership of cattle by Tswana has always been unequal. Periodic droughts have caused dramatic stock losses, notably around 1914, 1933, the late 1940s, and the mid-1960s (q.v.). These, together with equally frequent outbreaks of foot-and-mouth disease, particularly hurt the farmers on marginal lands where the pasture was thin, and those who owned only a few head of cattle. This has resulted in a tendency towards increasing concentration of cattle ownership. Although there have been some mitigating factors, such as the action by Chief Seepapitso of the Ngwaketse in 1914 to allow younger tribesmen to own cattle separately from their parents (UK, 1933: 26), and the tradition of 'mafisa' whereby persons tending cattle may be given the progeny of those in their care,[21] it has nevertheless remained difficult for farmers who never owned or who lost their cattle to establish a new herd.

The chiefs too have always been in a commanding position with regard to cattle ownership. Occasionally their subjects were required to pay levies for some public undertaking—such as building a dam or a a school—but also, in some cases, to meet the personal debts of the chief. The payment of these levies would often necessitate the sale of some possessions—which usually meant cattle. The annual obligation to pay taxes had the same effects (in the early years of this century the Hut Tax was equivalent to about one-fifth of the price of a good ox), and those with few cattle and little income were made considerably poorer as a result. The ten-per-cent commission which was paid to the chiefs for taxes collected in each reserve also contributed significantly to the concentration of cattle wealth in a few hands, and to the creation of the personal fortunes held by some of the leading families in Botswana today.

According to one source, Chief Seepapitso owned about 3,000 head of cattle in 1914, about 20 other Ngwaketse farmers owned between 150 and 1,200 head, with other members of the tribe (perhaps between two and three households) owning fewer cattle. In the 1930s Schapera estimated that amongst the Kgatla, whilst five persons owned about 20 per cent of the cattle held by the tribe, about 16 per cent of the adult males owned no cattle at all (Schapera, 1971: 118). More recent figures on the national distribution suggest that about one-third of all households owned no cattle in the early 1960s and that almost one-half were in that position ten years later.[22] Although all of these data are subject to wide margins of error, they are generally consistent with the picture of an increasingly unequal distribution of cattle ownership over the last century.

Administrative changes and political dissension

Although the undertaking made by Joseph Chamberlain in 1895 about the nature of the future British administration in the protectorate was vague, the chiefs envisaged 'a form of parallel rule, in which they would administer the internal affairs of the tribes without interference from the Administration' (Hailey, 1953: 324). Each of the chiefs viewed this interpretation as being of major importance—whilst they wanted protection of their lands by the British, they did not want any curtailment of their traditional powers, nor any interference with their domestic affairs.

The very establishment of the protectorate, of course, implied some change in the sovereign rights of the chiefs, not least because the administration soon began to introduce legislation. The tax laws, already discussed, were obviously an important example. But other legislation was introduced which demarcated tribal reserves (1899), regulated the activities of labour recruiters (1899), and prohibited circumcision without parental consent (1917). Nevertheless, these and other early laws did not directly weaken the position of the chiefs, and the Tswana continued to be governed primarily by their own laws and customs.[23]

Gradually, however, the range of issues on which action was required by the colonial administration was extended, and in 1919 a Native Advisory Council was established which was to involve the chiefs more closely in the formulation of its policies. The function of this council was 'to discuss with the Resident Commissioner all matters affecting native interests which the members desired to bring forward'. Previously, the details of new legislation had been explained to assemblies (Kgotlas) of each tribe separately. Now, the Resident Commissioner also met the chiefs and other tribal representatives collectively at council sessions which were held once a year. By 1928 it had been agreed that the council should not merely be a forum in which the commissioner would explain new legislation to the chiefs, but rather a consultative body in which draft legislation would be discussed. The council thus gave to the chiefs a means of securing amendments to legislation of which they disapproved.[24] Although the Resident Commissioner was not bound to accept the advice of the council, in practice its views could not be ignored.

In parallel with the Native Advisory Council, a European Advisory Council was constituted which held its first meeting in 1921. Comprising six elected members from the European population, then about 1,700 persons, its function was to advise the Resident Commissioner on matters which affected that racial group. Although the number of resident Europeans, who were mainly traders and farmers, was tiny compared to the African population (and, indeed, compared to the settler communities in African territories to the north) this council had a more than proportionate influence over the affairs of the protectorate.

The powers of the chiefs were not to remain unfettered for long: during the 1930s the administration introduced important legislation which regulated their authority much more closely than had been attempted previously. These changes were prompted by a growing uneasiness on the part of the British Government over the propriety of chiefly authority and control. It was well known that the chiefs were often very rich, and that they had profited greatly (and lawfully) from their tax collection activities on behalf of the administration. But in addition, the chiefs were also able on occasions to exploit their positions of influence to pursue their personal gain rather than that of the tribe as a whole. In some tribes, for example, it was not unknown for the proceeds of fines imposed in the Kgotla, of levies, rents, and mining subsidies to be absorbed into the personal income of the chief.[25] Equally, there were examples of the ancient practice of calling out 'regimental' tribal labour for public works being misused by the chiefs. Although there were broader international reasons which were prompting a reassessment of Britain's role in the colonies at the time (Sillery, 1974: 132) these were the main domestic issues which led to introduction of administrative reforms in the protectorate.

The Native Administration Proclamation (No. 74 of 1934) gave the Government power to suspend chiefs if they were not performing their duties 'adequately'. These duties were defined in detail by the legislation, which also provided for the nomination of 'councillors' in each tribe who were to be consulted by the chief in exercising his functions. Chiefs could no longer impose tribal levies without written approval from the Resident Commissioner and without the agreement of the tribe in Kgotla, and they were obliged to carry out all 'lawful' orders issued to them by the Resident Commissioner. Another proclamation in the same year (No. 75 of 1934) regulated the powers of tribal courts and provided for appeals against their verdicts to be made to courts set up by the Government.

The proclamations were not, however, accepted without a fight. At the centre of the controversy was Tshekedi who, since the death of Sekgoma II in 1925, had been acting as regent over the Ngwato, pending the majority of Seretse, Sekgoma's son and heir, who was then only four years old. Tshekedi and Chief Bathoen II of the Ngwaketse had strongly criticized the draft proclamations when they were before the Native Advisory Council, on the grounds that they severely encroached traditional law and custom, and were thus contrary to the spirit of the Order in Council of 1891. After their subsequent enactment, chief and regent challenged their legality in the courts. However, the judge ruled that the High Commissioner must respect, but need not be bound by, native law and customs, and the case was lost. But the authorities had been sufficiently challenged by Tshekedi as to be careful to involve him, together with Bathoen, closely in the formulation of future legislation.

Although Tshekedi's attempt to prevent the introduction of administrative reforms ceased in the early 1940s his greatest conflict with the colonial authorities was still to come. This was over his role in the events arising from the marriage of Seretse Khama to Miss Ruth Williams in 1948. At that time, Seretse was 27 years old and studying for Bar examinations in London. The news of the impending wedding came as a shock to Tshekedi, not merely because the tribe had not been consulted, but because the marriage of a chief to someone from outside the tribe was unprecedented and marriage to a European woman seemed unthinkable. In spite of Tshekedi's opposition the ceremony took place, after which Seretse went to Serowe to attend tribal meetings in which the matter was discussed.

Seretse's right to the succession was at no point challenged either by Tshekedi or by the tribe. The dispute concerned whether Seretse should be allowed to exercise that right in view of the irregularity of his marriage. Initially, the tribe sided with Tshekedi, who remained firm in his commitment to prevent Ruth Khama from coming to the country. But gradually the tribe began to shift towards supporting Seretse, and a final meeting of the tribe in June 1949 voted decisively in favour of Seretse as Chief with his European wife.

In response to this loss of support, Tshekedi, with a small number of followers, left Serowe, to take up residence in the Kwena Reserve. At the same time, however, he challenged the decision of the Kgotla, and requested a judicial inquiry which should examine whether Seretse —who had now returned to London—should be recognized, and, if so, what would be the position of the children with regard to the future succession.

At this point the views of the British Government accorded strongly with those of Tshekedi, though for different reasons. The authorities in London were not in principle concerned that tribal custom had been circumvented by Seretse's marrying outside the tribe, but rather with the effects that inter racial marriage would have—were Seretse to be recognized as chief—upon Britain's relationship with South Africa. Accordingly, rather than accepting the majority view of the tribe in Kgotla, a judicial inquiry was held which—though the document was never published—was said to have 'unanimously advised against the recognition of Seretse' (UK, 1950: 5), on the grounds that his absence from the protectorate 'was essential to the peace and good order of the Bamangwato Reserve and . . . further advised that Tshekedi should not be permitted to return'. It was on these grounds that the British Government decided to withold recognition of Seretse as Chief for a period of at least five years, during which time he would not be allowed to return to the protectorate without special permission. Tshekedi too was exiled from the Ngwato Reserve, and the District Commissioner was placed in control of the affairs of the tribe for the time being.

The British Government's attitude was shown to be less than honest in 1952, when Tshekedi and Seretse settled their differences and were reconciled. At that time Tshekedi was allowed back into the Reserve, but the ban on Seretse was maintained. In fact, the British position was very heavily influenced by the condemnation by South Africa of Seretse's marriage. In spite of British protestations to the contrary, they were simply not prepared to flout South African sensitivities in such an open manner. The British Government's main priority remained the preservation of good relations with South Africa, even when it involved the adoption of a clearly hypocritical policy on the question of the Ngwato succession.

The British finally allowed Seretse and his wife to return to the protectorate in 1956, on condition that Seretse and Tshekedi would both renounce their claims to the chieftainship—a condition to which they both agreed. By that date there was a belated realization in Britain that Seretse had been treated very badly, but even then it is doubtful if the ban would have been lifted if it had not been for a refusal by the Ngwato to negotiate a mining agreement with Roan Selection Trust in the absence of Seretse and Tshekedi. On his return Seretse was made vice-chairman of a newly formed Ngwato Tribal Advisory Council, with Rasebolai Kgamane[26] —who had replaced the District Commissioner as tribal authority in 1953—as chairman. Tshekedi was made secretary of the tribe in 1958. The Khamas were therefore able to become active again in local politics, and the fact that neither formally held the chieftainship did not prevent them having a decisive influence upon the future direction of tribal as well as national affairs.

In point of fact, Tshekedi had remained active even during his exile from Ngwato territory. He had been appointed as a regular representative of the Kwena on the African Advisory Council. When a Joint Advisory Council was established in 1951, comprising members from both the European and African Councils, Tshekedi became a member and his views continued to be heard. In this forum he campaigned tirelessly for the establishment of a legislative council, a fight that was also taken up by Seretse after his return to the country. The British at first firmly resisted this proposal even though such councils had already been established in other territories for several decades, and Africans had long been members of those in Kenya (1944), Tanganyika and Uganda (1945), Northern Rhodesia (1948), and in Nyasaland (1949). The transfer question was still not finally settled, and South Africa would have been dismayed by the increased power and influence this would give to the African leaders in Bechuanaland. Nevertheless opinion in Britain was increasingly moving away from support of South Africa as racialism in that country became more and more entrenched. With the appointment of Sir John Maud—a strong supporter of self-government —as High Commissioner, in 1959, it began to look as though an existence separate from South Africa was assured for the High Commission Territories. Shortly afterwards the Joint Advisory Council established a committee to look into constitutional questions. This committee recommended the establishment of a legislative council, which was at last accepted by the administration and the British Government. The formation of this council in 1961 marked the first major and irreversible step towards political independence for Botswana.

The colonial legacy

In 1885 the High Commissioner had stated that Britain's intention with regard to the administration of Bechuanaland was to do as little as possible. Throughout most of the following eighty years of British rule this promise was kept—so much so that at independence Botswana was worse off in terms of both social and directly productive infrastructure than any other ex-British territory in Africa. One consequence of these policies was that in the mid-1960s, the per capita income of Botswana was one of the smallest in the world. A brief examination of the main dimensions of this colonial legacy shows how severely it constrained the policy options of the Botswana Government during the immediate post-independence period.

Public expenditure during the colonial period was mainly financed from domestic sources. Grants-in-aid were received from Britain for eight years during the 1930s in order to compensate for the revenue loss arising from the closure of the Union market to cattle exports from Bechuanaland. Between 1933/4 and 1940/1 these grants financed about one-third of the recurrent expenditures of the administration. Otherwise, no recurrent subventions were received from the British Government between 1911/2, when the increased rates of poll tax and the ending of the railway subsidy allowed the budget to be balanced for the first time, and 1956/7, when grants-in-aid recommenced. It is true that development loans and grants began to be made by the British Government from 1932/3 onwards. But these were very small until two or three years before independence, and it was not until the final decade of the colonial period that they increased to as much as one quarter of total expenditures (Table 1.1). Thus a large part of the Government's expenditure prior to independence was paid for by the African population.[27]

The attitudes of the British Government concerning its role and responsibilities in Bechuanaland are well illustrated by the expenditure pattern of the local administration. It can be seen from Table 1.1 (columns 1 and 2) that during the first quarter of the twentieth century over 90 per cent of government expenditure was accounted for by routine administrative functions, and that, of this, well over one-third was spent upon the police force. Initially the police were established as a small army, and in the 1890s they comprised about 500 men. The force was reduced somewhat, to about 350, in 1897, and further reductions were made during the following decade. Nevertheless, prior to 1920 between 50 and 60 per cent of annual expenditures were absorbed by the police, and they accounted for a very high proportion of established posts. In 1913/4, for example, 147 of the 160 Africans employed by the administration were policemen, and the department included over 85 per cent of all established posts at that time.

By contrast, as will be shown in Chapter 8, the development of education was viewed by the government as a tribal responsibility, and even the health service was left largely to the missions. When, for

TABLE 1.1 *Functional breakdown of expenditures by the protectorate administration 1900–1966*
Percentages

Period	General administration[1]	Police	Medical	Education	Veterinary and agriculture	Public works extraordinary[2]	Total recurrent	Development expenditures[3]	Total expenditure
			Recurrent expenditures						
1900–25	54.4	37.1	1.7	1.2	3.4	2.2	100.0	–	100.0
1926–35	51.8	20.0	7.5	3.4	10.9	5.8	99.4	0.6	100.0
1936–45	41.4	11.5	9.4	4.1	12.8	9.5	88.7	11.3	100.0
1946–55	35.3	10.8	9.9	4.8	12.6	12.9	86.3	13.7	100.0
1956–66	41.0	6.6	5.9	6.3	10.0	4.9[4]	74.7	25.3	100.0

[1] Includes the office of the Resident Commissioner, Justice, Audit, District Administration, Pensions, Posts and Telegraphs, etc.
[2] These were capital expenditures financed out of savings made on the recurrent budget.
[3] Financed mainly from British grants and loans.
[4] Includes capital expenditure on the construction of Gaborone during the last three years of the period, for which special British grants were made available.

Source: calculated from Hermans, 1974: Tables 2 and 3.

example, in 1932/3 the administration was employing 287 people in the police force, the medical, veterinary, and agricultural departments combined accounted for 81 employees, and the education department boasted a staff complement of only three.

Even those education and health expenditures which were undertaken by the administration were strongly biased towards benefiting the European rather than the African community. For example, in 1931/2, when about 8,000 African children were enrolled in primary schools, the administration provided no money out of general revenues for African education.[28] Nevertheless, several thousand pounds were provided to subsidize the education of less than 200 European children in the same year. Similarly, although by the early 1930s one hospital bed had been provided for every 250 European residents, the ratio for the African population was about 1:2,800 at that time—even though the health of Africans was much worse than that of the European population. A similar pattern is evident from expenditures in other sectors, and where funds for capital expenditures were available, they tended to be spent upon improving the housing and office accommodation for government employees. In view of the proportion of domestic revenues raised from poll taxes, it is clear that the costs to the Tswana of their protection were turning out to be very high.

There was, however, one area of public expenditure which did have some impact upon the incomes and productive capacities of the African population. This was veterinary expenditure, which was allocated between 10 and 15 per cent of the recurrent budget for most of the pre-independence period. Cattle exports were the basis of both the settler and Tswana economies, and a large part of the administration's domestic revenues was contingent upon the exports of cattle being maintained. Thus the colonial Government had a major incentive to reduce the incidence of cattle diseases in the protectorate, and this became the prime concern of the Veterinary Department's activities.

Although the most devastating outbreaks of disease occurred at the end of the nineteenth century, when the cattle population was ravaged by the rinderpest epidemic, the threat of other diseases has remained a spectre ever since. Each Coast fever and lung-sickness were eradicated from Bechuanaland during the 1920s, but foot-and-mouth disease continued to occur from time to time, and anthrax was also a persistent threat. Initially, the main method of controlling foot-and-mouth was to clear cattle from a strip of land around the affected area, thereby keeping the disease confined. This approach, however, was both expensive and impracticable in a country as large as Bechuanaland, and in the early 1950s a start was made on the construction of veterinary cordon fences and quarantine camps which, by the end of that decade, traversed the entire country. Henceforth, foot-and-mouth disease was easier to contain—particularly in the north-west of the country which was most vulnerable to outbreaks of the disease.

This emphasis upon veterinary expenditures for purposes of disease control was probably the single most important benefit of the colonial period. By contrast, arable agriculture, education, health, and physical infrastructure remained almost completely neglected by the central administration. What progress was made in developing these facilities was the result of expenditures made by the Tribal Treasuries, which raised their money from local taxes, or, in the health and education sectors, by the missionary societies.

As Hermans (1974) points out, there was some change in the attitude of the British Government towards Bechuanaland after 1955. In 1956 budgetary grants-in-aid were resumed, which within three years were financing one-third, and by 1963/4 one half, of the recurrent expenditures of the administration. The flow of development funds from Britain also increased rapidly, from less than £200,000 in 1955/6 to over £1 million ten years later. This allowed a considerable acceleration of government spending. Recurrent expenditures, which had been sluggish prior to 1955, increased more than fivefold, to about £5 million per year over the following decade. Similarly, the sources of development finance began to grow. In addition to grants and loans from the Colonial Development and Welfare Fund, Intercolonial Loans (from 1955 to 1960), and Exchequer Loans (from 1960 to 1963) were provided from the British Treasury. In the early 1960s, loans were raised from commercial banks within the country, and a credit from the International Development Association—mainly to finance telecommunications, power, water, and roads projects. In this way, development expenditure increased tenfold, to about £2.5 million over the decade ending in 1965/6.

All this, however, was rather little and rather late. For example, the fact that total expenditures by the administration doubled between 1963 and 1966 was almost entirely the result of the very belated decision to move the administrative headquarters of Bechuanaland from Mafeking in South Africa, to Gaborone, in time to accommodate the first elected Government in March 1965. Much of the increase in expenditure, therefore, was spent in providing office blocks, housing, and ancillary urban services for the new capital.

The number of regular wage-earning opportunities in the protectorate remained very small throughout the colonial period. Although the estimates are very rough and probably unreliable, total wage employment in the territory was put at about 7,000 persons in 1950, and about 10,000 in 1960. In both years, this represented only about

2 per cent of the resident population,[29] and probably three times as many Batswana were working in jobs in South Africa—mainly on the mines and farms—at both dates.

This dependence upon South African employment as a source of cash was strengthened during the early 1960s by the onslaught of the worst drought since the end of the nineteenth century. From 1961/2 until 1966/7 rainfall throughout Botswana was consistently well below the long-term average. A series of crop failures necessitated a sharp increase in imports of maize and sorghum, from a value of less than £100,000 in 1958 to about £750,000 in 1964. It is estimated that up to 400,000 cattle died during the drought, which was equivalent to about one-third of the estimated cattle population in 1960. The value of exports increased over the period because very large numbers of cattle were sent for slaughter to avoid starvation. But the productive capacity of the agricultural sector was seriously depleted, and almost every family experienced severe losses at this time.

By 1966, the year of independence, over 100,000 people (one-fifth of the population) were dependent for their food supply upon famine-relief programmes. Many of these had lost or sold all of their cattle and had no other means of securing cash incomes sufficient to meet their needs. The prospects for the future were bleak. Over 85 per cent of the country's export income and up to one-third of total output were normally generated by the cattle industry. Access to cattle was also important for ploughing and for making even a meagre income from the land. The drought was thus a major disaster which pauperized a very large number of rural people and hit at the heart of the country's productive capacity and potential. Incomes in the mid-1960s for many people were lower than they had ever been, and a large proportion of the population were no better off than their grandparents had been at the end of the nineteenth century. Incomes in Botswana had always been fragile. The drought demonstrated this in an extreme way, but it also showed that the years of colonial rule had done little if anything to protect the livelihoods of ordinary people.

CONCLUSIONS

The main economic change that occurred as a result of the years of British rule was that the self-sufficiency of the Batswana was undermined. The administration began to levy taxes at an early date, without providing people with the means of paying them. The widespread need for cash income which this created, which was further nourished by the growing availability of mass-produced and imported consumer goods, forced many people to take labouring jobs in South Africa. Self-sufficiency was also reduced by the fact that the distribution of cattle, which was the main source of income and wealth within Botswana, became more unequal. Although this was in large part a result of periodic droughts, it was also encouraged by the system of taxation employed by the Government. Since the poll taxes were regressive, the poorer people with no ready cash were forced to sell, or surrender, part of their assets, and the payment of commission on revenues collected considerably strengthened the wealth of the chiefs.

The Batswana received few of the benefits of 'modernizing' forces that could be pointed to in other territories. Investment in Bechuanaland was minimal throughout the colonial period, and the small number of regular jobs that were created were probably insufficient even to compensate for the decline in traditional sources of employment arising from the introduction of a cash economy open to imports from abroad. With the exception of expenditures upon veterinary disease control, and the construction of the abattoir—both of which did much to protect the territory's export trade—the administration was not very active in improving the welfare of the African population. Progress where it occurred was mainly a result of tribal initiative on the basis of local resources.

This extreme neglect arose because the British presence in Bechuanaland was not motivated by a search for exploitable resources but rather, in view of their interests to the north and south, to prevent the territory falling under the control of other colonists in the region. Initially, the main threat was from the Boers and the Germans, but after 1909 it was from the Union of South Africa itself. After that date, Britain's intention became to transfer the territory to the Union as soon as domestic politics in South Africa and in Bechuanaland made this possible. However, the promises made to the Tswana chiefs at the end of the nineteenth century were not broken, and the political independence of Botswana, gained in 1966, was a tribute to the consistency of British policy in the face of sustained South African pressure to secure transfer. The Batswana had gained the protection that they wanted. Nevertheless, they gained very little else, and they paid much for it in return.

CHAPTER 2

POLITICAL AND CONSTITUTIONAL CHANGE

As it became clear that Britain intended to give the Bechuanaland Protectorate full independence rather than handing the territory over to South Africa, and as more and more other African colonies were seen to be on the road to independence, so the pace of political change within the country accelerated. The Joint Advisory Council was superseded in 1961 by the Legislative Council which brought together in one legislative chamber representatives of all races. The European community directly elected ten members, the Asian community one, while the African Advisory Council, which continued in existence, nominated ten members to represent the African population.[1] This disparity in voting strength, given the relative sizes of the various racial communities, and the different methods of appointment caused some resentment among educated Africans (Gabatshwane, 1966: 23). Nevertheless, the Legislative Council was a useful transitional body prior to the introduction of universal suffrage in 1965.

At about the same time political parties began to emerge. The first on the scene was the Bechuanaland Federal Party, which was formed in 1959. But its existence was short lived and by 1961 it had dissolved. The Bechuanaland People's Party was formed in 1961. Its leadership and political philosophy had its roots in the racially charged atmosphere of South African politics, particularly the ANC and the PAC. Its politics tended to be radical, anti-colonial, and nationalistic. Before very long, however, it was riven with dissension. In 1962, the party secretary, Motsamai Mpho, was expelled. He formed a party of his own originally called the BPP (No. 2) but renamed in 1964 the Botswana Independence Party (BIP). In the same year there was a further split in the BPP when its Vice-President, Philip Matante, obejcted to the increasingly moderate line of Kgeleman T. Motsete, the founder and President, and broke away to start his own party, the BPP-Matante. The rump of the party has now disappeared but the two breakaway parties have survived to the present day under the same leadership.

In its early years the BPP achieved some measure of international recognition as Bechuanaland's liberation party. Matante twice addressed the United Nations Committee on Colonialism, in April 1962 and towards the end of the following year. The Organization of African Unity continued to support the BPP until as late as October 1965, even though it had already by then been soundly defeated at the polls (Stevens,

1967: 159). Some informed local opinion considered that a BPP government would be dangerously antagonistic to South Africa, and would stir up racial tensions within the country itself. In consequence Seretse Khama formed the more moderate Botswana Democratic Party in 1962. He was encouraged to do so by the British administration, which was anxious that a suitable national leader should emerge on whom the mantle of power could eventually descend, and was unhappy with the leadership of the BPP.[2] Seretse Khama was the obvious choice for this role. As the traditional heir to the chieftainship of the largest tribe he commanded wide popular support. He had shown his ability and his preference for modern democratic ideas in his participation in the Ngwato Tribal Advisory Council since returning to Bechuanaland in 1956, and more recently in the workings of the Joint Advisory Council which he had been instrumental in founding. His marriage, not many years earlier a considerable embarrassment to the administration, could now be taken as proof of his commitment to non-racialism. In addition he was an intelligent, moderate leader, and one of the best educated Africans in the territory, with moderate and 'responsible' views attractive to the colonial administration.[3]

The BDP drew support from a wide political base as soon as it was founded. The Ngwato rallied to a man behind their traditional leader, while in the country as a whole the new party found the political 'middle ground'. The chiefs, who were extremely nervous of the BPP's anti-chief policies, were attracted by the BDP's promise of constitutional role for the chieftainship after independence, interpreting this to mean that, at the tribal level, government would remain much as before. In fact, as will be seen in the next section, the BDP leaders actually had in mind some considerable constitutional restriction of the more autocratic powers of traditional authority. At the other extreme, an important section of the small but influential white-settler community began to support the non-racial aims of the BDP, which was obviously more attractive to them than the anti-white, anti-colonial position of the BPP. Nevertheless, there was a significant part of the white community which wished to have nothing to do with an independent Botswana. As late as 1964, white farmers in the Tati Area in the north-east petitioned the administration to be allowed to break away from Bechuanaland and join up with Southern Rhodesia.[4] The petition was unsuccessful, and many of these same settlers later took out Botswana citizenship.

Increasing political agitation by the BPP and the formation of the more moderate BDP in 1962, combined to cause the British Government to accelerate its timetable for constitutional change in the territory. Originally it was intended to hold a constitutional review in 1968, but in August 1962 the Resident Commissioner, Peter Fawcus, announced that this would be brought forward to 1963.

Preliminary discussions on a constitution for self-government began on July 1 1963 in Lobatse, and were complete by 18 November, after only six days of actual discussion. It was agreed that a National Assembly should be created to which members would be elected by universal adult suffrage. Executive power would be vested in a Cabinet with a Prime Minister but presided over by Her Majesty's Commissioner who 'exercised his powers in accordance with the advice of the Cabinet' but 'retained a general reserve executive power' (Gabatshwane, 1966: 51). Arrangements were made for a census to be held in the following year, so that constituency boundaries could be defined for an election in 1965.

DECLINE OF THE CHIEFS

The 1963 constitutional conference marked the beginning of the power struggle between the traditional ascriptive authority of the chiefs and the younger, more educated leaders of the BDP. In the coming years this struggle was to overshadow that between the political parties, especially after the BDP had asserted its dominant position.

Traditionally the chiefs had wide executive and judicial powers over their tribesmen. But they were not, and were not supposed to be, absolute dictators. A Setswana proverb has it that a chief is a chief only by the will of the tribe, implying that the tribe could if necessary remove the chief. In practice this meant that the chief had to govern with the consent of the Kgotla, the gathering of the tribe. The Kgotla does not have a fixed membership; on some important issues the whole tribe will gather in Kgotla, but the elder, more respected men, especially those with kin relationships with the chief, carry greater weight in the Kgotla than do others. Some argue that the countervailing power which the Kgotla represented against that of the chief was weakened during the colonial period. The British administration, not under-standing the subtleties of this traditional structure, regarded the chief as the sole representative of the tribe and on occasion supported him against the will of his own people. However much truth there is in this assertion it is clear that by the end of the colonial period many of the chiefs, including the great Tshekedi Khama and Bathoen II, were accustomed to behave in a very autocratic way. Stevens (1967: 144) reports for example that Chief Bathoen II of the Bangwaketse had taken land away from Quett Masire, who was later to become the country's Vice-President, and with whom he had long had a political struggle. While Gabatshwane (1966: 28), in a revealing little personal description of his own first meeting with Seretse Khama, remarks:

'contrary to my expectation, Mr. Seretse Khama, gave me his hand, notwithstanding the tendency of the Ngwaketse, Kwena and Ngwato tribal chiefs, never to shake hands with ordinary people'. It was clear to all at the Lobatse conference that in the new dispensation the traditional power of the chiefs would have to give way to some degree to democrative government. Yet the traditional form of government in the tribal areas could not simply be swept away and it was not desirable to do so. After considerable debate, it was decided that the authority of the chiefs should be given consitutional status by creating a separate chamber, the House of Chiefs, which could advise the Government on matters pertaining to traditional customs and institutions.

Elections under the new constitution were held on 1 March 1965. The results were not a foregone conclusion. The BPP organized a vigorous, stirring campaign which, however, tended to be concentrated in the towns. The BDP, in the meantime, had been quietly nurturing the rural constituencies, frequently with the tacit or active support of the local chief. It was here that the election was actually decided. The BDP won a landslide victory, taking 28 out of the 31 seats. The BDP Government immediately began to introduce a series of Bills to the National Assembly, some of which had been foreshadowed in the deliberations of the earlier Legislative Council, in order to restrict the power of the chiefs. Prominent among these were the Chieftainship Bill of 1965 and the Local Government (District Councils) Bill of 1965. The first 'regulated the appointment and removal of Chiefs, Regents, Deputy-Chiefs, Sub-Chiefs and Headmen, provided for the payment of salaries to Chiefs; and defined their powers and functions. Its effect was to strip the Chief of all his legislative powers and most of his executive authority' (Proctor, 1968). The second Bill 'provided for the establishment of popularly elected district councils which would assume many of the Chiefs' powers and exercise authority over all people in the district' (Proctor, 1968). Other legislation such as the Local Government Tax Act, which gave the district councils power to raise local taxes, the Matimela Act which tranferred powers in relation to stray cattle from the chiefs to the district councils, and, a few years later, the Tribal Land Act which established local boards to allocate and administer tribal land, all served further to diminish the power of the chiefs.

The House of Chiefs appears to have accepted the inevitability of such legislation though it attempted to use its advisory powers to modify some of the provisions. But its suggestions were largely ignored by the Government, and the ineffectiveness, arising out of illiteracy coupled with either old-age or inexperience, of many of the chiefs themselves limited their capacity to appeal to the growing educated élite which gave its support to the BDP Government. The era of the great chiefs had passed. Only Chief Bathoen II of the Bangwaketse was a really articulate spokesman and he soon perceived that he would be more effective in the national life by resigning his chieftainship and joining the parliamentary opposition, which he did in the 1969 general election.[5]

However, the BDP's tactics have been more subtle than this cursory analysis might suggest. Each modern, more democratic institution which was brought into existence to replace a chiefly function incorporated the chief as an ex-officio member or even chairman.[6] Chiefs were paid a stipend for the exercise of the traditional functions which they still retained. Thus the chiefs were individually faced with a dilemma. Either they could join the new bodies, which enabled them to continue to act as chief and for which they were paid, but which also constitutionally debarred them from party politics. Or they could resign the chieftainship and go into a political wilderness, unless, like Bathoen II, they could get a parliamentary seat. Most chiefs chose the former course and have now settled down into a somewhat uneasy co-operation with the new order.

Yet, as Gillett (1973) has pointed out, although they are no longer a serious threat to the stability of the Government, the chiefs still exercise considerable local authority and influence which can act as a check on too precipitate action by the Government and can even swing local elections. Thus when Bathoen II stood in the Ngwaketse district as a candidate in the 1969 general election he soundly defeated the BDP candidate who was his old adversary, Quett Masire, the Vice-President. The national status of the Vice-President was clearly less magnetic to the local voters than the local prestige of their ex-chief. The continuing influence and importance of traditional authority, represented by sub-chiefs and headmen, is more pronounced at the village level where district councillors, let alone MPs, have yet to impinge on the consciousness of the ordinary people.[7] Many people still look to their chief for leadership. Nevertheless, the opportunity seems to have been lost in Botswana for a creative role for the traditional institution of chieftainship in the formation of a modern society.

LOCAL GOVERNMENT

The BDP's motive in reducing the power of the chiefs and traditional leaders appears to have been more a desire for genuine local democracy, over which the party and the Government might have some control, than a fear of tribalism which has never been a major threat in Botswana. Furthermore, the educational and cultural background of most chiefs, with the exception of Bathoen II, of the Ngwaketse, and Linchwe of the Kgatla, had left them inadequately prepared to cope with modern institutions or the complexity of economic and social development, which the Government was determined to promote.

But one effect of the policy was that during the 1970s there were no less than three systems of local government operating in parallel. First, traditional authority, exercised through the chiefs and the Kgotla, still retains important judicial functions and some minor executive responsibilities. The Kgotla itself probably remains the most effective and important means of expression of views by a local community. National politicians still use it as a means of addressing the people and of discerning the popular will.

Second, and at the other extreme, the colonial district administration was carried over into independent Botswana. The District Commissioner was, in colonial times, the most important representative of central government in the district with considerable local executive authority. Since independence the powers of this office have steadily declined. Simultaneously, various departments of central government, notably the agricultural and other extension services, have built up their own regional and district organizations which are answerable only to Gaborone and not to the local District Commissioner. Although attempts to re-assert the importance of the DC have been made,[8] we are inclined to believe that the Government has been anxious merely to slow the decline of that office rather than to restore to it the status which it had in colonial times.[9]

Finally, by contrast, the enhanced importance of the elected District Councils has been the most striking political development since independence. Initially, their influence was limited. Although in theory the councils had authority from the beginning to provide a wide range of local services including primary schooling, health care, sanitation, water supplies, and the maintenance of district roads, in practice they originally lacked both the financial and manpower resources to do much more than provide primary education. 'The result is that the district councils still bear the character of local education boards' (Tordoff, 1973), and in 1969 education expenditures accounted for 68 per cent of District Council budgets.[10] The councils, other than those in the towns, were dependent on annual subventions from central government to balance their budgets and so had no prospect of expanding their activities except with the support of the Government.

But a number of events and decisions in the early 1970s began to transform this situation. In 1970 a Presidential Circular established in each district a District Development Committee (DDC). The DDC brought together, under the chairmanship of the District Commissioner, local representatives of government departments and of the District

Council, together with prominent private individuals to plan and co-ordinate development activity in the district.

Scarcely had the new DDCs been established when the Government faced the unprecedented prospect of having surplus funds. How this occurred is taken up in Chapter 4. Suffice to say that with an election on the horizon, it was decided to expend some of the surplus on building rural infrastructure under the Accelerated Rural Development Programme (ARDP) which was launched at the end of 1973. By chance the (largely expatriate) district and council staff necessary to manage the programme at the district level had just been recruited; without them the ARDP would not have been implemented.

These events facilitated a considerable increase in the development activities of the councils. It can be seen from Table 2.1 that their

TABLE 2.1 *District and town council budgets*[1]

		P millions		
		1966/7 [2]	1969/70	1975/6
Recurrent budget				
Expenditure:	Towns	0.32	0.53	2.72
	Districts	0.88	1.64	7.21
	Total	1.20	2.17	9.93
of which education		0.61	1.47	4.70
Revenue: Towns	(Local revenue	0.26	0.52	2.77
	(Govt. grant	0.03	0.04	0.05
Districts	(Local revenue	0.69	1.28	2.16
	(Govt. grant	0.10	0.32	5.05
	Total	1.08	2.17	10.03
Development expenditure		3	3	
Towns	(Own account	n.a.	0.03	0.10
	(From government	0.06	–	0.60
Districts	(Own account	n.a.	0.08	–
	(From government	n.a.	0.01	4.72
Totals			0.12	5.42
As percentage of govt. capital expenditure			2	14

[1] All figures based on estimates not final accounts.
[2] Districts only operated for 6 months of this year, but these figures based on 12 month estimates. As this was the first year of operation for councils, estimates are particularly uncertain and probably understate actual revenue and expenditure.
[3] Information on development activities undertaken by councils at this time is sparse. The tentative figures here probably understate development expenditure.

Sources: MLGL, 1966; MLGL, 1969; MLGL, 1975a; MLGL, 1975b.

recurrent expenditures grew more than eightfold between 1966/7 and 1975/6,[11] while development expenditure increased from virtually nothing to more than P5 million a year. Most of the increased expenditure has been financed by grants from central government.

The creation of elected District Councils has taken the democratic political structure in Botswana one step closer to the people. Councillors are usually men or women of some local influence and prominence, who represent in council the interests of their ward.

Nevertheless, the BDP, unlike say Chama Cha Mapinduzi (CCM), formerly TANU, in Tanzania, is not a mass party with local cells, indeed it scarcely exists between elections.[12] To many people in the villages the District Councils must therefore seem almost as remote as the central Government in Gaborone (Parson, 1977). In addition, councillors and MPs are generally drawn from an élite group, wealthier and better educated than the populace as a whole and frequently with close kin ties with the traditional aristocracy of chiefs and headmen.[13]

ELECTIONS AND POLITICAL PARTIES

Botswana is one of the few countries in Africa which continues to have free multi-party elections on a universal franchise. Since the 1965 election under the self-government constitution, there have been two further national elections, in October 1969 and September 1974. The voting patterns in all three are summarized in Table 2.2. In 1965, as in the two subsequent elections, the BDP emerged with a clear and overwhelming majority. Mainly because Seretse Khama was its leader, the BDP was able to draw more than ninety per cent of the votes cast in the three largest Tswana tribal areas—those of the Ngwato, Kwena, and Ngwaketse. The more radical Botswana People's Party, led by Philip Matante, did much less well than expected and only managed to secure three seats. Two of these were in the north-east where all the land was owned either by white-settler farmers or by the Tati Concession Exploration and Mining Company which had originally acquired ownership as a concession granted in 1882 by Chief Lobengula of the Matabele and subsequently confirmed by Proclamation 2 of 1911. Since then the Tati Company had retained a firm grip on the area, refusing to sell or transfer land to Africans, and, even when it did make sales, it imposed restrictive covenants. In the circumstances it was inevitable that the anti-colonialist policies of the BPP should have strong appeal in that part of the country. The BPP's third seat was in the Kgatla tribal area in the south-east, where a popular local candidate received the influential support of the young Chief Linchwe who was opposed to the BDP. The Botswana Independence Party, led by Motsamai Mpho, failed to win any seats but drew considerable support in the north-west, the home

TABLE 2.2 *Botswana elections*

Party	No of seats won [1]		
	1965	1969	1974
Botswana Democratic Party (BDP)	28	24	27
Botswana Peoples Party (BPP)	3	3	2
Botswana National Front (BNF)[2]	–	3	2
Botswana Independence Party (BIP)	–	1	1
Totals	31	31	32[3]
Percentage of registered electorate voting	74	55	31
Total votes cast	140,789	76,858	64,011
For BDP:	113,168	52,518	49,047
% for BDP:	80	68	77

[1] Excludes the seats of 'specially elected members'.
[2] BNF did not exist in 1965.
[3] One new constituency was created by 1974.

Sources: Winstanley, 1965; RB, 1970c; RB, 1974b.

of a number of non-Tswana tribes, to one of which Mpho belongs.

Accordingly, in 1965, the BDP formed the Government with Seretse Khama as Prime Minister. The BPP took three seats, and Matante as Leader of the Opposition was, quite properly, invited to London to participate in the discussions on an independence constitution in February 1966. However, Matante argued that there should be further internal consultation and another general election before the granting of independence, and when this demand was not met he walked out of the conference, which must then have taken on the appearance of an exclusively BDP affair.

The proposals which were agreed in London did not differ radically from the existing constitution, except in those details which related to full independence rather than self-government. Thus the post of Prime Minister was abolished and executive responsibility was vested in the President, who is also Chairman of Cabinet. The President, although an MP, is not directly elected but each prospective parliamentary candidate has to declare his support for one of the presidential candidates. Thus the one with majority support from the elected MPs becomes the President. This electoral-college system was devised to avoid the potentially divisive situation of a President not being able to command the support of a majority of the National Assembly. Some minor changes were made to the constitutional position of the House of Chiefs: it was more closely linked to the National Assembly and was strengthened by enabling the eight ex-officio members to co-opt three additional members. But it still retained only advisory powers.

The 1969 elections were called, somewhat unexpectedly, six months earlier than was constitutionally required. Negotiations for the Selebi-Phikwe and Orapa mining projects had reached a critical stage, and the President was no doubt anxious to assure the potential investors of the country's political stability. Once again support for the BDP was solid, though the BPP retained its three seats in the north-east and Kgatleng, and this time the BIP won one seat in the north-west. However, a new party also contested this election. The Botswana National Front had been formed to unite opposition within the country, an objective which has yet to be achieved. The impetus behind the BNF came from a small group with more radical views than those in the BDP hierarchy. But its major coup came as a result of attracting the great traditionalist, Chief Bathoen II, into its ranks when he resigned his chieftainship of the Ngwaketse. Bathoen himself stood for Parliament in one of the Ngwaketse constituencies, drew most of the tribe behind him, and was elected together with two other BNF candidates in the same district. The BNF won no other seats though it had a good following in the rapidly growing towns. The BDP was considerably embarrassed by the BNF success, especially as Bathoen had himself defeated Quett Masire, the Vice-President. However, Masire was brought back into the National Assembly by using the constitutional provision which permits the National Assembly to co-opt or 'specially elect' four additional members to its numbers.

Because of its losses in 1969, and because of a feeling that the BNF had since then been gathering further support especially in the towns, the BDP approached the 1974 election somewhat nervously. It prepared its ground more carefully than for the previous election and now had the advantage that some of the fruits of development, especially in the form of budgetary surplus, were beginning to be available. Inducements were given to both the urban and rural electorates. The former received a large increase in the general wage level (see Chapter 7), and the latter benefited from the initiation of the Accelerated Rural Development Programme (ARDP). There is little doubt that both actions enhanced popular support for the BDP. The negotiation for and purchase of land from the Tati Company and the re-development of Francistown, the main population centre in the north-east, which had been progressing for a few years, won it further votes in that part of the country. Campaigning was heavily concentrated in the seats which had been lost in the previous election, particularly in the Ngwaketse and Kgatla tribal areas. As a result Masire regained his seat, though in this election he did not stand in the same constituency as Bathoen, and the BDP won the Mochudi seat from the BPP. But the BPP retained its two seats in the north-east, and Bathoen and Mpho were both returned in their constituencies. In all, the BDP won 27 out of 32 seats, the BPP and the BNF won two each and the BIP one.

A disconcerting feature of this series of election results is the declining proportion of registered voters who actually turned out to vote: the proportion fell from 74 per cent in 1965 to 31 per cent in 1974. Three possible explanations of this trend have been suggested. First, the voter register may have become out of date. Second, there may be a widespread belief that to vote once is sufficient—that political parties, like the chiefs they replaced, do not need the repeated endorsement of the people in order to stay in office. On this hypothesis, declining turnout can be taken as a mark of approval for the Government and its policies. Third, it may be that 'non-voting is a measure of apathy in face of intractable poverty or actual dissatisfaction but without any perception that this may be expressed through the behaviour of voting' (Parson, 1976). At present insufficient research has been done to reach a conclusion on this question, but any explanation implies some misunderstandings of the nature of the new political system on the part of the people of Botswana and that they may not fully appreciate the value of the political system which they possess.

It might appear from the pattern of election results that party politics in Botswana is dominated by tribal or regional loyalties. But this would be too simple an explanation. It is true that where the opposition parties have won seats it has been the result of local personalities or issues swinging the electorate in their favour. But the opposition parties themselves, with the exception of the BIP, are more nationally based than the central government election results would suggest. This is illustrated most readily with reference to the results of District Council elections (Table 2.3). Nevertheless it is clear from that Table that the BDP has dominated the outcome of local government elections as completely as it has those for the National Assembly, especially in 1974. In only two councils—those for Francistown and the North-East District—have the BDP elected members been in a minority, and in both cases the BDP has retained actual control by the use of the power the Government has, under the Local Government Act, to nominate additional members to each council.[14] The existence and use of this power has been resented and somewhat discredits the Government's claim that the councils are democratic bodies. But it is doubtful if the BDP Government would have given so much encouragement to the flourishing of the councils without it.

Given the BDP dominance at both national and local levels it is pertinent to enquire how genuine is democracy in Botswana and how committed is the BDP to its maintenance. Are there any important differences between the situation existing in Botswana and the one-party

TABLE 2.3 *District and town council election results*

District or town	1966				1969					1974				
	BDP	BPP	BIP	Ind	BDP	BPP	BIP	BNF	Ind	BDP	BPP	BIP	BNF	Ind
North-West	7	1	5	—	7	—	6	—	—	9	—	4	—	—
Ghanzi	10	—	—	—	9	—	1	—	—	10	—	—	—	—
Kgalagadi	11	4	—	—	10	—	—	—	1	11	—	—	—	—
North-East	2	1	—	1	2	5	—	—	—	2	5	—	—	—
Central (Ngwato)	31	1	—	—	31	1	—	—	13	32	—	—	—	—
Kgatleng	8	6	—	—	7	6	—	1	—	1	—	—	1	—
Kweneng[1]	17	—	—	—	16	—	—	1	—	21	—	—	1	—
South-East	11	2	—	—	8	3	—	2	—	11	1	—	2	—
Southern (Ngwaketse)	24	—	—	—	13	—	—	11	—	14	—	—	10	—
Gaborone	7	—	—	1	4	—	—	4	—	8	—	—	—	—
Francistown[1]	2	6	—	—	2	6	—	—	—	5	4	—	—	—
Lobatse	6	1	—	1	4	—	—	4	—	7	—	—	1	—
Selebi-Phikwe[2]	—	—	—	—	—	—	—	—	—	6	—	—	—	—

[1] Number of seats increased for 1974 election.
[2] New council for the 1974 election.

Sources: Vengroff, 1977: 88; RB, 1970c; RB, 1974b.

system which has been introduced in other parts of Africa?[15] First, although the opposition is numerically weak its very existence has caused the BDP to cultivate the electorate either on local issues, such as the control of the Tati Company in the north-east, or nationally through, for example, the launching of the ARDP. While these manœuvres might be seen as electioneering it is also possible to regard them as a genuine attempt to satisfy some of the aspirations of the electorate. Second, our own judgement is that both Seretse Khama and Quett Masire are personally deeply committed to the concept of multi-party democracy, though we doubt whether the same can be said for all of their advisers. This judgement is difficult to substantiate by reference to political speeches, not because they have not explicitly asserted this commitment but simply because all politicians are inclined to proclaim their belief in democracy. Perhaps the best evidence for this view is the extraordinary respect for the constitutional rule of law which the country's leaders have always shown. In colonial times the characteristic response of traditional leaders to dissatisfaction with the administration was not to foment discontent but to take legal action. Tshekedi Khama in particular initiated several actions against the administration. Since independence the same attitude has prevailed. The few minor changes to the constitution which have been made have been approached with considerable reluctance and caution, while the constitution itself has rarely been flouted.

However, the daily business of the National Assembly is conducted in a manner closer to the best of the African one-party states than to the Westminster model. The alignment is not so much the government benches against the opposition as Ministers against the backbenchers. Sometimes, indeed, opposition members are seen to support the Government when its own backbenchers are critical. Thus the role of the National Assembly, like that of the traditional Kgotla, is to audit proposals made by those in authority: to approve them and occasionally reject them. The ministers respect this function of the assembly. When it comes to a vote on an issue, again as in the Kgotla tradition, support is unanimous, except for the rare occasion when a government measure is overwhelmingly defeated. This has happened two or three times in recent years,[16] but it is not a call to the Government to resign, rather it is notice given by the National Assembly to the Government to think through an issue again. More commonly, however, such dissatisfaction has led to draft bills being withdrawn before the voting stage.

It is difficult to speculate with any confidence on the future for political parties in Botswana, though we believe that all will be allowed to continue in existence at least so long as Seretse Khama is in power. The BNF now forms the main focus for opposition in the country, though it is not so well organized as the BDP. It is also an uncomfortable alliance between traditionalists, under the leadership of Bathoen, and more radical elements. Its manifesto (BNF, 1974) proposes on the one hand measures such as the abolition of freehold land, more protection and benefits for employed workers, and the nationalization of 'all the essential means of production, communication and distribution', and on the other hand a federal type of government in which the House of Chiefs would be replaced by a House of Nationalists to which the various groups and tribes in the country should send equal numbers of representatives and which would be superordinate to the National Assembly.

Of the two elements from which the BNF derives its support organized labour is likely to become more of a threat to the quiet equanimity of the BDP than the forces of traditionalism. In 1975 there was a major strike which turned into a riot at the Selebi-Phikwe mine, following which the President spoke darkly of 'political subversives' (Khama, 1975) who were trying to wreck Botswana society. More recently, towards the end of 1977, it seemed that the BDP Government was becoming impatient with left-wing criticism emanating especially from the idealist, Patrick Van Rensburg, and from Kenneth Koma, the Prague-educated intellectual leader of the BNF.

As for the BDP itself, it is not easy to define those sections of society from which it derives its support when that support is so widespread. Sillery sums the matter up concisely when he describes the BDP as: 'the party of the countryside, of the farmers, cattle owners, herdsmen, the men of the tribes, who form the great majority of the people of the territory. In the towns the party appeals to the moderates, the professional and middle classes' (Sillery, 1974). Certainly the BDP is the country party, deriving its support from the rural population with whom the party leaders still retain strong links. But the prominent personalities in the party, including both Seretse Khama and Quett Masire, are big cattle farmers. There are increasing conflicts of interest between large cattle farmers and the mass of the rural population (see Chapter 5). Suffice to say here that the interests of the cattle owners are being given political priority. In many ways the BDP is not acting in the interests of the mass of the rural electorate from which it derives its support. Whether and when the BDP will begin to lose that support, or change its policies, is an important political question for the future.

FOREIGN POLICY

When Botswana became an independent nation on 30 September 1966, some observers considered the country to be so economically dependent on South Africa that its political independence was something of a facade, not very different in practice from the status of the homelands within South Africa itself. This pessimism was not shared by the Botswana leaders, who personally believed in the creation and nurturing of a viable, non-racial state despite the shadow of South Africa. They were determined to break with the pattern of recent history and assert the reality of their independence from South Africa.

Botswana immediately set out to overcome international scepticism, which was particularly widespread within Black Africa itself.[17] A diplomatic offensive was mounted. Foreign relations were early established with Zambia and Tanzania, which have been African opinion leaders in the protest against apartheid and the regime of Southern Rhodesia. Botswana joined the United Nations, the Organization of African Unity, and the Commonwealth, and participated in these organizations more actively than is normally expected of such a small nation. In all these forums the President distanced his country politically from South Africa. Addressing the UN General Assembly in September 1969 he summarized Botswana's attitude towards apartheid in these words:

We have made no secret of our detestation of apartheid. Although for obvious reasons we are obliged to interpret strictly the principle of non-interference in the affairs of other sovereign states we have not hidden our views. Our voice has been heard in this Assembly, and in other international forums, in favour of universal self-determination, in support of peaceful solutions to international conflicts throughout the world, and in pleas for a realistic appraisal of what can be achieved by this organisation. Living as we do face to face with the realities of apartheid, we have little sympathy with token demonstrations and empty gestures. Yet we have unequivocally condemned the theory and practice of apartheid and we do deplore its intensification. . . (Khama, 1969b)

The attitude of South Africa itself towards the independence of Botswana, as of Lesotho and Swaziland, has also evolved. Three phases can be distinguished.[18] The first phase covers broadly the first half of the twentieth century, when, as seen in the previous chapter, the three High Commission Territories were considered to be similar to tribal territories within South Africa itself, available to be exploited for their labour, though not yet for their land. The second phase began with the publication of the Tomlinson Commission report in 1956 in which the apartheid policy was first formulated. The three territories were now seen as essential elements in the policy. They could constitute the nuclei of three of the eight proposed tribal bantustans, having the effect of raising the bantustan land allocation from 14 per cent to more than 40 per cent of the total, thereby giving the policy some credibility.

The subsequent doubts which many African countries had about the genuiness of the three territories' independence when it came may well have been caused by the publication of these proposals linking them with the bantustans. Nevertheless, incorporation into South Africa, whether as bantustans or not, was fast becoming unlikely. The tide was running the other way and preparations were soon begun to grant the territories political independence. Thus the third phase of South Africa's attitude began in 1961 when Verwoerd finally acknowledged that the three countries would become independent. From that time on, South Africa's main concern has been that the Botswana, Lesotho, and Swaziland (BLS) should be effective buffer states between itself and the rest of Black Africa, and that the governments which emerged there should be, if not pliant, at least peaceable.[19]

In order to achieve its objective in this third phase South Africa has used both carrot and stick. In the period just before independence there were veiled threats against the emergence of radical anti-South African governments. But as the character of the new governments in the High Commission Territories began to emerge these threats gave way to more conciliatory, if often patronizing, gestures to encourage good relations. After the 1965 election, the ban on Seretse Khama, who had been a prohibited immigrant in South Africa on account of his marriage to a white woman, was lifted. Some political refugees from South Africa, who had been kidnapped in and abducted from Bechuanaland by South African police, were again quietly returned to Bechuanaland. Offers of aid, both capital and technical assistance, were made. These were consistently declined by Botswana, though not by Lesotho and Swaziland where, since independence, South African influence over domestic affairs has been much greater. The most striking conciliatory gesture was the renegotiation in 1969 of the Southern African Customs Union Agreement on terms more favourable to the three BLS countries.[20] Although the new agreement can be considered an equitable one, which goes a long way to compensate the weaker parties for the dominating effect of their economically stronger neighbour, it seems certain that South Africa, after long negotiations, finally accepted the new terms for the essentially political reason that they draw the economies of the four countries more closely together. Nevertheless, the new agreement has endured precisely because all the parties have underplayed its political implications.

On a few occasions the stick has also been brandished by South Africa, sometimes following some particularly critical speech of President Khama. Typically, South African Railways refrigerated waggons would suddenly become unavailable at the Lobatse abattoir, or inexplicable difficulties would be experienced in routing international telephone calls through South Africa (Hermans, 1973). Similarly, when the proposal was announced to build a road between Botswana and Zambia, South Africa disputed whether the two countries actually had a border across the Zambezi river, even though a small ferry service between the two countries was in existence. The political significance of the road— a new transport route through more friendly countries—was obvious. But as with other instances of this kind, once the threat was made it was not pursued. There was an exchange of diplomatic notes on the BotZam road question during 1970, in which the parties simply disagreed with each other, and the matter was let drop. The road was built and the ferry service enlarged. As one of those best able to observe these and similar incidents has commented: 'It would be wrong to imply that the South African Government has taken advantage of Botswana's physical vulnerability to any significant extent' (Hermans, 1973). Rather, South Africa has come to realize the advantages of having an independent neighbour, both stable and peaceable, and has become careful not to upset this situation.

In many respects Botswana's relations with white-ruled Southern Rhodesia after UDI paralleled those with South Africa. Previously, northern Botswana obtained many of its imports from Southern Rhodesia though this trade has never been as critical as that with South Africa. More importantly, the railway, which runs through Botswana from north to south and on which Botswana now depends as much as Zimbabwe itself, was owned and operated by Rhodesia Railways. Imposing full economic sanctions after UDI, which would have implied closing the railway, was therefore impracticable without doing great harm to the domestic economy. Instead, with UN endorsement, only limited sanctions were applied, diverting some trade and banning the transport of oil and arms through Botswana. Southern Rhodesia realized that to retaliate against these partial sanctions would have prompted a complete border closure between the two countries, as happened with Zambia, and thus a stalemate persisted for more than a decade.

Thus Botswana's political relations with its neighbours can be described as a stand-off, characterized by a certain amount of interdependence between Botswana on the one hand and Southern Rhodesia and South Africa on the other, and in which all the parties have had an interest in maintaining the status quo.[21] Although there have been no formal diplomatic relations between Botswana and Southern Rhodesia, and diplomatic representatives have never been exchanged with South Africa, some political contact has obviously been necessary to maintain this precarious stability frequently by resorting to 'telephone diplomacy'. In the meantime, Botswana has, from the moment of independence, exploited the stand-off to diversify its foreign relations away from South Africa. Diplomatic relations were opened with a number of Communist countries—Czechoslovakia soon after independence, later the USSR, and more recently China—much to the discomfort of South Africa. This diplomacy may be contrasted with that of Lesotho or Swaziland, which both flirted with South Africa after independence rather than keeping a clear diplomatic distance. Consequently neither country has achieved the same respect and support, especially within African circles, which Botswana now enjoys.

Of greater importance for Botswana's development has been its broadening relations with Western countries. Initially, and especially while still receiving budgetary support, dependence on Britain, the former protecting power, was second only to that on South Africa and Southern Rhodesia. But British assistance, other than technical assistance, has been declining. The most prominent role is now taken by the Scandinavian countries which have included Botswana in their very selective aid programmes because it appears to be more democratic, efficient, and uncorrupt than almost any other country in Africa and because of its vulnerability in southern Africa.

The single most important diplomatic event since independence arose out of Britain's accession to the European Communities in 1972, and its consequent acceptance of the European Common Agricultural Policy. Effective control over the continued export of Botswana beef to the UK, and over the price paid, moved from London to Brussels. The principle of European agricultural self-sufficiency, which is enshrined in the CAP, has become a major threat to this trade, as it has for a number of other beef-exporting countries such as Kenya, as well as for the sugar-producing countries of the Caribbean. Fortunately, when in 1975 Botswana along with about fifty other small countries became associated with the EEC under the Lome Convention, a framework was created within which it has been possible to negotiate the continued sale of beef on the European market. But the new arrangements have been *ad hoc* and fragile and what was a long-standing free-trade arrangement has now come to be portrayed, notably by European propaganda, as a magnanimous concession by the EEC. Botswana's future will depend, to a considerable extent, on the goodwill of the European countries and their interest in supporting its economic and political development.

SOUTHERN AFRICA: BOTSWANA'S ROLE

Although President Khama made his country's views on apartheid and on the minority regime in Southern Rhodesia clear, it is neither his style nor his inclination to incite violent change. But equally, Botswana has not been among those African nations, such as Malawi and the Ivory Coast, which have at various times advocated 'dialogue' with South Africa. Botswana's position, like that of Zambia and Tanzania, has been that any dialogue should be on the basis of the 1969 Lusaka Manifesto, which, of course, South Africa does not accept.[22] Despite rejecting violence at one extreme and dialogue at the other, the country's leaders have nevertheless hoped that they might be able to influence political change in the region by creating a non-racial society which could become a model for the rest of southern Africa.

A second and much more obvious role has been the acceptance of refugees from throughout southern Africa—including some from Lesotho. The PAC and ANC refugees of the late fifties and early sixties, who in some senses first politicized the Batswana, were followed a few years later by a wave of several thousand apolitical peasant farmers fleeing from Portugese Angola. This group has now been successfully assimilated in the north-west. But it is since 1976 that refugees have flooded through the country as a result both of the disturbances in Soweto and other towns in South Africa, and increasingly of the war in Zimbabwe.[23] Although many of the latter only pass through on the journey to guerrilla training camps in Zambia or Mozambique, a significant minority has remained and could ultimately constitute a threat to the country's stability, not to mention a drain on its resources.

The commitment to non-violent solutions of southern Africa's problems, and the concomitant absence of permanent guerrilla bases in the country, is the single most important concession that Botswana has had to make to secure the continued goodwill of and non-interference by South Africa. This policy of non-violence was not difficult to maintain so long as the country was behind the front-line, while the conflict was waged further north in Angola and Mozambique. Neither the OAU nor the liberation movements could at that time have seriously expected Botswana to become a launching pad for guerrilla incursions into either South Africa or Southern Rhodesia. But the front line has now moved southwards, closer to Botswana, and the country's non-violent stance has become impossible to sustain. After a decade in which there had been no peaceful solution to the problem of Southern Rhodesia, Botswana finally aligned itself, along with the other Front-Line countries with the Patriotic Front, which is committed to taking power in Zimbabwe if necessary by force. The guerrillas themselves have begun to use Botswana as a staging point for raids into Southern Rhodesia, although there are apparently still not permanent guerrilla bases within Botswana itself. Similarly, detachments of the Rhodesian Army have crossed the Botswana border and attacked nearby villages, allegedly, in pursuit of guerrillas. These raids in turn caused Botswana itself to establish its own small army early in 1977. Since then there have been several small engagements between the two forces. Thus has Botswana been drawn into the war.

As Zimbabwe emerges from Southern Rhodesia, Botswana will, for the first time, have the possibility of transport routes to the sea, through Zimbabwe and Mozambique, which do not depend on white-controlled minority regimes. It should therefore be able to sever some of the economic links which now tie it to South Africa. But by then the full force of the southern African liberation movement will have turned onto South Africa itself. The Botswana Government, whatever its own wishes may be, will come under intense, probably irresistible, pressure to provide facilities and bases for these movements. The period of precarious stability, which the country has enjoyed so far, will have come to an end.

CHAPTER 3

ECONOMIC GROWTH AND STRUCTURAL CHANGE

Independence brought immediate and profound political change, but in the economic sphere Botswana faced critical problems in the mid-1960s, and the prospects for rapid progress appeared to be slight. With a per capita income of about P60 per year (then equivalent to about US $80), Botswana was one of the poorest countries in the world. Widespread absolute poverty had become entrenched as a result of five years of serious drought. By 1966, one third of the national herd of cattle had died, and in the same year one fifth of the population were receiving famine relief.

During the years immediately prior to independence a number of economic-survey missions had visited the protectorate to assess aid requirements and development prospects.[1] Each of them concluded that the likelihood of achieving a rapid growth of domestic income was negligible—so much so that the Government would be unable to raise sufficient revenue from local sources to cover even its recurrent expenditures within the foreseeable future. By implication, aid would have to be sought to finance not merely the future investment programme, but also to help cover the basic consumption needs of the society. If this aid was not forthcoming, it seemed that the Government would have to remain a skeletal institution along colonial lines, with a continued emphasis upon regulatory rather than developmental functions.

From the point of view of the new Government, the most important of these survey missions was that of the British Ministry of Overseas Development, which completed its report in November 1965. In that year, almost half of the total recurrent and development expenditure of the protectorate was financed directly by the United Kingdom, and it seemed certain that Botswana would continue to seek the major part of its aid requirements from the same source. Not surprisingly then, the British survey team was mainly concerned with the problem of how to achieve development in a way which would not significantly increase the budget deficit. Mineral deposits of copper, soda-ash, and coal were known to exist. But the survey team believed that the exploitation of these resources could affect economic growth and government revenues only in the long run. It was clear that the Government had insufficient resources to engage in any direct physical investment for mining development, but the report did not seriously consider how the Government might stimulate or benefit from private initiatives in the minerals sector.[2] It was thought that economic growth would have to be based upon agricultural development, and the strategy envisaged by the British team concentrated upon measures to rebuild the national herd of cattle and regulate offtake from it, together with stronger measures in support of arable production. There was a firm emphasis in the report upon the need for stringent economic and financial management, reflecting a pessimistic view of the prospects for economic growth. As a result, its budgetary projections painted a depressing picture. The mere maintenance of public services at pre-independence levels would involve only a small narrowing of the recurrent deficit over a ten year period—from P4.7 million in 1966/7 to P3.8 million in 1975/6, in constant prices. The addition of even a modest development programme was expected to increase the recurrent deficit to P6 million by 1970/1 (RB, 1966b: 101, 108).

This early pessimism has since been shown to be unfounded. The Botswana Government's revenue from domestic sources increased from P4.5 million in 1965/6 to P28.1 million in 1972/3, in which year the recurrent budget was balanced. Over the same period public-development expenditures increased sixfold, from P5 million to almost P30 million, of which more than 10 per cent were financed from domestic resources in 1972/3.[3] Domestic production measured in constant prices almost quadrupled within the first seven years of independence, allowing income per capita to triple over the same period. In real terms, the rate of economic growth appears to have been in excess of 15 per cent per year between 1966 and 1973, though growth was slower than this in the early years and faster in the later ones.

Botswana has obviously benefited from a remarkable change in her fortunes. History appears to have rebutted the sceptics—not merely in the narrow sense of the Government being able to balance a much expanded recurrent budget earlier than most observers had imagined would be possible but, more important, that a major increase in production and in productive potential has occurred. This chapter examines how this change has been achieved and provides a macro-economic analysis of its impact on the nation.

ECONOMIC GROWTH AS A MEASURE OF PROGRESS

In almost all countries economic growth is necessary if welfare gains for the majority of the population are to be made. This was particularly obvious in Botswana in the mid-1960s, where foreign aid was required to provide famine relief to a large proportion of the inhabitants and to support government services. The overwhelming need was to create and sustain a domestic-production capability to support these basic consumption needs: growth was vital if development was to proceed. Nevertheless, as discussed in the Introduction, the ways in which the gains from growth were distributed is a critical question: in countries where most of the income accrues to a small minority of the population, further increases in total income may be irrelevant to the welfare of most of the people, unless accompanied by appropriate re-distributive measures.

Equally important are the ways in which the increases in income are generated—for example, whether from output increases in high-employment sectors, such as agriculture, from high-income enclave developments, from terms-of-trade gains, or from the sale of assets such as minerals. These various vehicles for growth are significant in that they may each have different implications for future performance: they may imply different savings ratios, investment and employment opportunities, types of dependence upon foreign interests, and vulnerabilities to external events.

In addition, structural change is usually an accompaniment of economic growth. This may involve a real diversification of production and a reduction of dependence upon a small number of export commodities. Or it may result from an expansion of services or of other sectors which are not directly productive, financed perhaps from an expansion of primary exports. Thus, economic growth alone cannot be accepted as an unambiguous indicator of progress. Its components must be analysed in order to judge whether real development has occurred.

PRODUCTION ACCOUNTS IN BOTSWANA

It is well known that the accurate estimation of national income and its rate of growth in Third World countries is fraught with difficulties. These tend to be of two main kinds: first, those arising from the generally incomplete registration of business establishments—particularly those in rural areas—and the consequent practical difficulty of designing an adequate census frame; second, the valuation of the output of the majority of the economically active population, including most self-employed agricultural workers and many of the workers in the formal sector, is theoretically difficult because a large part of their production is not marketed. As a result, the official production data for many poor countries include highly arbitrary estimates which undermine the reliability of both time-series and inter-country comparisons.

Until very recently, Botswana has been even worse off than most other countries in this regard. Apart from a rough estimate made for the calendar year 1955 (Erasmus, 1963), production estimates prior to 1965 are not available. Since then, national accounts have been prepared for eight of the first eleven years of independence, and these are shown in Table 3.1. In spite of several revisions of data, the estimates for the early years are still very unreliable, and part of the growth indicated over the 1960s arises purely from an increase in the statistical coverage of the production surveys.

An equally important problem for the interpretation of Botswana's production data arises from the lack of estimates in constant prices. Though an attempt was made in 1973 to construct indices for sectoral price changes over the previous three years (CSO, 1973: Ch. 14), the available data were very unreliable, and it is doubtful that the effort was worth-while. For this reason, subsequent national-accounts publications either reverted to current price series, or used a very rough and ready approach, deflating the total GDP estimates on the basis of an aggregate cost-of-living index based upon a combination of South African and Botswana data. Given that the original current price estimates, at least until 1970, are subject to considerable margins of error, and that price information was not collected on a scientific basis in Botswana until about that date (and then only for consumer items), this is the best that can be done at present. But it does mean that constant price estimates of sectoral contributions to value-added cannot be produced.

Nevertheless, production increases in Botswana since independence have been so large that the above problems are not significant enough to invalidate an analysis of the major economic changes that have occurred. A general awareness of the weakness of the data is sufficient and attention will be drawn to more specific problems where this is necessary.

THE OVERALL RATE OF GROWTH

The data presented in Table 3.1 show that Botswana's economic growth has been fast and accelerating for most of the decade. Growth rates in real terms increased from around 7 per cent per year at independence[4] to 15 per cent at the end of the 1960s. But for the five years 1968/9 to 1973/4 rates of growth in excess of 20 per cent per year in real terms were sustained, before giving way to more variable progress later. The real value of domestic production doubled between 1965 and 1970, and it had almost doubled again by 1973/4.

1965–1968/9

The years between 1965 and 1968/9 were dominated by rapid output increases in agriculture owing to an improvement in the weather cycle, and by the growth of the government sector. For the rural areas, this

TABLE 3.1   *Industrial Origin of the GDP, current market prices (P millions) and aggregate real growth estimates (percentages), 1965–1976/7*[1]

Industrial sector	1965	1966	1967/8	1968/9	1971/2	1973/4	1974/5	1975/6	1976/7[2]
1. Agriculture, forestry, hunting, fishing	11.1	14.5	18.3	23.2	34.2	69.2	61.2	64.2	70.8
2. Mining, quarrying & prospecting	0.2	0.0	0.7	0.2	11.2	15.9	15.2	33.9	43.3
3. Manufacturing	3.8	2.9	3.6	2.8	5.1	10.1	15.5	20.9	21.0
4. Water & electricity	0.2	0.3	0.3	0.3	1.3	3.3	6.9	11.1	10.9
5. Building & construction	2.1	2.1	2.0	1.9	10.0	21.1	21.2	20.3	17.5
6. Wholesale & retail trade, restaurants, & hotels	6.2	6.8	5.0	5.1	17.5	35.1	43.0	53.9	57.9
7. Transport, storage, communications	2.7	3.0	2.4	3.4	3.8	5.3	5.5	7.6	1.7
8. Banking, insurance, real estate, ownership of dwellings, & business services	2.1	2.4	2.9	3.5	5.3	13.2	14.2	17.8	23.4
9. General government	} 4.5	} 4.9	7.7	9.5	11.9	18.2	24.9	36.1	47.3
Other services			1.0	1.3	3.5	6.8	8.8	13.1	12.1
10. Errors & omissions	–	–	–	–	–	-0.7	-3.3	-2.7	-6.8
GDP at current market prices	32.9	36.9	43.9	51.2	103.8	197.5	213.1	276.2	299.2
GDP at constant 1974/5 prices	59.0	63.0	73.0	84.0	148.0	227.0	213.0	245.0	235.0
Average annual rate of growth (%)		6.8	10.3	15.1	20.8	23.8	-6.2	15.0	-4.0

[1] Data for 1965 and 1966 refer to calender years. All other data are for the period July to June of the years shown.
[2] Preliminary figures.

Sources: CSO, 1976d: Tables 0.2.c and 0.2.5; CSO, 1978: Table III.

was a time of recovery and restocking after the dreadful droughts of the early 1960s. These had caused many farmers to increase their slaughter in order to offset the losses from mortality and crop failures. Thus the throughput of cattle at the Botswana Meat Commission (BMC) increased by 80 per cent to 140,000 head between 1960 and 1965. However, as is commonly found elsewhere in southern and East Africa, farmers in Botswana allow the size of their herds to build up during years of abundant rainfall, and the annual slaughter fell back again to about 100,000 head by 1968. Accordingly whilst agriculture made rapid progress, mainly as a result of the growth of the cattle herd, in the manufacturing sector—which is dominated by the operations of the BMC—output was unstable over this period owing to the variable rates of slaughter.

These were also years of rapid expansion in the public sector. The move from Mafeking to Gaborone in 1966 and the establishment of the new capital town and of new government departments required an early increase in government employment. In addition, the administration of a much expanded development programme, made possible by the large amount of aid negotiated in the late 1960s,[5] necessitated a considerable increase in the government establishment. As a result of these pressures, employment in the central government increased by 70 per cent between 1964 and 1969. In other sectors, the slight downswing in construction, transport, and trade after 1966 resulted from the completion of most of the construction activity at Gaborone in 1966/7. At this stage the mining sector was insignificant.

Thus, during the first three years of the independence period there was a fairly healthy increase in total output. But this was almost entirely due to factors that were products of chance. First, the ending of the drought in 1966/7 allowed some recovery in the national cattle herd. Second, greatly enhanced aid flows—including budgetary support from Britain—sustained a big increase in government employment. In the absence of these two factors, the GDP would have remained stagnant at this time.

1968/9-1973/4

There was a sharp change to unprecedentedly high rates of economic growth between 1968/9 and 1973/4. During this period the two mines and townships at Orapa and Selebi-Phikwe were completed and gross fixed investment—excluding changes in cattle and other stocks—increased to more than half of the value of GDP. As a result, value-added from the construction industry rose tenfold over the five years and performance in the mining sector was transformed. Net outputs of less than P1 million from small amounts of asbestos and manganese before

1968/9 were increased to P16 million, mainly from diamonds, in 1973/4.

Succeeding years of good rainfall sustained the agricultural progress. With the growth of the cattle herd and the lower variability of income from crops offtake rates varied around 7 per cent of the herd. This allowed a steady increase in the number of cattle slaughtered each year between 1968 and 1973.[6] Incomes were also supplemented, by a rapid improvement in international beef prices. These developments caused the value of meat production by BMC to double between 1971/2 and 1973/4, and explain about three-quarters of the growth of the manufacturing sector between these two years.[7]

Income from cattle sales accounts for over half of the increase in the gross output of agriculture over this period. Arable production received additional stimulus from the exceptionally abundant rainfall, 74 per cent higher than the long-term seasonal norm, during the 1973/4 agricultural season. There was a bumper harvest, and crop production (sales plus own consumption) probably more than doubled in that year, to more than P13 million.[8] Most of this increase accrued to tribal farmers, and less than half of the total was marketed in that year—the remainder being held for future home consumption. Much of the remaining growth of the agricultural sector, however, is accounted for by the larger number and value of live cattle held by farmers. In most years since independence, stock increases have represented about one-fifth of total agricultural output. There is a danger, then, of overstating —or misrepresenting—the agricultural growth that has occurred. Although it is correct to value cattle stocks at world-market prices for the purposes of national accounts, in the event of another drought many of these cattle might die before being sent to slaughter, and their value would not be realized. Part of the recent agricultural recovery, therefore, is still only potential output, much of which would be lost with a change in the weather cycle.

The government sector, too, benefited during this period from the large inflow of foreign capital to finance the infrastructure for minerals development. Owing to the new Customs Union revenue formula, which had been renegotiated in 1969,[9] almost one-fifth of the value of all imports came back to the Government as customs revenue two years later.[10] The enhanced revenues allowed a faster growth in recurrent expenditures, which led to the large increase in value-added of the Government, shown in Table 3.1—a reflection both of a sustained growth in government employment and a generous revision of public-sector salaries in 1974.[11]

1973/4-1976/7

Such rapid growth could not continue for long. But the severity of the drop in performance the following year exceeded expectations. Again, this was caused by a combination of factors affecting different economic sectors. The rains proved to be only slightly less exceptional than those of the previous year.[12] The pasture continued to improve and offtake remained at the high levels of the previous two years. The output of beef thus increased from P34 million to P43 million in spite of a slight drop in producer prices in 1975. Arable production, however, was cut back sharply. The output of freehold farmers was maintained. But on the tribal lands, farmers reduced their planting, apparently because of having sufficient stocks from the previous season to meet their own consumption needs. Consequently, value-added in the agricultural sector as a whole fell by about 12 per cent, measured in current prices—which was a fall of about one-fifth in real terms.

There were additional problems in the mining sector. Although diamond output moved slightly ahead of its 1973/4 level, the copper-nickel mine sustained heavy losses because of a series of technical difficulties in the mining process. As a result, the production of copper-nickel matte fell seriously behind schedule, the mine was operating at much less than full capacity, and some expensive changes to the plant were required. This led to a fall in the net output in mining of five per cent in current prices, and necessitated considerable foreign borrowing.

The final factor was that the level of investment, particularly that undertaken by the Government, fell after the completion of the mine and town at Selebi-Phikwe. Thus the increase in the output of the construction industry was not sustained. In 1974/5 value-added from construction was only fractionally higher than the level of the previous year, which represented a fall in real terms. Although good progress was made in other sectors, with output in trade and manufacturing increasing by about 30 per cent in current prices, this was nevertheless insufficient to compensate for these problems. As a result, GDP fell by an estimated 6 per cent in real terms during 1974/5.

Real growth in GDP began again in 1975/6. The dominant influence in this year was the copper-nickel mine which finally began to produce on a significant scale. Diamond production also increased and the output of the mining sector as a whole almost tripled—rising from P13 million to P34 million between 1974/5 and 1975/6. In other sectors, growth was fairly evenly spread. This general recovery, however, was not sustained through 1977. Investment fell back in that year, and the output of the construction industry declined to the levels of the early 1970s. Severe losses on the Botswana section of Rhodesia Railways badly hit the transport sector, and an outbreak of foot-and-mouth disease probably caused agricultural output to remain depressed through 1977/8. Overall, growth rates in the mid-1970s were much lower than those of the boom period at the beginning of the decade.

National income, which takes account of remittances to and from other countries, was not so strongly affected by these changes. In recent years, substantial sums have been earned in South Africa by migrant labourers from Botswana. Wages in the South African mining sector increased sixfold between 1969 and 1976, and the number of recruits from Botswana increased by about one-third over the same period.[13] As a result, factor payments from abroad have been strongly positive. For example, in 1974/5 remittances from migrant workers in South Africa more than compensated for the fall in crop production in that year. Moreover, 85 per cent of the equity capital of the copper-nickel mine is owned by foreigners, and its losses mainly fell on their shoulders. Thus, whereas GDP fell back in 1974/5, national income improved by about one or two per cent in real terms.

Nevertheless, the fragility of this recent growth pattern is very marked. The recurrence of drought, political changes in South Africa, and fluctuations in international commodity markets—none of which are unlikely—could have disastrous effects upon incomes and production in Botswana. Thus, there is an important question as to whether the structure of domestic output is changing in a way which in future will provide sufficient security, or production alternatives, should any or all of these events occur.

STRUCTURAL CHANGES

Tables 3.2 and 3.3 show the changing composition of output over the period, together with the investment pattern that has created it. The lack of GDP series in constant prices somewhat hampers these comparisons unless the inflation over the period affected all sectors equally. In fact, there have been relative price movements between the different sectors, and because of this, the current prices series somewhat overstate the contributions of agriculture, manufacturing, and trade to the real structural change of the period, and similarly underestimate those of other sectors.

It is clear from Table 3.2 that the agricultural sector has had a very significant role in the growth of total output, even excepting the effects of price changes—over the decade the national herd more than doubled, and the annual slaughter increased by over 50 per cent.[14] Fully 21 per cent of the increase in total domestic output came from agriculture compared with only 16 per cent from mining.[15] These facts have often been overlooked by observers of Botswana's development, who tended to put exclusive emphasis upon mining as the leading sector of the

TABLE 3.2 *Percentage contribution of different economic sectors to the increase in value-added at current market prices 1965–1976/7*

Agriculture: Crop production, own consumption, and sales	16.5	
Increase in the cattle herd	5.3	
Mining	15.8	
Primary activities		37.6
Manufacturing & Utilities	10.2	
Construction & Transport	5.3	
Secondary activities		15.5
Trade and hotels: Net of indirect taxes[1]	9.2	
Indirect taxes[1]	9.8	
Government	16.0	
Other services[2]	11.9	
Tertiary activities		46.9
	100.0	100.0

[1] Customs, excise, and sales duties, collected by South Africa, are transferred to the Government in a lump sum. National Accounts allocate all these to the trade sector, which gives a false picture of the size of its contribution to the GDP (see footnote 10).

[2] Includes financial, community, and business services.

Source: calculated from CSO, 1978: Tables II and III.

economy and to underplay the agricultural recovery which occurred.

However, other criteria, apart from the direct contribution to increased production, can be used to distinguish a leading sector.[16] The first of these concerns the extent to which the growth of a sector has occurred autonomously, rather than being derivative of growth elsewhere in the economy; the second would focus upon the degree to which the growth of one sector has stimulated the growth of other industries or sectors.

Applying the first of these, it is clear that both the mining and the agricultural sectors have grown autonomously. Both are based on the exploitation of natural resources, though in the case of agriculture these are renewable resources—grazing and water—provided good husbandry is practised. However, there is also another important difference. The type of agricultural growth which has occurred, being based upon good fortune with the weather and with the prices of beef rather than upon changes in technology, rural skills, or agricultural policy, implies that the output of this sector is highly vulnerable. The recent gains could be reversed at short notice and they are less significant for the long-run growth of the economy than the extraction of minerals, which can be expected to continue for a long time.

The importance of mining as a leading sector emerges even more clearly when the final criterion is applied. During the early 1970s minerals development provided a major stimulus to other sectors—with

TABLE 3.3 Sectoral allocation of investments and shares in GDP at current prices, 1965–1976/7[1]
Percentages

	Shares of gross capital formation, 1965–1976/7[2]			Shares of GDP 1965–1976/7			
	1965–1968/9	1971/2–1976/7	1965–1976/7	1965	1968/9	1971/2	1976/7
Agriculture, forestry, hunting, fishing[3]	6.8	14.7	14.0	33.8	45.3	33.0	23.1
Mining, quarrying, & prospecting	6.3	23.3	22.0	0.6	0.4	10.8	14.2
Manufacturing	2.8	4.0	3.9	11.6	5.5	4.9	6.9
Water & electricity	0.3	9.1	8.4	0.6	0.6	1.3	3.6
Building & Construction	0.8	5.0	4.6	6.4	3.7	9.7	5.7
Wholesale & retail trade, restaurants, & hotels	5.3	9.1	8.8	18.9	10.0	16.9	18.9
Transport, storage, & communications	5.5	2.4	2.6	8.2	6.6	3.7	0.6
Banking, insurance, real estate, ownership of dwellings, & business services	14.6	6.0	6.6	6.4	6.8	5.1	7.6
General government	48.9	24.0	26.0	} 13.7	18.6	11.5	15.5
Other services	0.5	2.5	2.3		2.5	3.4	3.9
Unallocated	8.3	–	0.7	–	–	–	–
	100.0	100.0	100.0	100.0	100.0	100.0	100.0

[1] Percentages may not add to 100.0 owing to rounding off.

[2] These averages are based upon the available national accounts data which cover only nine of the twelve years and hence are not strictly accurate. However, the broad picture of the sectoral allocation of investments would remain unchanged by the addition of the missing years. Possibly slightly more investment has gone to the mining sector and less to Government and agriculture over the period than the table suggests.

[3] Over nine-tenths of gross capital formation in agriculture since 1965 has been the growth of the cattle herd. Thus, the amount of *real* investment resources devoted to agriculture is considerably less than the figures in the first three columns might suggest.

Sources: calculated from data in CSO, 1978: Table IV, and from Table 3.1.

the striking exception of manufacturing—by creating a demand for their output. The capital inflows to Botswana for mining and associated infrastructure investment massively increased the output of the construction and utilities industries after 1968/9. Subsequently, the sector has stimulated services, including the government sector, though there were important independent consequences of the phasing and magnitude of government expenditures, which are analysed in the next chapter.[17]

For these reasons, although mining output was still only a comparatively small contributor to the total value of domestic production in 1975/6, the developments in this sector can be considered to have led the economy since the late 1960s. It can be seen from Table 3.3 that the most significant structural changes over the period to 1976/7 were a decrease in the shares of agriculture and manufacturing in GDP and a concomitant increase in the share of the mining sector. On the other hand, the major output increases from minerals *per se* were yet to come, and it is likely that this sector will contribute about one quarter of GDP by 1980/1, with a real value of up to six times its level of 1974/5. But the mining sector is highly capital-intensive, and is unlikely to provide jobs directly for more than 6 to 8 per cent of the active labour force and still has only very weak links with the manufacturing sector. The economic and social impact of mining will therefore largely depend upon whether the Government uses its share of the surplus generated by mining to create self-sustaining livelihoods for large numbers of people, especially in the smaller and poorer villages. The potential benefits for the rural people are great, but they will not be realized if most of these resources are spent upon the enhanced provision of urban services and higher remuneration for the wage- and salary-earning élite.

THE SUPPLY AND ALLOCATION OF RESOURCES

It is important to understand the main sources of the resources available to Botswana and the uses to which they were put. The extent of dependence of the economy upon external resources and the question as to whether this dependence is increasing or decreasing can be examined as part of this analysis. The relevant data are provided in Table 3.4. The analysis begins by considering investment because of its importance in determining the growth of the economy. It is also convenient to link this discussion with an analysis of the trade balance, since the movement of imports has been strongly determined by variations in the investment ratio.

TABLE 3.4 *Supply and use of resources, 1965–1976/7, at current prices*
P millions

	1965	1966	1967/8	1968/9	1971/2	1973/4	1974/5	1975/6	1976/7
Resources									
GDP at factor cost	30.8	34.9	41.3	49.1	92.4	182.1	194.6	252.9	271.3
Indirect taxes (net)	2.0	1.9	2.6	2.1	11.2	15.4	18.5	23.3	27.9
GDP at market prices	32.8	36.8	43.9	51.2	103.6	197.5	213.1	276.2	299.2
Exports	10.4	10.8	10.2	11.7	39.8	76.4	93.8	135.2	155.8
Imports	16.6	18.8	27.8	32.0	65.7	116.7	142.3	175.0	207.4
Net imports	6.2	8.0	17.6	20.3	25.9	40.3	48.5	39.8	51.6
Total resources available	39.0	44.8	61.5	71.5	129.5	237.8	261.6	316.0	350.8
Allocation									
Gross fixed investment	7.2	8.1	9.9	9.9	53.1	77.5	56.8	79.1	77.1
Changes in stocks[1]	-5.2	-1.4	2.1	7.3	1.3	26.0	44.8	35.1	18.1
Public consumption	7.9	9.3	11.6	11.3	16.0	28.3	39.2	50.6	70.5
Private consumption	29.1	28.8	37.9	43.0	59.1	107.1	125.3	150.0	185.1
Errors & omissions	–	–	–	–	–	-1.1	-4.5	1.2	–
Total expenditures	39.0	44.8	61.5	71.5	129.5	237.8	261.6	316.0	350.8

Shares in GDP at market prices (%)

Gross fixed investment	22.0	22.0	22.6	19.3	51.3	39.2	26.7	28.6	25.8
Gross investment[2]	6.1	18.2	27.3	33.6	52.5	52.4	47.7	41.3	31.8
Public consumption	24.1	25.3	26.4	22.1	15.4	14.3	18.4	18.3	23.6
Private consumption	88.7	78.3	86.3	84.0	57.0	54.2	58.8	54.3	61.9
Net imports	18.9	21.7	40.1	39.6	25.0	20.4	22.8	14.4	17.2
Domestic savings[3]	−12.8	−3.5	−12.8	−6.1	27.5	32.0	24.9	26.9	14.6
Indirect taxes	6.1	5.2	5.9	4.1	10.8	7.8	8.7	8.4	9.3
Imports	50.6	51.1	63.3	62.5	63.4	59.1	66.8	63.4	69.3
Exports	31.7	29.3	23.2	22.9	38.4	38.7	44.0	49.0	52.1

[1] Including increases or decreases in the cattle herd.

[2] Fixed investment plus changes in stocks.

[3] The share of domestic savings equals the share of investment minus net imports.

Sources: computed from data in CSO, 1976d: Table 0.2b, and in CSO, 1978: Table II.

Investment and the balance of trade

It is clear from Table 3.4 that Botswana has maintained a consistently high investment ratio since independence: fixed investment has in almost all years been greater than 20 per cent of domestic production, and gross investment, which includes changes in cattle and other stocks, has been considerably greater than this since 1967/8. The recorded peak for the fixed investment ratio came in 1971/2, when over half of the GDP was invested. Though data are not available, it is possible that the ratio moved even higher than this in 1972/3, when construction of the copper-nickel mining complex was at its height. In the following years this remarkably high investment ratio was not sustained, and, although the value of fixed investment continued to increase until 1973/4 as a result of the tail-end of urban construction at Selebi-Phikwe together with large investments in power and water-supplies, it fell significantly both as a proportion of GDP and in absolute terms in 1974/5.

Throughout most of the decade there has been a very close association between the movement of the GDP and that of imports and fixed investment. Botswana has no domestic capital-goods-producing industries of any size; consequently the sharp increase in investment spending between 1968/9 and 1973/4 was largely responsible for the increase in imports over the same period. The years of very high investment ratios stretched Botswana's implementation capacity and abilities to mobilize the necessary resources to their limits. Within the country this was a period of relative austerity. Public-sector salaries remained relatively unchanged until 1974, and an incomes policy was introduced to limit private-sector wage increases. Between 1968/9 and 1971/2 consumption increased only slightly in real terms, in spite of rapid employment increases. Accordingly both public and private consumption fell markedly as a proportion of GDP. After 1973/4, however, the belts of the urban élite were loosened: a very generous public-sector salaries review was introduced, which was passed on to other parts of the formal sector during 1974. This, together with the increased wages paid by the South African mines, brought a considerable increase in consumption, and the savings ratio fell back from a peak of 32 per cent to 26 per cent of GDP, and was reduced even further to less than 15 per cent by 1976/7. Meanwhile, the import bill continued to increase in spite of a fall in the level of investment. This means that there was a considerable shift in the composition of imports from capital to consumption goods after 1973/4.

The rise in the share of gross investment in GDP was not initially matched by a similar rise in the share of exports. Consequently, since most capital goods have to be imported the gap between savings and investment became substantial.[18] The deficit in the balance of trade rose to 40 per cent of GDP in the late 1960s, since when it has fallen back steadily to about 17 per cent in 1976/7 (Table 3.4).

As Botswana was part of the Rand monetary area at the time, the balance-of-payments implications of the trade deficit was not an explicit policy concern. But, in reality, the deficit was financed in much the same way as it would have been even without the use of the South African currency. The rapid rise in Botswana's import requirements from 1968/9 onwards was caused mainly by the construction of the two mines and towns at Orapa and Selebi-Phikwe. The purchase of the imports needed for these projects was financed by foreign aid and by private foreign investment—though mainly by the latter. Thus Botswana's own reserves would have been unaffected by the growing trade deficit since it was financed by inflows of long-term capital.

Future large projects, such as the new diamond mine at Jwaneng for which a Eurodollar loan was raised in 1978, will continue to be financed in the same way. But, with the departure of Botswana from the Rand monetary area in 1976 and the introduction of a domestic currency, the country now has to manage its own foreign-exchange flows. In general, in a situation of world inflation where loans are available at very low or even negative real interest rates, it makes sense to borrow abroad provided that the project concerned is likely to help the future balance of payments. But the costs of being wrong could be considerable. The point is not necessarily to minimize overseas funding, but rather to ensure that the terms on which investors come to the country are advantageous to Botswana and that those on which loans are secured are such as to involve minimal risks. The Government seems to be well aware of these dangers (RB, 1978b).

Over the decade, although exports did not keep pace with the country's growing import requirements, the foundation for much enhanced export earnings was laid. Until 1968 beef products accounted for more than 90 per cent of the country's exports, in the form of carcass meat and other products derived from livestock (Table 3.5). Since then, this extreme dependence upon one export commodity has been removed, and diamonds and copper-nickel now provide a substantial part of export receipts. By 1977 these products generated 30 per cent and 26 per cent respectively of export earnings—minerals had now replaced beef as the major earner of foreign exchange. With the subsequent rise in diamond prices and the expansion of production, the value of diamond exports as a proportion of the total is likely to have risen even further.

Although the country's dependence upon a limited range of export

TABLE 3.5 *Botswana's trade flows, 1964-1977*
P millions

	EXPORTS					IMPORTS[1]	
	Meat & Animal Products	Diamonds	Copper-nickel	Other	Total Exports	Total Imports	Trade Deficit
1964	7.8	–	–	0.6	8.4	14.5	6.1
1965	9.6	–	–	0.5	10.1	16.6	6.5
1966	10.4	–	–	0.3	10.7	18.8	8.1
1967	9.0	–	–	0.2	9.2	22.4	13.2
1968	7.0	–	–	0.5	7.5	23.2	15.7
1969	10.2	0.2	–	2.7	13.1	34.3	21.2
1970	n.a.	n.a.	–	n.a.	20.0	44.8	24.8
1971	17.0	11.7	–	2.3	31.0	60.8	29.8
1972	19.5	19.5	–	5.8	44.8	84.0	39.2
1973	32.5	20.0	–	6.5	59.0	111.7	52.7
1974	33.6	30.1	8.3	9.7	81.7	121.5	39.8
1975	38.0	32.1	22.0	13.0	105.1	157.2	52.1
1976	46.0	37.0	52.0	18.0	153.0	181.0	28.0
1977	48.0	47.0	40.0	18.0	153.0	227.0	74.0

[1] Import statistics are unadjusted for coverage and timing, and are inclusive of duties. These adjustments would give a trade deficit less than that shown in the above table for most years.

Sources: data on trade flows are unreliable in Botswana, particularly for the years before 1972. Moreover, the published statistics conflict in different sources. The data are from the following sources:

Exports: 1964–8 Dini *et al.*, 1970: 163; 1969 CSO, 1970a: Table 30; 1970–1 CSO, 1975: Table 37, and RB, 1973a: 24; 1972–5 CSO, 1976g: Table 7b; 1976–7 BB, 1978.

Imports: 1964–5 Dini, *et al.*, 1970: 163; 1966–75 RB, 1977a: 8; 1976–7 BB, 1978.

products has been somewhat reduced by the growth of minerals exports, the overall importance of foreign trade has considerably increased. It can be seen from Table 3.4 that export revenues rose from about one-third to over a half of GDP between 1965 and 1976/7, and that the share of imports increased from about one half to almost three-quarters of the value of domestic production over the same period. Thus the strong external orientation of the economy has become even more marked. The pattern of development has been dominated by the enhanced production of raw materials for export, and the internal linkages of this export sector have been very small.

Most imports have traditionally been purchased from South Africa. Although the Botswana Government is strongly opposed to the domestic policies of the South African Government, that country–largely because of the customs agreement–remains the cheapest available source for almost all Botswana's capital and consumer goods, and over

four-fifths of the country's imports are purchased from that market
(Table 3.6).

TABLE 3.6   *The direction of trade*
                       Percentages

IMPORTS

Year	South Africa	Other Africa[1]	UK	Other Europe	USA	Other	Total
1966	67.0	25.0	8.0	–	–	–	100.0
1976	81.0	12.0	2.0	2.0	2.0	1.0	100.0

EXPORTS[2]

Year	South Africa	Other Africa[1]	UK	Other Europe	USA	Other	Total
1974	38.0	4.0	43.0	3.0	11.0	1.0	100.0
1976	15.0	8.0	41.0	1.0	34.0	1.0	100.0

[1] Mainly Southern Rhodesia.
[2] Data for years prior to 1974 are not available.

Sources: RB, 1968b: 6 and data provided by the Ministry of Finance and
Development Planning.

There are obvious costs involved in Botswana having such an extreme import-dependence upon a country with which she is so anti-
pathetic. But Botswana's geographical position, together with the
existence of sanctions against Southern Rhodesia, have meant that no
alternative trade strategy could have been viable over the last few years.
Political changes, however, will alter the balance of costs and benefits
of a continued exclusive dependence upon South Africa, and the
introduction of majority rule in Zimbabwe will justify some restructuring of trade links with surrounding countries. This is desirable, not
merely as a means of developing new political alliances with countries
further north, but also as a way of reducing the considerable economic
power presently wielded over Botswana by her wealthy neighbour.

The markets for Botswana's exports have already changed. Prior
to 1970 a large part of the country's total exports, which mainly
comprised beef and animal products, were sold in South Africa. Since
that date there has been a significant shift away from the South African
market. Most beef exports are now sent to Britain; diamonds are
marketed in London, and copper-nickel matte is refined in the USA
and subsequently sold in Germany. Thus, the diversification of products
for export has brought a similar widening of market outlets: less than
one-sixth of Botswana's exports are now brought by South Africa,
compared with more than one-half in the mid-1960s.

From the point of view of trade links, therefore, Botswana's circumstances are similar to many other of the world's small and poor countries. Its economy is extremely vulnerable to changes in international prices, to the introduction of trade quotas (particularly by the EEC), and to shifts in the structure of international demand and technology. The discovery of copper, nickel, and diamonds has allowed an extension of Botswana's markets—away from South Africa and towards Europe and North America. But the country's dependence upon South Africa for almost all imports has been confirmed and strengthened over the decade.

Savings

One of the most remarkable features of the Botswana economy over the first decade of independence is the changing pattern of savings behaviour. Savings are important in that in most economies they provide a major source of investible resources which, in their absence, have to be provided from foreign sources—either borrowing, aid, or private foreign investment. The data in Table 3.4 portray a striking picture given the high rates of investment sustained in Botswana over the period, in that over the years 1965 to 1970 domestic savings in Botswana were actually negative. This implies not merely that foreign sources financed all the fixed investment of this period, but also that they financed a significant part of domestic consumption.

The major source of this support was the United Kingdom Government which provided grants-in-aid to Botswana for recurrent expenditure purposes until 1971/2. In addition, important famine relief was received from a variety of agencies, most notably the World Food Programme. Quite apart from the Government's needs, however, at least during the early years of the period, many families in the rural areas were dissaving as a result of the drought: their cattle were dying in large numbers, and it was necessary to sell them to the abattoir both to realize their capital value whilst this was still possible and to provide the income that was lacking as a result of crop failures.

The sharp change in the savings pattern in the early 1970s, from negative to strongly positive savings ratios, was generated by three main developments. First, exports began to pick up: the combined effects of diamond production and buoyant beef prices allowed exports to increase faster than both GDP and imports between 1970/1 and 1973/4. Though the import ratio remained roughly unchanged this allowed the trade deficit to decline as a porportion of GDP between these years. Second, the share of consumption declined as a proportion of output— at least until about 1974. Though in absolute terms it continued to grow at a real rate of about 10 per cent, this was much less than the real rate of output growth over the period. Third, the series of good rains allowed big increases in the national herd of cattle—the traditional form of saving for most Batswana. A major source of savings has therefore been the increase in the number of cattle-on-the-hoof, reflected in the significantly positive 'stock change' item for mid-1970s shown in Table 3.4.

It is important to note, however, that savings net of changes in stocks were reduced from 37 million to 8 million between 1973/4 and 1974/5. The main reason for this was the large operating loss experienced by the Selebi-Phikwe mine, which reduced operating surplus in the nation as a whole and, consequently, national savings. However the decline was aggravated by the growth of consumption by 16 per cent over the year, measured in current prices, in spite of the negligible growth of total output in that year. The consumption trend was led by the public sector, primarily as a result of the large increase in salaries which became effective in April 1974. This decision, at a time when the economy was starting a downswing,[19] was taken for political reasons, a few months before the third general election. Although it bought the Government enhanced popularity, it was an important factor in the decline of the savings ratio and postponed the day when dependence upon overseas sources for the supply of investible resources could markedly be reduced.

Given the size of the public and private investments required for the mining projects relative to GDP it has always been clear that most of the necessary funds would have to be mobilized from abroad. But, perhaps as a hangover from the very severe budgetary problems which were inherited at independence, the Government appears to have been excessively pre-occupied with raising additional capital, even over and above its immediate spending requirements, as the analysis of the next chapter demonstrates. The ready availability of foreign capital to Botswana has meant that very little attention has been given to structural changes which might enhance the level of real domestic saving. With the exception of a short period in the early 1970s, growth has been achieved without any constraint on the level of consumption expenditure and the Batswana have not been called upon to make major sacrifices in the interests of national development. Such savings and investment institutions which currently exist are small and not very effective. But the establishment of the Bank of Botswana in 1976 may prove to be the first of a series of institutional changes which will ultimately strengthen and develop the financial institutions of the economy, perhaps stimulate the level of domestic savings, and permit a more self-reliant financing of new investment.

CONCLUSION

Botswana was extremely fortunate during the first decade of independence. Total output increased enormously, and real national income per capita tripled to reach about P450 by 1976/7. Botswana had been amongst the 20 poorest countries in the world in 1966, as measured by per capita incomes. Ten years later, however, there were more than 50 countries in the world which were poorer than Botswana, and per capita product was higher than the average for Africa and Asia, excluding Japan (IBRD, 1977).

This growth was made possible by a diversification of the economy into minerals production on a large scale. Major investments in mining infrastructure created a boom between 1968 and 1973 which, after more recent set-backs, now holds promise of being sustained by a growth of minerals output and the prospect of new investments in the diamonds sector. During this period the share of minerals output rose from less than one per cent to more than 15 per cent of GDP. Although production is still focused upon a limited number of products, the range of productive activities undertaken in Botswana is now much wider than it was, and this must be counted as a considerable achievement by the Government over what has been a comparatively short period of time.

But luck has played a large part in the growth that has occurred. Primarily because of a change in the weather cycle—from a succession of drought years to ones of good rains—the growth of the agricultural sector was also remarkable over the period. This was based upon the growth of the cattle herd, which, by 1978, had increased to more than three times its 1966 level. There are two aspects of this which are particularly important. First, this recent agricultural progress is fragile— a recurrence of drought could remove the output gains within two or three years. Second, its benefits have been largely confined to those who owned cattle which survived the drought. This group comprise only slightly more than half the total population. Of course, most rural dwellers benefited in some measure from the good rains: provided cattle could be borrowed for ploughing, arable incomes increased. Families no longer needed famine relief, so things were better than before. But the fragility and the unbalanced nature of the agricultural recovery mean that this progress may be short lived; they raise, too, major questions about the extent to which economic growth in Botswana has fundamentally affected the incomes and prospective opportunities facing the poorest rural groups. These questions are addressed in the chapters which follow.

CHAPTER 4

GOVERNMENT
AND PLANNING

Implicit in the analysis of the last chapter has been the important role played by the Government in Botswana's recent development. In the mid-1960s the country's total output was overwhelmingly dominated by beef and its associated products. The rest of the formal sector was very small and mainly comprised tertiary activities. The subsequent diversification of production towards a much greater contribution from other primary and secondary industries has been achieved partly as a result of a massive investment programme led by the Government: about half of total investment over the decade 1965–1975 was undertaken directly by the public sector, and by the end of the period the Government's budget was equal to almost half of the value of the GDP. This chapter analyses how these resources were mobilized and absorbed.

Consideration of the government sector is important for other reasons. First, at the time of independence, half of Botswana's public expenditure was financed directly by the British Government. This implied not merely an extreme financial dependence upon the metropolitan power, but also that changes in many aspects of domestic economic and social policy were subject to the approval of a foreign government and the interests it represented. It is important to ask, therefore, whether the subsequent removal of this dependence on Britain has brought real budgetary independence or merely a switch to other external sources of support and influence.

The second reason for treating the Government as a separate sector is that in Botswana, as in other poor countries, the pattern of government expenditure is critically important in raising the living standards of the majority of the population. Although most people may not have access to any form of wage employment, their welfare can be directly improved by the provision of education, health, rural infrastructure, marketing, credit, extension, and other services. The generation of the resources needed to provide these services has been a recurrent theme of government policy. Large amounts of domestic revenue have been raised since independence. Thus, an analysis of the Government's expenditure allocations as between rural and urban areas, between service and directly productive sectors, and between consumption and investment, will provide some indication of the success, or otherwise, of the Government's stated strategy.

The main focus of this chapter, therefore, is an analysis of government revenues and expenditure. Because the problem of how to raise money has been more pressing for most of the period—especially in the early days—than how to spend it, revenue matters are treated first. This is followed by a detailed consideration of patterns of both capital and recurrent expenditure together with some comment on the underlying planning and political process. A final section examines the important contribution which aid has made in Botswana, and concludes with some discussion of the future.

DOMESTIC REVENUE

The need to raise sufficient domestic revenue to balance ordinary recurrent expenditure was seen by the Government as its major problem at independence. In the Transitional Plan, published on Independence Day in 1966, the Government stated that 'in the absence of national income statistics it is not meaningful to talk about raising the per capita income five or ten per cent per annum'; income redistribution was regarded as a 'long range objective', but strong words were spoken of the need to promote budgetary independence:

Fundamental to the plans and policies of the Government is a determination to make the country a financially viable entity in the shortest possible period. No politically independent nation can or should depend for any lengthy and continued period on grants to meet ordinary recurrent expenditure on existing services. Such is the plight of Botswana now and for some time to come. But the Government intends that the affairs of the country will be handled in such a way as to expedite the reduction of dependence on foreign assistance for ordinary budget purposes.
(RB 1966a: 6)

The government establishment was still very small and there seemed no prospect of trimming expenditure; indeed in the long run this would have been counter-productive. Attention turned rather to raising additional revenue, first from the Customs Union with South Africa, and later from the encouragement of mining ventures.

As mentioned in Chapter 1, the existing customs agreement between South Africa and the three High Commission Territories, which dated from 1910, had been based upon the simple principle that each country should receive as customs revenue the equivalent of the duty content of its own imports. The rates of duty were set by South Africa, which also collected the revenues. These were then allocated between the four partners on the basis of the estimated shares of total imports to the area that went to each territory between the years 1906 and 1908. Under these arrangements, Botswana received less than one-third of one per cent of the total revenues collected by South Africa.

The only adjustment made to the 1910 formula came in 1965, when the British Government, acting on the basis of the results of a brief statistical consultancy, reduced the share of revenue given to Lesotho and increased the shares of Botswana and Swaziland. This attempted to take account of the changed shares of imports between the three smaller territories, whilst leaving the South African share unchanged. Thus the fairness of the 1910 agreement was not questioned for the following fifty years. Even as late as 1965 the official British view was that it remained advantageous to the three junior partners and that to call it into question might result in a shift of the net benefits in favour of South Africa. This was based upon the belief that South African growth had been much faster than that of the three smaller countries and that its share of total imports to the area was more likely to have increased than to have fallen back from its share at the turn of the century. This, however, was by no means self-evident. Apart from its requiring considerable faith in the accuracy of statistical reporting of trade flows fifty years earlier, it also involved a presumption that South African growth had not significantly reduced its dependence upon imported goods relative to the other three territories.[1]

In addition, however, the British Government was concerned about the costs that would be incurred by the smaller partners if the Customs Union were to break up. Advisers from the British Ministry of Overseas Development felt that the additional advantages gained by such a development would be unlikely to cover the additional costs:

The available evidence suggests that under this arrangement the revenues . . . are not less than she [Bechuanaland] would raise if she had her own customs administration levying the same rates of duty. Bechuanaland is therefore spared the burden of administering her own customs and excise system and, given the enormous length of her frontiers and the practical difficulties of policing them effectively from a customs point of view, this is an undoubted advantage. (RB, 1966b: 88)

They concluded that 'it would seem doubtful in present circumstances if there would be anything to gain from a radical departure from the existing arrangements, and there might be much to lose' (RB, 1966b: 11).

Thus, the British argued for the maintenance of the status quo. They tended to see the main argument as being between leaving or remaining within the Customs Union, and because they underestimated the benefits gained by South Africa from the existing arrangements they overlooked the case for renegotiation by the three smaller countries. The Botswana authorities took a very different line. In the Transitional Development Plan, the new Government set out its objections to the 1910 agreement. These were that at present Botswana (and likewise Lesotho and

Swaziland) did not receive compensation from South Africa for five adverse factors. First, the movements in customs-revenue receipts were related much more closely to changes in the South African economy than to that of Botswana. Second, South Africa set the level of tariffs, which served its own interests rather than those of Botswana. Third, Botswana suffered a loss of customs revenue because of the imposition of high protective duties for South African industries. Fourth, Botswana suffered a diversion of demand from cheaper overseas imports to more expensive South African products, and thus was subsidizing the growth of South African industry. Finally, the benefits of the agreement in terms of its providing a stimulus to industrial development were unequally distributed—most being captured by South Africa at the expense of the smaller countries. Accordingly, in the face of opposition from the British Government which, as provider of deficit finance to BLS, still had an interest in the affair, Botswana committed itself to fundamental renegotiation of the 1910 agreement, and the points mentioned above became central to the position adopted by each of the three smaller countries in their discussions with South Africa.

The negotiations were protracted and were not concluded until 1969. The new agreement became effective as from 1 April of that year. It differed substantially from the earlier arrangements in several respects. It was agreed that the revenue transfer to Botswana, Lesotho, and Swaziland would be based upon their actual annual imports, including imports originating from other parties to the agreement. This is an unusual provision in customs agreements of this kind, since it covers not only imports to the region, but trade between some of the partners. The great majority of such imports flow to BLS from South Africa and the provision considerably augments the revenues to the smaller countries at the expense of South Africa. Secondly, sales duties, an increasingly important source of revenue in South Africa, were to be included in the new revenue formula, which would significantly raise the size of the total revenue pool. These would be divided on the basis of each country's consumption of dutiable goods, which they either imported or produced themselves. Finally, the revenues calculated on this basis were then to be inflated by a factor of 1.42 in order to derive the total-revenue transfer. Though not explicitly stated in the agreement, it is known that this multiplier is intended to provide the peripheral countries with compensation for the costs, mentioned above, of entering into a customs-union agreement with a richer and more powerful neighbour.

The changes of a non-financial kind incorporated in the new agreement were less of a departure from the past. The South African authorities continue to enjoy the prerogative of unilaterally fixing the tariff of duties, except that consultation is now required when changes that may have major effects upon the economies of the other countries are contemplated. The main vehicle for this became the Customs Union Commission, comprising representatives from the four-member states, which meets at least once each year to review the operation of the agreement. In addition, South Africa accepted provisions in the agreement,[2] which allow BLS, though not South Africa, to protect new industries for a period not exceeding eight years. None of the three countries have in fact made much use of this clause. In Botswana's case infant-industry protection has been used only once, for the establishment of a brewery.[3]

The impact of these new arrangements on government revenue has been very substantial. It has been shown by Landell-Mills (1971: 275) that the changed basis of calculating the shares of customs and excise revenue alone almost doubled the receipts of Botswana, as compared with the 1910 agreement. And the inclusion of sales duties in the total-revenue pool resulted in the revenues increasing to more than double their previous levels. The net effect of the new agreement, with the rates of duty then in force, was to generate for the governments of the small countries a revenue transfer equal to about 20 per cent of the total value of their annual imports from all sources. The effects of this are shown in Table 4.1. Customs duties increased their share from one-fifth to almost one-half of Botswana's domestic revenue between 1968/9 and 1969/70. This proportional contribution was maintained until 1974/5, in which year the customs receipts of P30 million were more than twenty times greater than they had been six years earlier.

These developments were very important from a budgetary point of view, and were responsible for the Government becoming self-sufficient with regard to recurrent bugetary expenditures in 1972/3. Whether revenues of equivalent magnitude could have been collected by an independent customs administration, outside the framework of the Customs Union, has never been studied in detail. It would be necessary to examine all the major imports to Botswana and to compare the prices of imports supplied from South Africa with what they would be from elsewhere. Initially the data for such an exercise were just not available. More recently the Government has appeared sufficiently satisfied with the present arrangements that alternatives have not been seriously considered. However, such work that has been done strongly suggests that purely from the point of view of government revenue independent customs arrangements would be less favourable (Mosley, 1978). It is possible that the financial benefits of the agreement are outweighed by its economic costs, most notably the difficulty of creating domestic import-substituting industries. But the problem of

TABLE 4.1 Domestic revenue,[1] 1966/7–1976/7
P millions

	1966/7	1967/8	1968/9	1969/70	1970/1	1971/2	1972/3	1973/4	1974/5	1975/6	1976/7
Direct taxes											
PAYE	} 1.62	} 1.27	0.43	0.46	0.60	0.89	1.57	2.91	4.66	6.02	5.73
Other income tax			1.44	1.53	1.21	2.23	3.83	5.22	10.97	16.78	16.73
Customs, excise, sales duty	1.13	1.74	1.40	5.14	4.58	8.29	12.47	20.94	30.40	24.61	15.44
Export taxes											
Cattle	0.35	0.19	0.25	0.22	0.26	0.36	0.25	0.44	0.42	0.41	0.42
Other	0.05	0.03	0.05	0.06	0.07	0.07	0.09	0.09	0.06	0.08	0.11
Other domestic revenue											
Mineral royalties & dividends	–	–	–	0.01	0.20	0.40	3.07	3.74	3.00	13.67	9.16
Other property revenue	0.64	0.64	0.72	0.71	0.93	0.89	0.88	0.87	1.45	2.02	3.16
Other revenue[2]	2.41	1.88	2.74	2.67	3.86	4.28	5.96	7.58	13.09	18.34	30.92
TOTAL	6.20	5.75	7.03	10.80	11.71	17.41	28.12	41.79	64.05	81.93	81.67

[1] Excludes UK grants and loans for recurrent expenditure purposes and treasury-bill issues.

[2] Mainly loan repayments, interest, and revenue from departmental services; also includes posts and telecommunications revenue.

Sources: *Annual Statements of Accounts* (RB, 1967–RB, 1977).

industrialization is complex, and for reasons which are amplified in a later chapter, we would judge that at the present time, without a major reorientation of a range of policies, continued membership of the Customs Union is desirable for Botswana.

The agreement does, however, serve to integrate the three peripheral states more closely into the South African economy and increases their dependence upon South Africa itself. The revenues are all collected and distributed by the South African Government, which also sets the level of duties. Although the agreement in theory provides for consultation in this matter, in practice there have been problems. For instance, in the early 1970s the average rate of duty on imports into the region declined—largely for technical reasons[4]—with consequent effects on the level of revenue to the three smaller countries. In response to this, an amendment to the agreement was negotiated in 1976 which provides for transfer payments to be made as before, but subject to a minimum rate of revenue of 17 per cent and a maximum of 23 per cent of the value of all dutiable goods imported by the three smaller countries. It is significant that, as in the original negotiations, a solution was found in terms of financial compensation, instead of devolving more authority for the design and determination of the level of duties to the three smaller partners.

Whatever reservations may be made about the 1969 agreement, however, there is no doubt that it made a major contribution to achieving budgetary independence, which was one of the Government's earliest objectives. The additional customs revenue, being provided on a formula basis, is now much more secure than were the budgetary grants-in-aid from the British Government, which had to be renegotiated each year. The Customs Agreement, then, provides a large and dependable supplement to domestic revenue which is no longer dependent upon foreign goodwill or charity.

The second major means by which the Government sought to increase its financial strength was through the promotion of mining in Botswana. This was particularly important from 1973/4 onwards and it subsequently provided a useful financial surplus over and above the requirements of the recurrent budget. In fact, part of the revenue attributable to mining development has come through the mechanism of the new customs formula as a result of the substantial capital imports required for the mining infrastructure. But since the customs-transfer payments to the three smaller countries in any one year are based upon the total value of imports two years previously, the imports for mining development, which began on a large scale from 1970/1, contributed only marginally to the move towards budgetary independence. These expenditures did however generate the large increase in customs receipts that took place after 1972/3. The subsequent budgetary surpluses, and the growing availability of domestic funds for development expenditure purposes, were in large part generated by this interaction between the new revenue formula and the much enhanced levels of imports for mining development.

The diamond mine at Orapa, though not yet the copper–nickel mine at Selebi-Phikwe,[5] has also contributed more directly to the growth of government revenues. The payments from diamond royalties and dividends are shown explicitly in Table 4.1. Published tax revenues are not, of course, disaggregated. However, using company accounts, it is possible to construct a reasonably accurate estimate of taxes paid by the diamond company. Between 1973/4 and 1976/7 tax revenues together with royalties and dividends from diamonds amounted to approximately P50 million, or about 18 per cent of total domestic revenue over the same period.[6] On these figures, it could not be argued that the Botswana Government has yet been excessively dependent on the earnings from mineral exports. By contrast, the Zambian Government, for example, relied on copper for 70 per cent of its revenue in the mid-1960s (Bostock and Harvey (eds.), 1972: 4). But the recent and planned expansion of diamond production is likely to increase dramatically the proportion of government revenues coming from this source. This is likely to be of some concern in the future.

Botswana's other major primary industry–livestock–provides two main sources of revenue, an export tax and the income taxes paid by the BMC. Export duties on cattle and other animal products were levied by the colonial administration continuously from 1942. These duties were an important source of revenue–particularly during the long period between 1940 and 1956 when Britain provided no budgetary support to the protectorate. Their contribution to domestic revenue grew markedly during the 1950s after the opening of the abattoir, as sales of cattle from Botswana in overseas markets began to increase rapidly. After 1962/3, however, when export duties comprised almost 10 per cent of domestic revenue, they continuously declined in importance. They now contribute only about half of one per cent of domestic revenue. Though, theoretically, this form of taxation is regressive, it is simple to administer[7] and has the advantage of reaching many people in the traditional farming sector who currently evade payment of income taxes–including some very rich farmers. It therefore provides a means of making the incidence of taxation less patchy, and an increase in export duties would tend to counteract what, in practice, are inequitable aspects of the existing tax system. But it is because such a tax particularly hits the traditional and political élite of the country that proposals to increase the rates of duty have been short-lived. At present, it seems likely that this tax will decline further in importance in the future.

The total revenues from cattle-export taxes amounted to just less than P4 million between 1966/7 and 1976/7. Income taxes paid by BMC—again drawn from the annual BMC reports and accounts—have raised an additional P20 million. Hence the livestock industry has directly contributed less than 7 per cent of total domestic revenues over the period, a very small contribution given that the industry has accounted for about one-third of GDP since independence.

As Chapter 3 has shown, the development of the mining and livestock industries has had an important impact upon the growth of the trade, construction, and service sectors. This, together with the expansion of government service itself, has promoted a considerable increase in tax revenues. Since 1965, the main types of direct taxation in Botswana have been personal and company income tax. In that year, the discriminatory system by which Africans had paid both an 'African' and a 'Graded' tax, whilst Europeans paid an income tax and a 'Poll' tax, was abolished. Henceforth, all income earners, irrespective of race or nationality, became liable to the same rates of income and local government tax. Income tax on companies was levied at a rate of 30 per cent of taxable income until 1976, and 35 per cent thereafter.[8] In addition, some multinational firms where supra-normal profits were expected have been subject to individual taxation agreements, negotiated between the Government and the companies concerned.[9]

Excluding the special cases of the BMC and the De Beers diamond mine at Orapa, the revenue from personal income and company taxes has increased eightfold since independence. This has arisen partly from more intensified economic activity and employment in all sectors and partly as a result of more efficient tax collection. However, the contribution of this type of taxation to total revenue (net, in both cases, of taxes from diamonds and livestock) has declined from 21 per cent to 15 per cent over the same period. This is contrary to the more usual trend of an increasing contribution of direct taxation to total revenue. A more detailed analysis of personal taxation and its incidence is given in Chapter 7.

To conclude this review of revenue changes some comment should be made on the final two lines of Table 4.1. These items, which comprise 'Other Property Revenue' and 'Other Revenue', have apparently advanced twelvefold over the period. This reflects a much enlarged private, and predominantly urban, sector, with a greater ability to pay for the services offered by the Government. In addition, and probably of greater importance, is the repayment of loans made by the Government to parastatals in connection with the construction of Selebi-Phikwe and other urban expenditures. In so far as the Government has merely acted as an intermediary between some external lender and the parastatal in question, much of the increase shown in the Table is a purely financial transaction balanced by an increase in the public-debt commitment. However, these loans also reflect a policy of reducing the magnitude of urban subsidies by lending to cost-covering parastatals at 'commercial' rates of interest. This policy has been pursued with mixed results since the early seventies.

In summary, the raising of new revenue has been the most dramatic feature of Botswana's recent financial history. Its growth from P6.2 million in 1966/7 to P85.4 million in 1976/7, at an average annual rate of 30 per cent, was much faster than the expansion of either capital or recurrent expenditures, and it provided the means of eliminating budgetary aid from Britain much earlier than most observers had thought possible. Relatively fast growth of government revenues is not without precedent in Africa: Zambia's domestic revenues increased sixfold over the 1960s (Faber and Potter, 1971), and even Lesotho achieved a fourfold increase between 1966/7 and 1973/4 (Jones, 1977), largely because of the renegotiation of the customs agreement. Nevertheless few governments outside the oil-producing nations have been as successful as that of Botswana in transforming their domestic revenue sources so fundamentally within less than a decade.

EXPENDITURE: 1966/7–1969/70

Although both the renegotiation of the Customs Union Agreement and the outcome of mineral negotiations have attracted much comment and interest outside Botswana, revenue raising has not been a particularly controversial matter within the Government. Perhaps it would have been if there had ever been a serious attempt to make the live-stock industry contribute more equitably towards the fiscus. Fortunately for the ruling politicians, however, financial success came without that particular nettle having to be grasped. By contrast far more attention has been given to the planning and phasing of public expenditure. This aspect of the Government's economic management has become more controversial as the surplus has increased.

The almost complete lack of any productive investment undertaken by the colonial authorities, discussed in Chapter 1, provides an important part of the explanation for Botswana's parlous financial position at independence. Though a large injection of external funds began, for the first time, in the years immediately before independence, it was some years after that—and even then only indirectly—before these began to have major effect upon the Government's ability to raise its domestic revenue. Thus, until about 1969/70 when the enhanced revenues from the renegotiated Customs Union Agreement began to be received, expenditures remained acutely constrained by a shortage of funds.

Nevertheless, the transition to independence and the need for the elected Government to establish itself caused an upsurge of public investment in most sectors in the mid-1960s. There was a need to establish an administrative headquarters for the new Government, and it was decided to locate this at Gaborone, which had previously comprised a small government camp and trading centre with a population of less than three thousand people. Expenditures incurred in the construction of the new capital amounted to about P7 million between 1963/4 and 1966/7. The other major item of this transitional development programme was the provision of all-weather gravel roads between Francistown and Maun, Serowe, and Palapye, and Gaborone and the South African border. Accordingly, over these three years capital expenditures by the Government increased dramatically from about P1 million to P5.5 million per year,[10] and more was spent on development projects at this time than the total of all development spending during the previous colonial period.[11]

As the figures in Table 4.2 show, this peak of public investment declined during the first three years after independence, as the major works at Gaborone neared completion. Nevertheless, the budget continued to be dominated by the provision of urban facilities. Between 1966/7 and 1969/70 more than 60 per cent of capital expenditures were allocated to physical infrastructure and roads projects. By contrast social services, including education, received 16 per cent and agriculture only 11 per cent. This strong bias towards urban and infrastructure investment and the very low priority given to agriculture has continued.

The preparation for independence against a background of financial stringency also accounts for changes in the recurrent budget during this first phase. Following fairly rapid growth from 1963/4 onward, and a jump—fuelled mainly by establishment increases—of over 20 per cent in 1966/7, recurrent expenditure was sluggish for the following three years, with an average annual growth of less than 5 per cent. Table 4.3 shows that no single group of sectors was dominant in the growth of expenditure: over the four-year period 20 per cent of expenditure was accounted for by the health and education sectors,[12] 15 per cent by agriculture and physical infrastructure respectively, and a further 30 per cent by general administration.

Despite the slow growth of expenditure, it was during this period that the institutional foundations for future developments were laid. The Customs Union was being renegotiated and the framework for the expected mining development was being discussed. Within the

TABLE 4.2 *Capital budget expenditure,* [1] *1966/7–1976/7*
P millions

	1966/7	1967/8	1968/9	1969/70	1970/1	1971/2	1972/3	1973/4	1974/5	1975/6	1976/7
General services											
Administration	0.51	0.19	0.08	0.48	1.04[2]	0.48	0.72	2.42	2.24	2.57	2.95
Internal security	0.05	–	–	0.01	0.09	0.05	0.20	0.30	0.37	0.44	0.55
Economic services											
Agriculture	0.72	0.45	0.31	0.49	0.31	0.41	0.48	0.69	2.56	2.76	1.94
Minerals	0.02	0.09	0.03	0.07	0.04	0.01	0.06	0.05	0.12	1.17	0.38
Commerce & industry	–	–	0.19	0.09	0.14	0.32	0.06	2.67	0.27	0.74	0.61
Wildlife & tourism	0.01	0.05	0.09	0.06	0.03	0.02	0.02	0.04	0.07	0.11	0.06
Physical infrastructure											
Power	0.06	0.06	0.32	0.01	1.23	3.42	11.96	6.29	3.86	2.96	3.35
Water	0.77	0.34	0.31	0.76	0.87	2.53	8.07	5.53	3.15	2.67	2.80
Housing & urban	0.96	1.10	1.18	0.83	2.13	1.85	3.88	6.17	5.54	8.77	6.14
Communications											
Roads, airfields	1.36	0.59	0.25	1.64	1.31	1.68	2.43	5.90	9.69	8.98	15.89
Telecommunications	0.07	0.05	0.13	0.16	0.44	0.56	0.54	0.95	1.06	1.54	1.04
Government transport	–	–	0.02	–	0.14	0.48	0.04	0.08	0.05	0.61	0.29

	1966/7	1967/8	1968/9	1969/70	1970/1	1971/2	1972/3	1973/4	1974/5	1975/6	1976/7
Social Services											
Health	0.11	0.15	0.16	0.14	0.12	0.15	0.25	0.17	1.20	0.91	1.37
Education	0.95	0.72	0.26	0.16	0.57	0.31	1.31	2.38	5.43	7.30	5.47
Community development	0.07	–	–	–	0.05	–	–	–	0.01	0.08	0.02
Subventions & loans to councils	–	–	0.01	–	–	–	0.06	0.47	0.57	0.50	0.21
TOTAL	5.66	3.78	3.35	4.90	8.52	12.25	29.88	34.11	36.99	42.09	43.07
of which, Shashe Project	–	–	–	–	1.41	5.79	23.59	16.13	4.84	1.47	2.37

[1] Includes long-term loans made from the Public Debt Service Fund and Revenue Stabilisation Fund.
[2] Includes an IMF Gold Tranche payment of PO.36 million.

Sources: Annual Statements of Accounts (RB, 1967–RB, 1977).

TABLE 4.3 *Current budget expenditure' 1966/7-1976/7*
P millions

	1966/7	1967/8	1968/9	1969/70	1970/1	1971/2	1972/3	1973/4	1974/5	1975/6	1976/7
General services											
Administration[1]	2.00	2.09	2.34	2.60	2.99	3.46	3.68	5.47[2]	7.03[3]	8.94	11.21
Internal security	1.07	1.48	1.19	1.32	1.45	1.69	1.96	2.30	3.55	4.36	4.91
Economic services											
Agriculture	1.61	1.86	1.90	2.05	2.08	2.34	2.49	2.92	4.45	5.48	5.97
Minerals	0.17	0.17	0.18	0.37	0.43	0.66	0.78	0.96	0.95	1.10	1.16
Commerce & industry	0.15	0.27	0.16	0.18	0.21	0.29	0.41	0.47	0.79	0.94	1.08
Wildlife & tourism	0.06	0.07	0.08	0.11	0.11	0.14	0.20	0.24	0.33	0.40	0.37
Physical infrastructure											
Power[4]	0.07	0.08	0.09	0.10	0.11	0.14	0.13	0.14	0.19	0.30	0.37
Water	0.29	0.37	0.39	0.30	0.51	0.73	0.94	1.05	0.99	1.36	1.36
Housing and urban	0.14	0.50	0.49	0.63	0.73	0.86	1.95	2.66	2.69	2.66	3.33
Communications											
Roads, airfields	0.57	0.60	0.63	0.71	0.90	1.71	1.32	1.40	2.17	2.39	2.34
Telecommunications	0.59	0.60	0.58	0.65	0.72	0.84	1.19	1.33	2.47	3.01	3.45
Government transport[5]	0.18	0.12	0.13	0.14	0.16	0.19	0.16	0.22	0.39	0.52	6.89
Social services											
Health	0.71	0.82	0.83	1.00	1.10	1.27	1.53	1.84	3.08	4.00	4.89
Education	1.51[6]	0.86	0.84	1.01	1.32	1.88	2.19	2.64	4.06	5.57	12.97
Community development[7]	1.06	0.27	0.28	0.30	0.36	0.30	0.37	0.43	0.29	0.22	0.02

	1966/7	1967/8	1968/9	1969/70	1970/1	1971/2	1972/3	1973/4	1974/5	1975/6	1976/7
Subventions to councils	0.18	0.48	0.50	0.53	0.41	0.60	0.70	1.50	3.09	4.78	2.60
Financial obligations											
Pensions, etc.	0.69	0.81	0.95	0.83	0.91	0.83	0.70	0.63	0.76	0.95	0.85
Long-term public debt	0.68	0.71	0.71	0.79	0.94	1.07	1.19	1.15	2.74	4.42	6.28
OSAS	0.47	0.44	0.39	0.40	0.41	0.43	0.29	0.28	0.28	0.35	0.60
TOTAL	12.19	12.61	12.67	14.01	15.84	19.42	22.18	27.63	40.30	51.75	70.65

[1] Includes, *inter alia*, parliament, immigration, labour, audit, surveys and lands, meteorology, government buildings, libraries, museums, information and broadcasting, district administration, finance, and planning.

[2] Includes interim pay increase throughout public service of P1.32 million.

[3] Large increase from previous year reflects 1974 public-service salary award.

[4] Recurrent expenditures on power prior to 1972/3 are not separated in sources from those for transport. Data given for these years are authors' estimates, based upon the ratio of power/transport expenditures shown for 1972/3 and 1973/4.

[5] Personal emoluments only, until 1976/7. In that year the Central Transport Organisation Special Fund, whereby transport expenditures were allocated to each of the user departments, was discontinued. This explains much of the apparent increase in expenditure shown for 1976/7. In fact transport expenditures in earlier years are underestimates.

[6] Anomalously high education expenditure in 1966/7 may include some primary teachers' salaries which are paid by District Councils in other years.

[7] Includes famine relief and institutional feeding programmes. The Department of Community Development was discontinued in 1975/6. Though expenditures continued, they are not shown separately in the accounts. This explains the apparent decline in expenditures in the last years of the period.

Sources: Annual Statements of Accounts (RB, 1967–RB, 1977).

Government itself a small Economic Planning Unit had been established within the Ministry of Finance shortly before independence.
Apart from occasional visiting missions from London, this was the
first experience the territory had had of economic planning, and the
attitudes and approaches of the young expatriate economists in the
EPU did not appeal to the older more entrenched colonial civil servants.
But the politicans themselves were advocating a planned approach to
development, and soon after independence the Economic Planning
Unit became a small Ministry of Development Planning under the
leadership of Vice-President Quett Masire. His outstanding intellectual
ability, together with the fact that he lacked a significant political
base of his own, made for a good working relationship between himself
and President Khama. In fact, the President was inclined—particularly
in the early years—to leave all economic and financial decisions to the
Vice-President and to support his judgement in these aspects of government policy.

Thus from its inception, and contrary to frequent experience of
development-planning units of ministries in other African countries,
the Ministry of Development Planning in Botswana played an important
role. After the Transitional Plan itself, two further plans were written
by the ministry in 1968 and 1970. These are usually referred to, somewhat illogically, as the first and second National Development Plans.
Each was a five-year plan, but the intention was to update them by
publishing new ones every two or three years. These documents were
largely qualitative descriptions of the economy. But their strength lay
in their inclusion of extremely ambitious 'shopping lists', covering
projects which were considered to represent the country's most urgent
development needs. Such agenda are a prerequisite for negotiating
development aid, and the plans' concise, well-articulated arguments
for an enhanced development programme were undoubtedly influential
in the subsequent securing of considerable assistance from a range of
western countries and agencies.

EXPENDITURE: 1970/1–1973/4

Thus the second distinct phase of expenditure policies, from 1970/1
to 1973/4, covers the period of the second National Development
Plan, although by the final year it had been superseded by the third.
At the beginning of this phase there was an important institutional
change. Growing conflicts of interest and philosophy between the
rather conservative Ministry of Finance and the younger, more energetic Ministry of Development Planning led to the combing of the two
ministries under the Vice-President in 1971. In subsequent years, even
though some tension between the two sides of the new Ministry of

Finance and Development Planning (MFDP) remained, it emerged as a formidable power within government: the sectoral executive ministries found they could exercise little initiative without its approval. The strength of MFDP was built on three foundations. First, the provisions of the Finance and Audit Act gave it the right to prepare and control the budget. This included a provision that no ministry could initiate a new development project without its first being written into the current national development plan. Second, Dr Masire's considerable natural ability and the support of the President that he enjoyed enabled him to dominate Cabinet discussions of economic matters, and of many sectoral issues which had some economic or financial content. Third, much of the adminsitrative and creative talent in the civil service was concentrated within MFDP. Other ministers simply did not get the same quality of advice or technical support as that given to the Vice-President.

During this period, a major change in the size and composition of both capital and current budgets took place, mainly as a result of the construction of another new town—at Selebi-Phikwe. This was the site of the copper–nickel mining venture known as the Shashe Project. Construction began in 1970/1, following a series of long and frustrating delays.[13] It can be seen from Table 4.2 that during that year capital spending by the Government increased from about P5 million to over P8.5 million, and for the first time the capital budget exceeded the levels reached in 1966/7. Initially, less than half of this increase was caused by the start of the Shashe Project. However, during the next two years expenditures grew enormously. By 1972/3 the construction of roads, railway lines, water and power supplies, and housing at Selebi-Phikwe had increased expenditures to P24 million, which in that year represented almost 80 per cent of the Government's total capital expenditure.

Altogether, public investment in the Shashe Project amounted to about P55 million. The total investment in the mining sector over a three- or four-year period, including the private-sector component of the project and the concurrent mining investment at Orapa, was roughly equivalent to the value of total domestic output for one year.

At this time, the implementation capacity of the Government and of the economy in general was stretched to its limits, and the huge increase in development activity in connection with the Shashe Project caused other developments to be delayed. It is nevertheless remarkable that it was possible to implement a project which caused capital expenditures to increase from P12 million to almost P30 million over a space of only twelve months, without even greater disruption to the rest of the development programme. This was achieved because almost all the site construction was handled by private-sector contractors from South Africa. This was one of the occasions when Botswana's integration with the economy of South Africa proved to be an asset. Few developing countries are able to import construction capacity so easily. Without it, this sudden burst of activity would have been impossible.

Meanwhile, other categories of expenditure increased hardly at all. The only exception was in education, where secondary schools were enlarged to create 17,000 more school places between 1971 and 1973. That, together with the construction of a new training centre for artisans and technicians in Gaborone, helped to double capital expenditure on education in 1972/3 as compared with earlier years. However, even including the increase in expenditure of P0.5 million on education, the total capital expenditures excluding the Shashe Project fell back from P7.1 million to P6.3 million between 1970/1 and 1972/3. This was only 60 per cent of the 'target' for non-Shashe Project development expenditure which the Government had set itself in the second National Development Plan (RB, 1970b). An unpublished study also demonstrated that rural projects were being more delayed than urban or communications projects (McCarthy, 1972). As Tables 4.2 and 4.4 show, over the three years ending in 1972/3, less than 10 per cent of public investment had benefited the rural areas and only about 2 per cent had been specifically invested in agriculture.

In 1973/4, the last year of the period presently under review, construction activity for the Shashe Project had passed its peak and fell back to P16 million. Other capital expenditure tripled from P6 million to P18 million. But despite this increase in overall activity the allocation of capital finance between sectors did not change markedly. The main increases were in road building and urban development in Gaborone and Francistown, with some significant growth also in education and health expenditures. The rural areas continued to receive less than 10 per cent of the total and only one per cent of capital expenditures were spent in the agricultural sector. This pattern was not in accord with the Government's expressed intention of using the financial surpluses from mining on the development of the rural areas. Increasing attention at the political level was being given to the re-direction of public investment, but it was not until 1974/5 that its results appeared in physical terms.

From the point of view of the recurrent budget, 1972/3 was in many ways a watershed for the Botswana Government. Owing to the increased domestic revenues from the renegotiated Customs Union Agreement, which had been further boosted by the rapid growth of imports which began in 1968,[14] the recurrent budget was balanced for the first time without resort to British grants-in-aid. It was nevertheless recognized

TABLE 4.4 Capital expenditure[1] by location and/or main beneficiary group, 1966/7–1976/7
P millions (percentages)

	1966/7	1967/8	1968/9	1969/70	1970/1	1971/2	1972/3	1973/4	1974/5	1975/6	1976/7
Rural	1.44(26)	1.48(39)	0.85(25)	1.00(20)	1.39(16)	1.00(8)	1.63(5)	3.32(10)	12.31(33)	13.40(32)	11.70(27)
Urban	2.79(49)	1.69(45)	2.12(64)	2.19(45)	5.34(63)	9.03(74)	25.39(85)	23.86(70)	13.67(37)	17.69(42)	14.15(33)
Communications	1.43(25)	0.62(16)	0.37(11)	1.71(35)	1.80(21)	2.22(18)	2.86(10)	6.93(20)	11.00(30)	11.00(26)	17.22(40)
TOTAL	5.66	3.79	3.34	4.90	8.53	12.25	29.88	34.11	37.00	42.09	43.07

[1] Defined as in Table 4.2.

Sources: Annual Statements of Accounts (RB, 1967–RB, 1977).

that the financial surpluses expected for the years 1973/4–1976/7 would be particularly influenced by the unusually high level of imports needed for the Shashe Project, and that, after the construction period was over, there was a strong possibility that domestic resources would again be insufficient to cover the cost of recurrent services. The Vice-President was concerned to ensure that financial self-reliance for recurrent budgetary purposes would remain protected in the future. He therefore advocated caution in expenditure policies, and in 1972 two funds for the appropriation of domestic revenues in years of surplus were established, which would be used to cover future deficits and to finance the small but growing public debt.[15]

During the course of 1972/3, however, it was realized that domestic revenues would continue to grow. Substantial surpluses would be generated, and the growing pool of domestic resources would provide the capacity to initiate a limited number of development projects without seeking funds from abroad. In introducing his Budget Speech in 1973, the Vice-President indicated that the achievement of budgetary independence would now allow some change in economic strategy. As had been promised by the Government since independence, the time had come to concentrate 'not only on economic growth and its impressive physical manifestations, but also on the quality of the lives of all Batswana and the equitable distribution of the benefits of development'. This was to be accomplished 'by raising rural incomes, by providing better services in rural areas, by developing a rural infrastructure, and by creating wider opportunities for self-advancement through education' (RB, 1973b: paras. 2, 4). Accordingly, he announced much increased finance and staff for agriculture, education, health, and local government services in introducing the 1973/4 recurrent budget. He promised the introduction of a new Tax Act during the session, which would redistribute income in favour of the poorest groups.[16] He also indicated that the recent decision to reduce primary school fees substantially had only been made possible by the Government's improved budgetary situation, and that it marked the beginning of a wider redistributive policy.

In the event, however, these pledges had only a limited impact upon the structure of expenditures in that year. Table 4.3 shows that current expenditures increased by 20 per cent in 1973/4–a smaller increase than in any year since 1970/1–and that expenditures on health, community development, and agriculture increased less than this average for all sectors together. But urban expenditures forged ahead. Thus, in spite of the new statement of intent given by the minister at the start of the year, the pattern of spending–both on recurrent services and on development projects–remained strongly biased towards the urban sector.

EXPENDITURE: 1974/5–1976/7

The changes foreshadowed in the 1973/4 Budget Speech were also reflected in the third National Development Plan published in the same year. This was more specific than previous plans about the Government's objectives and how they would be achieved. The main aims were to expand job opportunities, to increase agricultural production, and to improve cash incomes and living standards in the rural areas. These objectives were to be promoted, firstly, by securing large returns to the nation from investment in mining and other export-based industries; and, secondly, by reinvesting the resulting revenues in education, agriculture, labour-intensive manufacturing, and the provision of rural services.

However, the plan contained very little discussion of the relative priorities of its objectives, and the 'shopping list' of projects which should have reflected the new priorities was in reality much the same mixture as before. One reason for this was that on this occasion the executive ministries themselves prepared the plans for each of their sectors, rather than merely approving drafts prepared by MFDP, as had been the case in the past. As a result, the plan was strongly oriented towards the public sector, containing long descriptive passages of the work and aspirations of relatively peripheral departments. It appeared as if MFDP had swung from the earlier extreme of taking responsibility for all medium-term planning work in government to the equally undesirable position of incorporating every ministerial suggestion into the plan document.

These problems were partly the result of a growing tension between the centre and the periphery of the administration. There was a move in the early 1970s towards decentralization—probably reflecting the President's own wishes—and planning staff were appointed both to executive ministries and to the staff of district councils. Although MFDP apparently favoured this development, it also fought against any diminution of its power by trying to keep these staff under its own control. It tended to regard decentralization as a means of spreading its influence more widely, rather than as a way of becoming more responsive to other opinions. But this rearguard action was largely unsuccessful and inevitably the power of the central ministry has declined.

A further factor was also at work. Masire had been defeated by the old Chief Bathoen II in the 1969 general election and had been brought into Parliament as a 'specially elected' member of the National Assembly. As the 1974 elections drew closer the political weakness of his position became more apparent, and his dominance of Cabinet began to diminish. In the event he fought and won a parliamentary seat in 1974

TABLE 4.5   *Capital budget expenditures by source of funds, 1966/7–1976/7*
P millions

	1966/7	1967/8	1968/9	1969/70	1970/1	1971/2	1972/3	1973/4	1974/5	1975/6	1976/7
Shashe project expenditures											
CIDA							10.37	5.30	0.99	0.36	0.20
USAID							3.14	0.99	0.31	–	–
IBRD/IDA					1.41	6.18	8.28	8.71	3.28	0.76	2.08
Other							1.79	1.08	0.27	0.33	–
Government grants & loans											
UK	4.16	2.72	2.62	2.95	4.07	4.56	3.71	3.63	2.80	5.17	3.41
SIDA			} 0.09	0.21	0.08	0.16	0.79	2.58	4.18	4.87	7.05
DANIDA								0.58	0.85	1.01	0.93
NORAD					0.16	0.18	0.14	0.26	1.22	1.73	6.43
CIDA									0.64	2.38	1.25
USAID								1.51	2.50	3.35	4.36
Other				0.04						0.12	0.12

	1966/7	1967/8	1968/9	1969/70	1970/1	1971/2	1972/3	1973/4	1974/5	1975/6	1976/7
Other non-domestic grants and loans											
IBRD/IDA	1.00	0.50	0.04			0.15	0.35	1.20	1.19	1.22	2.41
ADB/ADF		0.46	0.14	0.12			0.50	0.45	0.20	0.10	0.24
Other	0.50	0.10	0.46		0.26		0.26		0.45	0.84	0.80
Domestic grants & loans				1.57	0.61	0.32	0.25	0.58	0.72	0.96	0.54
Domestic resources–DDF[1]								3.38	13.16	12.19	7.48
Bond issues/other					1.92	0.69	0.29	0.04	0.04	0.07	0.30
PDSF/RSF[2]								3.84	4.19	6.64	5.47
Miscellaneous[3]					0.01						
TOTAL	5.66	3.78	3.35	4.90	8.52	12.25	29.88	34.13	36.99	42.10	43.07

[1] Expenditures from the Domestic Development Fund. This was formally established in 1973/4.
[2] Expenditures from the Public Debt Services Fund and from the Revenue Stabilisation Fund.
[3] Mainly misallocations.

Sources: Annual Statements of Accounts (RB, 1967–RB, 1977).

and was reappointed Vice-President, but he has never quite managed to regain his former authority.

Because of the inherent weaknesses of the plan itself, the growing diversity of policy initiatives, and also the impact of external events, the most important expenditures during this third phase were scarcely reflected in the third National Development Plan. Before the document had even been published the President launched the Accelerated Rural Development Programme (ARDP), under which more than P20 million was to be expended on the construction of rural infrastructure, primary schools, clinics, roads, and water supplies. Although the individual projects of the ARDP were part of the plan, there is no doubt that they would not have received the same priority had it not been for this political impetus. In consequence, as Table 4.5 shows, rural expenditures increased fourfold between 1973/4 and 1974/5 and this higher rate of rural investment has since been maintained.

At the same time the introduction of the embargo by the Arab countries on oil supplies to South Africa reawakened concern within the Government about Botswana's landlocked position and its consequent dependence on South African transport routes. A Lifeline Programme was initiated, which involved the construction of over one thousand kilometres of tarred road between Lobatse in the south and the Zambian border in the north of the country. As a result of this project, road building absorbed fully 30 per cent of the capital budget between 1974/5 and 1976/7.

The ARDP and the Lifeline Programme, together with the completion of the Shashe Project, were the main determinants of the shifting pattern of capital expenditure during this third phase. Other changes, though smaller in financial terms, were also important. Popular demand, together with acute skill shortages, led to an expanded education programme. The existing secondary schools were enlarged, and in 1975 it was decided to build six new ones. Although there was some expansion of the absolute level of public investment in the agricultural sector over these three years, it still accounted for less than 7 per cent of the capital budget. Thus agricultural production was still not accorded the priority it had been given even in the late 1960s, when it accounted for 10 per cent or more of capital expenditure.

On the recurrent side, the most significant development during this final phase of the period under review was the general revision of public-sector salaries introduced by the Government in April 1974. This had the effect of increasing expenditures considerably in all branches of government, but particularly so in the labour-intensive departments, such as the police, agriculture, public works, health, and education. Though it is true that the larger share of social infrastructure in total current expenditures at this time was influenced by the greater emphasis given to these sectors on the capital budget, they were equally influenced by the revision in salaries. This trend, then, was as much a reflection of the increased costs of providing social services, as an indication of their wider availability.

THE ROLE OF FINANCIAL AID

Financial aid has provided a crucial supplement to the Government's budgetary resources. Until 1972/3, about half of public expenditure was typically financed from aid sources. Since that date, aid has become proportionally less important owing to the much increased levels of domestic revenue, and by 1976/7 the proportion of total expenditures financed by foreign aid had been reduced to about one-quarter. Two other significant changes occurred over the period. First, there was a shift from recurrent-budget aid to capital-project aid. This gave much greater autonomy to the Botswana authorities, who previously had had to seek the approval of the British Government in order to increase current expenditures. Second, the sources of aid funds have become greatly diversified, and, in particular, British aid has become much less important. Thus, Botswana's dependence upon the British Government is now negligible. Nevertheless, total aid flows to Botswana continue to increase rapidly. Development aid increased fivefold between 1970/1 and 1976/7, which was equivalent to a doubling in real terms. It is important to examine the effects of these trends.

Budgetary aid

Within Botswana, much was made of the achievement of budgetary independence from Britain in 1972. It was seen as a major step towards economic independence and self-determination. Support for recurrent expenditures had been received since 1956, when the British Government had finally acknowledged that public services in the protectorate were inadequate, and that Britain would have to accept some responsibility for their improvement.[17] From that date, recurrent grants increased annually to a peak of P8.6 million in 1967/8 (Table 4.6), and by 1972 Botswana had received more than P52 million in this way over a sixteen-year period. That was almost twice as much as Britain had provided in the way of development grants or loans.

The high levels of budgetary support received by Botswana after independence were, however, rather reluctantly provided. The Ministry of Overseas Development did not like budgetary aid. Little political capital could be made from subsidizing the current budget of ex-colonies, and owing to the nature of current expenditures ODM could not easily point to concrete evidence of the benefits brought by this

TABLE 4.6 *Budgetary operations and deficit financing, 1966/7–1976/7*
P millions

	1966/7	1967/8	1968/9	1969/70	1970/1	1971/2	1972/3	1973/4	1974/5	1975/6	1976/7
Current expenditure	12.19	12.61	12.67	14.01	15.84	19.42	22.18	27.63	40.30	51.75	70.65
Domestic revenue	6.20	5.75	7.03	10.80	11.71	17.41	28.12	41.79	64.05	81.93	81.67
Current surplus (+) or deficit (−)	− 5.99	− 6.86	− 5.64	− 3.21	− 4.13	− 2.01	+ 5.94	+14.16	+23.75	+30.18	+11.02
Capital expenditure	5.66	3.78	3.35	4.90	8.52	12.25	29.88	34.11	36.99	42.09	43.07
Overall deficit (−)	−11.65	−10.64	− 8.99	− 8.11	−12.65	−14.26	−23.94	−19.95	−13.24	−11.91	−32.05
Financing of deficit											
Government grants & loans											
UK grants-in-aid	4.70	8.56	7.61	5.97	0.50	1.92	–	–	–	–	–
Other UK	5.03	0.74	0.86	3.67	4.40	5.75	3.32	3.18	3.08	5.32	3.66
Other governments	–	–	0.11	0.20	0.44	3.35	14.00	11.28	10.63	14.34	19.84
Other non-domestic grants and loans	1.39	1.38	0.30	0.17	1.69	3.34	10.69	11.47	5.25	3.33	5.75

	1966/7	1967/8	1968/9	1969/70	1970/1	1971/2	1972/3	1973/4	1974/5	1975/6	1976/7
Domestic grants & loans[1]	0.49	0.03	0.52	1.65	3.43	–	0.45	0.02	–	1.80	11.53[2]
Miscellaneous[3]	0.01	0.07	0.03	0.05	0.05	0.05	0.07	0.02	0.09	–	–
Net change in other assets (increase –)[4]	0.03	– 0.14	– 0.44	– 3.60	2.14	– 0.15	– 4.59	– 6.02	– 5.81	– 12.88	– 8.73

[1] Includes a Government Bond Issue of P3 million in 1970/1.
[2] Includes net sales of Treasury Bills amounting to P10.79 million.
[3] Includes sales of produce and receipts where source is unspecified.
[4] This table was prepared before the Government itself published a similar consolidated analysis of the budget. Small differences appear in the figures for the net change in other assets between this table and that published by the Government (RB, 1978: Table V), as follows: first, the exclusion of interest accruing to the PDSF and RSF and RSF and short-term loans from the RSF; third, grants and loans are shown when credited to the development fund, as opposed to when received by the Government. These differences in the method of calculation lead to an understatement of about P3.5 million in the net increase in cash balances between 1973/4 and 1976/7 in the above Table.

Sources: *Annual Statements of Accounts* (RB, 1967–RB, 1977).

kind of assistance. Its general policy was, therefore, to curtail budgetary aid as rapidly as possible. Though it quickly reduced the amounts given to Swaziland and Lesotho, however, the opposite happened in Botswana, where more budgetary aid was received between 1966 and 1969 than during the whole of the previous ten years.

Botswana had argued strongly that the only way to ensure higher domestic revenues in the future was to create a much expanded and more efficient administration which could plan and implement an expanded development programme. The taxable capacity of the economy could be increased only by higher expenditures in the short run. The ODM's Economic Survey Mission had already set the stage for some widening of the recurrent-budget deficit after independence (RB, 1966b: 108), but its proposals were modest compared with the increases in support negotiated by Botswana from 1966 onwards.

Negotiations were conducted on a triennial basis, with the provisional-aid ceilings being adjusted in the light of subsequent annual estimates of revenue and expenditure provided by the Botswana authorities. In general, ODM approved of Botswana's development strategy and of the expenditure programmes needed to implement it—particularly after the transition to independence had been made. Although the prospect of possible censure by ODM may have influenced the items included in the estimates before their submission to London, there is no evidence that the large amount of discretionary power held by the British Government was ever used to Botswana's disadvantage.

Nevertheless, the fact that it could have been so used was of constant concern to the Botswana Government, because a contraction of recurrent services could have been much more politically damaging than a similar reduction in development spending. This same feature, however, made ODM equally uncomfortable: the provision of aid for the recurrent budget, since it comprised expenditures which represented continuing commitments, exposed the British to strong moral pressures to maintain past levels of support. The key to Botswana's success in negotiating large amounts of budgetary aid was probably that ODM was satisfied of the country's ultimate economic and financial viability. Unlike the case of Lesotho,[18] there appeared to be no danger that the expanded level of services could not be financed in the future by enhanced local resources. The vindication of this judgement came in 1972, when Botswana was able to dispense with budgetary aid, much earlier than had been expected in the mid-1960s. We have shown that this was made possible by the renegotiated Customs Union Agreement with South Africa. However, even without the renegotiation, the royalties and tax revenues from minerals development would have secured budgetary independence within two or three years.

Development aid

Over the decade following independence, but particularly since 1970, Botswana received a very large amount of aid for development-expenditure purposes. Between 1972 and 1975 Botswana's net development-aid receipts per capita from all sources were about twenty times the average for all Commonwealth developing countries. Amongst mainland African countries, only Congo and Gabon received more official aid per capita over the same period.[19]

Britain has had a special place in these development-aid flows. It can be seen from Table 4.5 that between 1966 and 1970 Britain was the only substantial donor, and she provided over 80 per cent of the foreign development grants and loans during these first four years. The UK was also willing to provide development aid for a large variety of mainly small projects. No particular sectoral preferences were shown in these early years, mainly because Botswana had few alternative sources of development finance and looked to the British to finance most of the development programme.

From 1971 onwards, however, the picture changed dramatically. During the following years large amounts of aid were received in connection with the construction of the mining town at Selebi-Phikwe. This project absorbed over P50 million, which was provided mainly by the governments of the United States and Canada and by the World Bank. Although the British were only marginally involved in this project, they continued to be a major source of aid funds, particularly for education, health, general infrastructure, and security projects. The other important development was the expansion of the Swedish aid programme, mainly for projects in the education and water sectors. By 1974 Sweden had become Botswana's main bilateral donor, and it became clear that the Swedes were prepared to give Botswana special treatment in their allocation of aid, alongside a small number of other favoured countries.[20]

Perhaps the most remarkable feature of the mid-1970s was the fact that the fall in aid receipts resulting from completion of the Shashe Project was compensated to a large extent by a big increase in foreign aid for other projects. This was mainly because the interest of the donors associated with the Shashe Project was retained after its completion. The Canadians and the Americans seemed prepared to have a long-term involvement in Botswana's development. In addition, aid from the World Bank and from the Scandinavian countries continued to increase. Only the British kept their aid to the levels of the early 1970s.

The reasons for this large, and sustained increase in the amount of aid received by Botswana are complex. Each of the nations providing bilateral aid have had different economic and political interests in the region, and their objectives in giving aid are likely to have been different. A full discussion of these aims goes beyond the scope of this book. In what follows we indicate the more influential factors that have helped to shape the attitudes of the main donors.

A recent analysis of the achievements of British aid in southern Africa (Jones, 1977) concludes that the main reasons why BLS received so much more British aid, on a per capita basis, than most other developing countries were, first, that large amounts of aid were needed after independence by these three countries in order to ensure their economic viability—an obligation which automatically fell on Britain's shoulders as the erstwhile colonial power; second, that Britian also felt obliged to provide compensation for having neglected the development of these countries in the past; third, that Britain was anxious to avoid the political consequences of abandoning BLS at a time when their financial weakness would encourage an unhealthy dependence upon, and possible incorporation with, South Africa. Now that the economic circumstances of BLS have changed, Jones argues (1977: 60–4) that the most important determinant of the continued flow of aid from UK is the weight of precedent. This arises from the fact that it is difficult to reduce aid without appearing to give a political snub to the countries concerned. All of these pressures have certainly been important in affecting the pattern of British aid over the period.

There is, however, an additional factor that has influenced the magnitude of aid from some European countries, including Britain, and from the United States. This arises from their economic and commercial interests in South Africa. The frequency of United Nations resolutions condemning the excesses of the South African regime, and the growing international concern over the extent to which Western capital supports these policies has caused some rich nations to reassess their long-term strategy in southern Africa. Those nations with substantial South African interests are for the most part committed to the objective of securing peaceful change within South Africa, and they see aid to BLS as being likely to promote rather than to work against these aims. Though it is difficult to document this judgement, it is almost certain that this has been an important factor in the continued large bilateral flows to Botswana (as well as Lesotho and Swaziland) since 1970—in particular those from Britain and North America. The case of the Scandinavian countries is slightly different in that their investments in South Africa are much more limited. But public feeling against South Africa is stronger—particularly in Sweden—than in many other European countries and their Governments are keen to be seen as hostile to apartheid. During the 1970s the Swedes increased their aid to BLS with the explicit purpose of helping them to be more independent of South Africa (Ohlin, 1973: 54). Here too, then, aid to Botswana is in part motivated by political, if not politico-economic, self-interest.

The reasons why Botswana did particularly well in comparison with Lesotho and Swaziland, which, in similar circumstances, received smaller amounts of aid, however, relate more to the efficiency, planning capacity, ability to spend, and negotiating skills of the Botswana administration, than to political, regional, or economic factors.

These features were as important in attracting aid from the British as from other bilateral and multilateral donors. However, it is arguable that they have resulted in Botswana over-emphasizing a project approach to planning to the neglect of wider issues of social and economic strategy. This emphasis in domestic planning was nourished by the practice—adopted by most donors—of giving aid on a project, rather than a programme, basis. It was additionally encouraged by the terms and conditions attached to aid. In this respect, British procedures were in some respects worse than other donors. For example, the convention of not allowing unspent British funds to be carried over the following financial year encouraged the preferential allocation of resources to sectors and projects where expenditure could occur quickly, rather than to those sectors where the need was greatest. Moreover, the placing of a premium on speedy implementation resulted in a more extreme import-dependent and capital-intensive approach to some projects than was desirable. It is to be hoped that the recent changes of emphasis in donor policies, towards a preference for more rural- and poverty-focused programmes, will also be accompanied by a rethinking of aid procedures.

Finally, financial factors have also had a strong influence upon the availability of aid to Botswana. This is not meant in the crude sense of donors wanting to establish a market for their exports or a guarantee of raw-material imports; rather, that the mining projects at Selebi-Phikwe and Orapa gave a promise of prosperity for Botswana where, earlier, the future had appeared bleak. This meant both that donors ran fewer risks of default on their loans to Botswana, and that, in being associated with rapid increases in living standards, the benefits of aid were easier to see and high allocations were easier to justify.

This, however, raises the question of the desirability of Botswana continuing to seek aid on the scale of the recent past. There are significant costs in this which are often overlooked. A large proportion of financial aid is spent on imported capital goods, in support of projects that are located in the urban areas, or which mainly benefit them. Even when allocated to the rural areas the awkwardness of communication between rural projects and the financing agency can be counter-productive. There are grave dangers of local initiatives and interest being stifled by long delays and by the apparently arbitrary requirements imposed by unseen donors. Experience in Botswana suggests that the benefits of a switch towards poverty-focused aid will remain elusive unless donors are prepared to relax considerably their project-approval and disbursement procedures. This generally implies a need to shift from project to programme financing. Moreover, at present, increased aid tends to imply more expatriates, both in the embassies and high commissions in Gaborone and as administrators and professionals in the projects financed by aid. In addition, securing more aid almost always requires more time being spent by the most capable economists and administrators in the preparation and negotiation of projects and programmes. This diverts scarce energy and talent away from tackling the more fundamental problems of how to benefit those people who really need government help: the majority of the population who live in rural areas, who depend upon agriculture for their livelihood, and who remain—in spite of the expenditures we have described—very poor indeed.

With regard to future strategy, these arguments are somewhat strengthened by an analysis of the Government's budgetary operations and deficit financing over the period. It can be seen from Table 4.6 that, after taking into account all sources of revenue and aid and all expenditures and investments, the Government has in fact enjoyed a series of financial surpluses since 1971/2. These have recently increased markedly—in 1975/6, for example the Government's cash balances and other financial assets increased by over P12 million, which was almost as large as the total grants and loans received from other governments in the previous year. Thus the Government has raised more foreign aid than it in fact required.

On the other hand the annual accumulation of reserves was sensible, in view of the uncertainty of the Government's revenue forecasts. The problems with the copper-nickel mine at Selebi-Phikwe and the fall in customs-revenue receipts in 1975/6 underlined the vulnerability of domestic-revenue sources in the face of these largely unpredictable internal and external events. If the revenues from diamonds had increased less quickly than actually occurred, the budget could easily have moved back into deficit in 1976/7.

In this case, the reserves would have been needed to finance the revenue shortfall. In addition the existence of substantial financial assets strengthened the position of the new currency in 1976, since at that time the Government's Rand-denominated financial assets automatically became holdings of foreign exchange.

In the end, deciding on the appropriate level of reserves in an open and vulnerable economy such as that of Botswana has to be a matter for local political and economic judgement. The security which reserves confer has to be weighed against the costs involved, whether those of forgoing productive investment or of submitting to onerous foreign-aid requirements for projects which could have been financed domestically.

CONCLUSION

The Government's allocations of development expenditures as between rural and urban areas and communications projects (which overlap both of these categories) are summarized in Table 4.4. As will now be clear from earlier paragraphs, over the whole period since independence, a very high proportion of these expenditures have gone to urban development. These, in turn, have been dominated by the construction of the new town of Selibe-Phikwe, and it can be seen that between 1970/1 and 1973/4, more than three-quarters of capital expenditures were absorbed by urban construction. In contrast, over the whole period, less than one-quarter of expenditures have been in the rural areas, where about 80 per cent of the population still live. The adoption of this expenditure strategy was seen by the Government as the only means whereby domestic revenues could be rapidly increased. Provision of the urban infrastructure was necessary if the mining complex was to be developed. And securing the revenues from copper–nickel exports was thought to be crucial to the long-run financial independence of the Government. In the event, it was the renegotiation of the Customs Union Agreement rather than revenues from minerals that secured the Government's release from dependence upon grants-in-aid. The revenue generated by the imports of capital goods for the mining sector greatly strengthened the Government's financial position, and it was this, together with greater than anticipated diamond revenues, that allowed some change in investment strategy from 1974/5 onwards. Table 4.4 shows that from that date there was some shift away from urban investment, with the rural areas now receiving up to one-third of total expenditure. This change was not exactly dramatic: the proportion of capital investment going to the rural areas between 1975 and 1977 was still not much greater than that achieved in the mid-1960s. Nevertheless, it did suggest that the Government was willing, at least in principle, to keep its pledge to switch the focus of investment to the rural areas, once its own financial position had improved. Whether this trend will continue, or be strengthened, however, is a different issue. The temptation will be for the Government to remain preoccupied with sustaining the growth of domestic revenues, and to continue to postpone the day when a real and fundamental switch in economic strategy is made.

The Fourth National Development Plan (MFDP, 1977), which was published at the end of the period under review, does give some indication of future government strategy. In many ways this is a much more mature document than earlier plans. The macro-economic content is stronger, the rural-development proposals are better articulated, and the plan is not quite so obsessed with the growth and activities of government departments. Both the document itself and the manner in which it was formulated reflect a greater concern than hitherto with the establishment of priorities. Before the plan was drafted ministers and senior officials were convened on a regular basis to discuss development issues so that the plan might more strongly reflect the political perspectives. In the event these discussions were not very conclusive, but there was undoubtedly a much greater openness in the planning process than ever before.

Nevertheless, the Fourth Plan like the Third seems likely in many respects to be overtaken by events. For example, the situation in Zimbabwe necessitated the establishment of a small army at about the same time as the plan was published. Although this has become a significant user of national resources its creation was not anticipated in the drafting of the plan. Moreover, a decision was taken in 1974 to take over the operation of the railway line from Rhodesia Railways. Implementation of this decision will ultimately cost between fifty and a hundred million Pula, but the plan is silent as to how this will be financed. Nor is there any provision for the settlement of refugees which in mid-1978 were entering the country at the rate of several hundred per week. On the credit side, the diamond mine now being established at Jwaneng will further strengthen the revenue base, but this too was scarcely anticipated in the plan.

Perhaps being overtaken by events is inevitable for plans prepared in the context of the present political situation in southern Africa, especially when they are drawn up for a period of five years. In retrospect the late 1960s and the early 1970s in Botswana are likely to be seen as a rather unusual period of stability and growth. The Government's plans, particularly with regard to new sources of revenue, were largely achieved; external relations with South Africa, although not cordial, were at least stable, and the agricultural sector enjoyed a sustained period of good weather. But in a country as vulnerably situated as Botswana, this undisturbed existence cannot last for long. As confrontation between black and white in Africa moves steadily south, it is inconceivable that Botswana will not become more involved than hitherto. A consequence of these social and political imperatives will be that economic progress is likely to be impeded—perhaps for a number of years.

One response to this danger, which the Government seems to be adopting, is to launch a series of emergency and contingency projects or initiatives in order to reduce national vulnerability—especially the vulnerability of the modern sector. The Lifeline Programme, the railway takeover, and the establishment of the Botswana Defence Force are all part of this trend. But these contingency responses themselves call for greater resources, which in the short term can only come from expansion of the mining sector, and particularly of diamond mining. The danger is that a vicious circle may thus be created, with the mining sector being rapidly expanded to provide new resources which are then largely invested in its own protection.

But this response overlooks the fact that the country's greatest resource is its own people and their knowledge of survival in the rather harsh environment in which they live. Future chapters will examine in more detail the nature of Botswana's economic dependence on South Africa, the distribution of the economic gains which have been made, and the agricultural and human potential of the country. From this analysis an outline will be suggested for an alternative strategy in the face of future uncertainty, which would be both more redistributive and which would leave the people of Botswana, if not strictly the national economy, less vulnerable to external events.

CHAPTER 5

AGRICULTURAL PRODUCTION
AND INEQUALITY

Botswana is a cattle country. Cattle now outnumber people by four to one and provide a fundamental part of the livelihood of the majority of Botswana families. Even those fortunate enough to have a secure job in the modern sector of the economy generally also hold a cattle herd. Until recently beef was the most valuable export and in 1974/5 cattle rearing contributed over one-fifth of GDP. Botswana is also an arable country, although the value of arable production is much lower than that of livestock. Nevertheless crop production is vital for many of the poorer people and it is the single most common productive activity.

Unlike much of Africa, where arable cultivation is traditionally carried out by hand on relatively small plots which are intensively cultivated for a few years and then abandoned, in Botswana the ox-drawn plough is used for repeated cultivation of extensive areas of arable land with rather low yields per hectare. There is thus an important link between cattle rearing and arable production, and access to oxen for ploughing is essential for any arable farmer.

Furthermore, mixed pastoral and arable production provides some security against the extreme uncertainties of Botswana's rainfall. Livestock rearing, which depends more on the total rainfall in any year than on its seasonal variation, is a more resilient activity in the face of climatic uncertainty than is arable farming. In years of good rainfall, when crops grow to harvest, people live off their arable produce while the numbers of cattle, sheep, and goats increase. In bad years, when the crops almost totally fail, livestock are available either for consumption—especially smallstock—or, more usually in the case of cattle, for sale to purchase food. Only in times of successive and severe drought, such as was experienced during the mid-1960s, does a significant proportion of the cattle herd die as a result of lack of grazing or water.

Traditional Tswana society had other mechanisms to provide security against drought and to support the poorer households. In good years a portion of the crop would be stored, for subsequent redistribution to the tribe by the chief when the need arose. The extended family provided a measure of support to everyone for food, money, draught power, and agricultural implements. The distribution of cattle ownership, which was probably never very even, was improved by the 'mafisa' system whereby the cattle owner would allocate some or all of his herd to his relatives and friends. For the owner of large herds this provided a source of management and reduced risk, while the recipient could use the cattle for ploughing, and for milk, and would sometimes be given a calf from the cattle he held. Finally, the abundant herds of game were also a source of security in times of drought. Hunting provided a significant source of protein in the diets of tribesmen and their families and, in the more remote parts of the country, it still does so.

While opinions differ on the rate and extent of recent social change, it is generally believed that these traditional methods of security are now breaking down. Certainly there are no longer any tribal stores of food, and cattle grazing is pushing the wildlife herds further and further from the centres of population. Much of the analytic content of this chapter is concerned with the extent to which these changes are undermining the security of the rural people as a whole and promoting the impoverishment of particular groups.

To provide a framework for the analysis, the rural population will be considered, throughout this chapter, in three groups—those who own no cattle, those who own small- to medium-sized herds, and those who own very large herds. These categories are used because access to cattle is critically important both as a source of wealth and security and as a means of undertaking arable production. Some of the more important social and economic characteristics of each group are these:

(1) Cattle ownership and wealth are highly correlated and the group which owns no cattle generally suffers from absolute poverty. The group is disadvantaged in arable production because of the need to borrow or hire oxen for ploughing.[1] Hectarages planted are lower than those planted by cattle owners and thus, the average crop production of this group is also lower (MOA, 1973: Tables 2.5 and 5.5). A high proportion of this group of households have women as their effective household head. These women are either unmarried or their husbands are absent, usually as migrant labourers in South Africa (Bond, 1974: Tables 2.1 and 3.3, and FAO, 1972b). Thus households without cattle are also characteristically short of labour, and ploughing, which is traditionally regarded as men's work, is often difficult.

(2) The second group consists of all cattle owners having up to about fifty head. On the whole these households have little difficulty in ploughing their lands, using their own, exchanged, hired or mafisa'd cattle. Thus they face fewer physical constraints to arable production. On the other hand, these farmers are not wealthy enough to acquire exclusive ownership of a borehole for watering their cattle, and consequently have to use the heavily overgrazed areas surrounding communal watering points.

(3) For the big cattle owners, with more than fifty head each, arable agriculture tends to be a more peripheral activity. This group is quite small but includes some enormously wealthy individuals including the President, the Vice-President, and many other leading figures in the BDP.

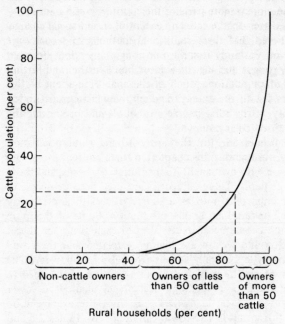

Fig. 5.1 Distribution of Cattle Ownership, 1974/5
Source: The Rural Income Distribution Survey (CSO 1976f)

The distribution of cattle ownership is shown in Fig. 5.1, which is based on the Rural Income Distribution Survey of 1974/5.[2] It can be seen that:

(1) non-cattle-owning households comprise about 45 per cent of all rural households, or over one-third of rural households actually engaged in agriculture;

(2) a further 40 per cent of rural households own up to 50 head each, accounting for one-quarter of the total national cattle herd;

(3) the remaining 15 per cent, who are the large cattle owners, own three-quarters of the national herd.

Thus although it is right to characterize the Batswana as a cattle-owning people this is true of only slightly more than half of the population, and there is a very heavy concentration of ownership among a small group of households. Apart from luck and individual ability, the main historical explanation for this concentration is that chiefs and local headmen were able to acquire considerable numbers of cattle by fines and by the custom of appropriating strays.

This tendency towards concentration of ownership became strongly dominant during the prolonged drought of the mid-1960s. At the height of the drought, when the traditional grazing areas were badly depleted, the administration opened up new grazing potential further west by drilling boreholes in areas which hitherto had no source of water. These boreholes were then allocated to the larger cattle owners on a long-term repayment basis so that they would relieve the pressure on the overgrazed areas by moving their cattle away. Thus at the end of the drought period the large owners frequently found themselves with *de facto* exclusive rights to large tracts of new grazing; meanwhile, many of the smaller cattle owners had lost all their herd. By 1966, the size of the national herd had declined since 1960 by about 400,000 head, approximately one-third of the total (RB, 1968b: 18).

TABLE 5.1   *Proportion of agricultural households without cattle*

Year of Survey	No. of Agricultural Households[1] '000	Owning no cattle %	Holding no cattle %
1968/9	48	n.a.	29
1970/1	52	25	23
1971/2	64	32	30
1974/5	80	37	32
1975/6	80	n.a.	36

[1] Estimates of the number of households which engaged in agricultural production in each year, as given by each survey.

Sources: MOA, 1970a: 30; 1971: 29–30; 1973: 53–4; 1975a: 3; 1978: 19.

There is evidence from the Agricultural Surveys carried out since independence that the trend towards a more unequal distribution of ownership has continued. Table 5.1 gives the relevant figures. The proportion of agricultural households not owning or not holding cattle appears to have increased in recent years.[3] The difference between the 'owning' and 'holding' columns—generally about 2 per cent—reflects the 'mafisa' custom. It is worth noting that although between 10 and 20 per cent of the national herd is mafisa'd (MOA, 1973: 57, and FAO, 1974: 66), it is predominantly those families which already own cattle that benefit. The 'mafisa' system does not greatly reduce the proportion of agricultural households who have no immediate access to cattle (FAO, 1972b: 12).

CATTLE REARING

Since the end of the rinderpest epidemic at the turn of the century the cattle population of Botswana has grown fairly steadily, albeit with set-backs from time to time as a result of the outbreak of disease. A veterinary department was established in 1905. As a result of its work the major contagious livestock diseases were steadily eradicated and the tsetse fly became confined to a small area in the north-west, more or less coterminus with the Okavango Delta. In order to control foot-and-mouth disease a system of cordon fences has been built. Cattle are not permitted to pass from one cordon zone to another without going through quarantine. This system, together with regular vaccination campaigns, has brought the disease under control. There has been only one major outbreak of foot-and-mouth disease since independence. This occurred towards the end of 1977 and it seemed to have been controlled by the middle of 1978.

The important veterinary work undertaken by the colonial adminis-tration laid the foundations for the modern livestock industry. Because the cattle are disease-free, meat exports from Botswana (as from Kenya but unlike those from most other African countries) are per-mitted into the lucrative European market.

The most dramatic increase in the numbers of cattle in Botswana occurred after independence. In 1966, at the end of the drought, the cattle herd numbered less than a million head. Ten years later it had increased to nearly three million. (MFDP, 1977: 138). The offtake rate for commercial slaughter varies considerably but rarely exceeds ten per cent per year, tending to be higher in drought years when the cattle are threatened by lack of grazing, and lower in good years when owners are anxious to build up their herds. Although this offtake rate is low and could be doubled at least, it is high compared with other African countries. The Batswana appear to stand out from other pastoral peoples in that cattle are increasingly regarded as a commercial com-modity, not just as a symbol of traditional wealth and status.

Apart from about 300,000 cattle in the freehold-farm areas (MOA, 1975a; CSO, 1972b), most cattle are raised in the tribal areas. Tradition-ally, land within the tribal areas in the common property of the tribe and is allocated by the chief or the local headman. In practice, however, land is usually passed from father to son. Land which is close to the villages is generally allocated for arable production, and is referred to as 'the lands', with the more distant locations being used for grazing. But the two land uses are very intermingled and the eastern part of

Botswana is generally a mixed pastoral-arable farming region. Further west, however, the land is more completely turned over to grazing. Those who graze their cattle in these remoter regions frequently also erect a dwelling in the area, termed a 'cattle post'. The small cattle owners depend on communal water sources, such as a well or a council-operated borehole, to water their cattle. In consequence, cattle herds tend to concentrate around water sources and severe local overgrazing can occur. The owners of large herds often finance their own boreholes, and for reasons which will be discussed later, they acquire *de facto* exclusive grazing rights in the area. Overall nearly 30 per cent of farmers (about half of all cattle owners) have a cattle post (MOA, 1968), although there is considerable regional variation. Perhaps only 5 per cent of farmers have their own borehole.[4]

Since 1970, when the Tribal Land Act came into force, the responsibility for allocating land has been taken over by the new Tribal Land Boards. These comprise the chief, one nominee of the chief, two members elected by the District Council, and two government nominees. The Boards are expected to keep records of their proceedings and allocations, the principal aim of the new legislation being to make the process of land allocation more democratic and less arbitrary.

PROPOSED CHANGES IN LAND TENURE

Disease eradication and increasing commercialization of the agricultural sector have encouraged an enormous growth in the cattle population of Botswana. The extension of grazing areas has in turn caused great ecological change. Large trees have tended to disappear from the landscape and in some places, particularly around watering points, the grass cover has almost completely disappeared. It has been replaced by scrubby acacia thornbush on which only goats can browse. But this is a slow secular change, only observable by those who have watched the coutryside over a period of many years, and easily masked by rainfall-induced variations from one year to another. In consequence the seriousness of the problem is not always recognized.

Nevertheless overgrazing of tribal land has been a concern of the administration since before independence. The 1965 Porter Report commented as follows:

Control over grazing is one of the most important single factors in the development of the livestock industry. We would go so far as to say that if adequate control is not secured within a reasonable period there will be a serious threat to the survival of the livestock industry and with it the economy as a whole. The opening up of new grazing areas without adequate controls merely spreads the devastation. It is thus of primary importance that energetic efforts be made at all levels to persuade the people to accept modifications to the present system of ownership of land in the tribal territories which will adapt it to present conditions. (RB 1966b: 10).

Since then the theme has been reiterated in each of the five national development plans, but it was difficult to see how to proceed. The problem is that for each marginal increase in the size of the national herd the benefits flow to the owner of the marginal animal, while herd the costs, in the form of deterioration of the range, are borne by the community as a whole. Thus an individual cattle owner always has a net incentive to increase the size of his herd.

One possible solution would have been to move from communal to individual land tenure. Under this system—as happened in Kenya— each individual would become responsible for the conservation of his particular piece of land. But how should the land be divided up and distributed? If each tribesman were to get an equal share, individual holdings would be uneconomically small, and some families would have land and no livestock while others would have too many animals for their allotted land. A market in land would have to develop and eventually land ownership would become as skewed as cattle ownership now is, whatever the initial distribution might be. Eventually, fifteen per cent of the rural population would own three-quarters of the grazing land, and nearly half—those with no cattle—would end up with none. Apart from the practical difficulties, such a solution is quite alien to the traditional system of land tenure, and the Government judged it to be politically infeasible—and inequitable—even though BDP politicians would have been among the principal beneficiaries.

At the other extreme, an alternative solution was that the State, or the local Tribal Land Board, should exercise greater conservation control in the interests of the community, thereby reinforcing and regulating the existing system of communal tenure. Such control would have to include periodic compulsory destocking of certain areas, as well as control over stocking rates and community management of grazing. The latter aspect is important because it is known that modern management methods, such as rotational grazing, can markedly increase the carrying capacity of the range. But this solution also would have met with popular opposition. Destocking, being associated with disease and drought control measures of the colonial era, is anathema to most Batswana. Equally, there is very strong resistance among farmers to surrendering the management of their cattle to someone else, except in the context of the traditional 'mafisa' system.

The Vice-President, reflecting on the dilemma in 1970, had this to say:

we should agree that whilst individual fencing of grazing is quite indefensible, communal fencing should not only be permitted but encouraged.

If the people who live in a particular area are willing to co-operate in the erection of fences leading to communally organised grazing control, much larger numbers of cattle may be safely accommodated within a given area. (Masire, 1970)

Such advocacy of voluntary communal grazing fell on deaf ears. When some experimental-group ranches along these lines were initiated a few years later only three got started and none has so far really worked.

TABLE 5.2   *Borehole allocations in Central District*

Year	Number of Allocations[1]
1971	83
1972	149
1973	138
1974	126[2]
1975	2
1976	10
TOTAL	508

[1] The figures refer only to new borehole approvals for cattle-watering purposes. Boreholes for other uses, transfers of boreholes from one owner to another, and registration of existing boreholes etc., are excluded.

[2] Of these, 122 were approved in a five-day session of the Tribal Land Board in Febuary 1974. The 'freeze' on further approvals was imposed soon afterwards.

Source: Records of the Ngwato Tribal Land Board.

In the meantime the problems were getting worse. Apart from the ecological deterioration, *de facto* changes in land tenure, amounting in effect to a land grab on the part of the owners of large herds, was already underway. Following the precedent established as a drought-relief measure in the 1960s, a growing number of applications were being made to the Tribal Land Boards for permission to sink individual boreholes for cattle watering. In the early 1970s the number of such allocations was accelerating rapidly (Table 5.2). Although Table 5.2 refers only to the large Central District, the home of the Ngwato, most of the big cattle herds are to be found here and the land rush in this area was on a larger scale than elsewhere. A conventional rule, probably established in the drought-relief exercise, was that each new borehole had to be at least eight kilometres from its nearest neighbour, so each allocation implied exclusive access to grazing over an area of more than 60 square kilometres. Thus, between 1971 and 1974, no more than five hundred individuals (there were several multiple applications) acquired *de facto* grazing rights over nearly a quarter of the whole of the Central District. Eventually the Government attempted to control the situation by imposing a freeze on new applications which accounts for the sudden decline in allocations between 1975 and 1976. This however amounted to closing the stable door after most of the horses had bolted.

But this is to run ahead. An international conference in Gaborone on Sustained Production in Semi-Arid Lands (BNR, 1971) at the end of 1971 and a consultants' report on Rural Development (Chambers and Feldman, 1973) in the following year created a much greater awareness of the conservation aspects of the problem and finally stimulated some action. The latter report also suggested a solution. The essence of this was a controlled opening up of new grazing land, which would be leased to individual owners of large herds for commercial ranching. The resulting movement of cattle out of the existing communal areas would relieve the pressure on the overgrazed land, which would henceforth be reserved for the small owners who might ultimately be persuaded or obliged to operate a system of communal management.

These proposals, which amounted to an ingenious mixture of the two extreme solutions outlined above, excited considerable interest. The politicians, being owners of large herds themselves, were pleased with a scheme which made individual, albeit leased, tenure not just respectable but also a positive mechanism for providing better grazing for the small man. After considerable discussion the essence of the consultants' proposals was made official policy, and a white paper dealing with these matters was published in July 1975 (RB, 1975b).

For the present discussion, the details of this policy are not of great importance and will no doubt change with time. More important is that the concept on which the policy was based, the opening up of new grazing land, soon proved to be a mirage. A land-use planning exercise revealed that many of the areas which it was thought could be utilized for grazing were found either to be already in use or to be unsuitable. This was most frequently because there was neither surface water nor ground water locally available for cattle watering. In other areas there were competing interests for the use of the land, either from the few remaining wandering bands of Sarwa (Bushmen) or for wildlife conservation.

Nevertheless the policy is being pursued. The opening up of new lands for commercial ranching has largely become a conversion of the *de facto* rights which owners of large herds had already acquired around their boreholes into *de jure* rights enshrined in a lease. But in this form and without the availability of significant areas of new land, the Tribal Grazing Land Programme, as it has come to be called, contains several internal contradictions. These suggest that the rhetoric of an equitable solution, which characterizes the Government's policy papers on the subject, will not be reflected in practice.

First, without major changes in the management of cattle and without significant new areas of grazing land, there are now more cattle in Botswana than the range can support on a long-term basis. Government publications (MOA, 1976b: 7, 12) show that there are approximately 220,000 square kilometres of grazing land now in use in Botswana, and that this area is capable of sustaining two million cattle, under traditional management practices, in an average rainfall year. At the end of 1976, there were in fact about three million cattle together with almost two million sheep and goats. The carrying capacity does, of course, vary from year to year. In 1976 and the years immediately preceeding there had been good rains and the range seemed to be supporting the extra million cattle reasonably well. It is equally clear that in the severe drought just over a decade earlier the range could barely support one million head. In short the total livestock population under any approach to land tenure which is presently conceivable is now larger than can be supported in the future. Either new methods of management, or destocking, or both, are urgently required. The latter does not form part of government policy;[5] the former implies communal or group management of cattle holdings on a scale which would affect virtually every owner, and neither the resources nor the will to undertake this presently exist.[6]

Second, there is a danger that in the implementation of the policy the pressure of the excess cattle will become steadily worse in the existing overgrazed communal areas, quite the reverse of the original intention. Pressure to establish the commercial ranches will be considerable and they may well be given priority. Stocking limits will be imposed as a condition of the leases. But since the total cattle population is already too great, the excess cattle will concentrate even more heavily in the existing overgrazed communal areas.

Third, the creation of commercial ranches out of tribal grazing land implies that tribesmen with few or no cattle are surrendering their traditional right to the use of this land. The rent to be paid on the leases is considered to be compensation for the loss of this right. But the rent will actually flow to the Tribal Land Boards and not to the tribesmen concerned, nor will there be any automatic mechanism to ensure that an economic rent is and continues to be charged.

Perhaps the best that can be said of the policy is that it is not as inequitable as it might be. The move to a system of freehold tenure has been resisted and, in view of the land grab, some important safeguards for ordinary tribesmen have been written into the policy documents. The execution of these policies is still at an early stage. The influence of the particular politicians and civil servants who have promoted the safeguards—often against their own interests—will decline. As this happens the safeguards will probably come to be disregarded in a political system entirely controlled by large cattle owners. In the meantime, because the need to limit the total number of livestock in the country as a whole, or in particular areas, has been side-stepped, it seems unlikely that the programme will help to conserve the extremely fragile ecology of the land.

In fact, another solution has been proposed, though not yet considered by the Government, which would go a long way towards meeting the objectives of both equity and conservation (Reynolds, 1977: 12–19). Under this scheme, tribal grazing land would be turned over to a public company in which each tribesman would have a single inalienable share. The company would assess each year the grazing potential and then auction off grazing rights for the year. In this way the land would always earn an economic rent which would accrue, through dividends, to the traditional holders of grazing rights whether or not they owned cattle themselves.[7] While the rich and powerful would no doubt quickly gain control of the company's management the proposal would be much less susceptible to manipulation and distortion than the vague guarantees of the present policy.

BOTSWANA MEAT COMMISSION

Apart from the series of disease-control measures undertaken during the colonial period, the other major foundation on which the modern livestock industry has been built is the export abattoir established at Lobatse in 1954. This has reduced dependence on the historically unreliable South African cattle market, increased the value-added of the cattle industry in Botswana, and lowered transport costs by halving the average distance which cattle had to be trekked or railed before slaughter. (Previously cattle for slaughter had to be consigned to abattoirs in South Africa or Zimbabwe).

The original investment was initiated by the Commonwealth Development Corporation, which took 50 per cent of the equity and provided the management. In 1965 legislation was introduced setting up the BMC as a parastatal corporation, which, it was agreed, should take over the ownership and operation of the abattoir from early 1966. The legislation gave the BMC a monopoly on the export of all cattle and beef but also required that the BMC 'secure that so far as it is reasonably possible all livestock offered or available for sale to the Commission are purchased' (LB, 1974). Six members of the ten-man board were to be appointed directly by the President, the remaining four were to be chosen from a panel submitted by the Livestock Advisory Committee, set up for the purpose.

The BMC purchases cattle only at its own front gate and in accordance with pre-arranged quotas. As it is rather difficult for the small cattle owner, for whom the sale of an animal is an occasional business, to rail or trek his cattle to the abattoir itself, or to handle the complexities of the quota system, a series of internal cattle-marketing arrangements has grown up within the country. Such farmers either sell to the BMC through an agent or a marketing co-operative, or, more often, to a local trader or 'cattle speculator'. The latter are frequently owners of freehold farms who fatten cattle before slaughter. As a result, although about half the cattle delivered to the BMC come from freehold farms and half from the tribal farming areas, in reality the proportion which comes indirectly from the tribal areas is much greater.

Complex though the arrangements may be they are undoubtedly facilitated by the fact that cattle owners have a marketing outlet in all corners of the country. Whether the small owner, who frequently has to sell a beast in order to meet some emergency requirement for cash, always gets a fair price is much more doubtful. Local traders are often monopoly buyers and agents can readily exploit their clients (MOA, 1975a). In order to encourage better returns for the small man the Government has fostered the growth of voluntary cattle-marketing co-operatives. In recent years this movement has flourished and now accounts for about a quarter of all sales to the BMC. There have been additional small measures to improve internal marketing—most notably the formation in 1973 of the Botswana Livestock Development Corporation, which purchases cattle mainly from farmers in the north-west of the country.

The operations of the BMC since its establishment are summarized in Table 5.3. The BMC came into existence at the end of the long drought period of the mid-1960s, and consequently the numbers of cattle being processed through the abattoir (143,000 in 1965 and 132,000 in 1966) were higher than ever before. Throughput declined dramatically in the following year as a result of better rainfall. Since then an upward trend has been maintained, with the number of cattle slaughtered increasing at approximately the same rate as the growth of the cattle population. Producer prices, including the variable bonus which the BMC pays to its suppliers at the end of each trading year, increased by 150 per cent between 1966 and 1976, reflecting world-wide increases in the price of beef.

During the decade the product sold has been made more sophisticated with more processing being undertaken in Botswana. Initially, most sales were of whole frozen carcasses or canned meat, with less than a third of the throughput being deboned before export. In 1970,

TABLE 5.3 *The livestock industry, 1966–1976*

	Year										
	1966	1967	1968	1969	1970	1971	1972	1973	1974	1975	1976
National cattle herd (millions)	1.2	1.5	1.7	1.9	2.0	2.1	2.2	2.1	2.3	2.6	2.9
BMC throughput (thousands)	132	89	104	93	127	167	157	209	186	188	212
Average producer price including bonus (P/100kg. cdw)	29	32	34	34	35	36	46	56	73	69	73
Total payments to producers (P millions)[1]	6.9	6.4	8.1	7.4	9.2	12.1	15.1	26.5	28.0	27.4	31.8
Values of BMC sales (P millions)	8.6	12.3	11.6	10.2	13.8	17.1	22.6	36.1	38.0	41.9	53.4

[1] Includes payments for smallstock, which are probably less than five per cent of the totals.

Sources: cattle figures from the *National Development Plan, 1976–81* (MFDP, 1977: 138). Other data from *BMC Annual Reports* (BMC, 1967–1977).

the proportion of throughput being deboned jumped to more than half and has continued to rise, to 85 per cent in 1976.

Since the BMC was formed the principal markets have been the United Kingdom and South Africa, each of which have taken just under 40 per cent by weight of total throughput. For most of the period Botswana has had a quota to sell 1,000 frozen carcasses a week in the South African market, together with some boneless beef, and although this quota has not always been filled this market has remained fairly steady. By contrast, the proportion of meat sent to the United Kingdom market has tended to increase, peaking at 68 per cent in 1973, and being 52 per cent of throughput in 1976.

Britain's accession to the European Economic Community caused considerable marketing problems. Because of over-production of beef in Europe in 1974, the EEC imposed levies on the import of beef to the member countries, including the United Kingdom, and eventually banned all beef imports. It was fortunate that the South African market was at the time undersupplied and Botswana was able to exceed its usual quota and export two-thirds of its output for the year to South Africa at good prices. The European market was reopened to Botswana early in 1975, following the signing of the Lome Convention, but an import levy was imposed which at a peak of nearly one Pula per kilogram would have halved the incomes of producers. Following intensive negotiations agreement was reached with the EEC to rebate 90 per cent of the levy in July 1975. The agreement has been extended periodically, but only at the expense of almost continuous and time-consuming lobbying and negotiation.

Blessed with a certain measure of good luck the BMC has done its job creditably well. Increases in revenue have generally flowed back to the cattle producers, rather than being syphoned off in taxation as so often happens in Africa, which in turn has stimulated further production. Indeed, if anything, the industry has contributed too little in taxation for obvious political reasons. But there remains a continuing debate whether the BMC could, as it is statutorily required to do, handle all the cattle which might be offered for sale in a drought. This is a critically important issue in the light of the earlier conclusion that the country is overstocked. Recalling that in a severe and prolonged drought the range in Botswana can carry perhaps no more than one million cattle it would not be surprising to see more than half a million cattle, worth P75 million to producers, offered for sale each year to the abattoir in the event of drought recurring. This is considerably in excess of the abattoir's capacity.

The BMC management has always been reluctant to invest in additional capacity, whether in Lobatse or elsewhere, simply to cushion the effects of a severe drought. But history has shown that periodic drought is one of the major dangers to which Botswana's vulnerable economy is susceptible. It is surprising that the harsh experiences of the 1960s have been forgotten so quickly and that this contingency investment has not so far been made.

SMALLSTOCK

Cattle rearing largely accounts for the monetized sector of the rural economy, which in this respect is dominated by fifteen per cent of rural households with the occasional involvement of a further forty per cent. Much of the rest of this chapter concerns the rural subsistence sector and arable agriculture. But, before leaving the discussion of livestock, some mention should be made of the important role of smallstock—sheep and goats—in the subsistence economy.

The smallstock population has, like that of cattle, tripled between 1966 and 1976, from about 600,000 to 1,800,000, with goats outnumbering sheep by about three to one. In many ways smallstock are the poor man's cattle. Ownership is more widespread than that of cattle; in 1974/5 three quarters of farming households owned smallstock (MOA, 1978: Table 19) and the distribution of ownership is much less skew. Smallstock fill a similar economic function to cattle in that they represent a reserve of wealth and especially of food which can be called upon in times of need. In fact, while cattle are only very occasionally slaughtered for the owner's consumption, most smallstock are killed and consumed within the rural areas, and are thus an important source of protein. Only a small number, averaging 25,000 a year since 1966, are sent to the BMC, with considerable variation from one year to another. Although capacity exists to slaughter four times this number, and markets for the meat could be found, there has been very little attempt to make the production of smallstock more commercialized.

Indeed, so strong is the emphasis on cattle in Botswana, both among the people themselves and among government agriculturalists, that the importance of smallstock to the well-being and security of the rural community is generally overlooked. Smallstock owners tend to be much less concerned about the welfare of their flocks than of their cattle, while the Government has, until very recently, devoted virtually no resources to eradication of smallstock diseases, better smallstock management, or to improved breeds. Even now the resources which are being devoted to this sector are in no way commensurate with its importance. Meanwhile, the lack of any policy towards, or control over, smallstock grazing is exacerbating the problem of land conservation around the villages and watering places.

ARABLE FARMING

The crop cycle begins in November or thereabouts with the arrival of the first heavy rain. Families then begin to migrate from the villages to the surrounding lands areas where they remain intermittently until the end of the harvest. Formerly the local chief had to choose the day for the migration to start, but this custom has now almost completely died out. About three-quarters of farming households have a separate dwelling at the lands (MOA, 1973: 22). Six or eight oxen are usually required for a ploughing team, and if, as frequently happens, there is very little grass left from the previous season, the operation cannot really start until the oxen have had a chance to get into condition on the new shoots of grass. Thus the rainy season can be well advanced before the fields are ready for planting. This is especially so for families without cattle who have to borrow or hire a ploughing team after the owners have finished. Ploughing is done mainly by men; planting is shared between men and women, while the remaining crop activities —weeding, bird scaring, harvesting and threshing—are undertaken almost entirely by women (Bond, 1974: 16). After harvesting, in about May or June, the people return to the village. Sometimes it may be necessary to return even earlier if the rains have not been adequate to replenish the shallow surface water supplies which are characteristic of lands areas.

The principal subsistence crops are sorghum and maize, with millet and beans also being commonly grown. Table 5.4 summarizes the production of maize and sorghum for all the years for which data are available. The most striking feature of the Table is the enormous variation in production from one year to another such that production in a good year is several times greater than in a bad year. This feature underlines the need to have some type of food reserves from one year to the next.

The Table also demonstrates the increasing production of maize in recent years, even though sorghum is a more drought-resistent crop and better suited than maize to Botswana conditions. A number of explanations for this trend are posited. The most common is that there is an increasing consumer preference for maize. This is true in the urban areas but mainly because, the alternative, factory-produced sorghum meal has been an inferior product. There is no evidence that maize is preferred to hand-pounded sorghum, which is the norm in rural areas. In addition, maize consumed in the towns is usually imported from South Africa, though ground within Botswana, and thus there is no direct supply-and-demand relationship between maize production and consumption within Botswana itself. A more likely explanation is that growing sorghum requires more labour. This is because the sorghum head is open and therefore vulnerable to birds, while the maize cob is

TABLE 5.4 *Sorghum and maize production,[1] 1967/8–1975/6*

					Crop year				
	1967/8	1968/9	1969/70	1970/1	1971/2	1972/3	1973/4[2]	1974/5	1975/6
Hectarage planted (thousands)									
Sorghum	57	103	120	161	180	90	181	100	178
Maize	30	42	26	38	26	186	113	100	223
Average yield (kg./hectare)									
Sorghum	183	289	65	455	379	114	400	338	311
Maize	253	303	56	435	390	120	300	287	281
Production (thousands of tons)									
Sorghum	10	30	8	73	68	10	72	34	56
Maize	7	13	2	17	10	22	34	29	63
Average rainfall (mm.)[3]	437	428	360	467	617	291	722	695	662

[1] All data refer to traditional tenure areas only; production on freehold farms is excluded.

[2] No agricultural survey in 1973/4; estimates based on interviews with farmers and agricultural-extension personnel. There is also considerable variation in the quality of the data for other years.

[3] Approximate seasonal rainfall averaged over the crop-growing areas.

Sources: Agricultural Statistics 1977 (MOA, 1978: 25), which in turn are based on *Annual Agricultural Surveys.*

enclosed. Consequently, sorghum requires more bird scaring than maize. A third possible explanation is that the increased production of maize is commercial rather than subsistence production, a matter which will be considered later. Whatever the explanation it is quite possible that the trend towards maize production is a temporary phenomenon encouraged by several recent years of good rains, which could quickly reverse if and when drought conditions return.

The apparent upward trend in the total production of maize and sorghum over the period, which is also shown in Table 5.4, may too be a temporary phenomenon associated with better rains. However, we are more inclined to the view that there is a genuine underlying upward trend in arable production as a result of increasing mechanization and commercialization of a small number of successful and energetic farmers, especially in the south-east.

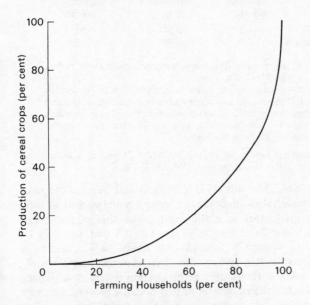

Fig. 5.2 Distribution of Crop Production, 1972
Source: Agricultural Survey 1971/72 (MOA 1973:47)

Fig. 5.2 shows the distribution in production of cereal crops in 1972. Although not as skew as the distribution of cattle ownership, it is nevertheless clear that arable output, like that of livestock, is dominated by a relatively small number of farmers. Thus twenty per cent of farmers accounted for sixty per cent of output; at the other extreme half the farmers managed to produce only just over ten per cent of the total cereal output.

To explain this pattern of production it is necessary to return to the three categories of rural households set out at the beginning of this chapter in order to consider the particular opportunities for and constraints on arable farming in each case. But the important distinction is now between cattle-owning households and non-cattle-owning households so the large cattle owners can be merged with the group of small cattle owners. Although there will be differences between and within these groups, the similarities are more important than the differences.

TABLE 5.5   *Arable production*[1] *by cattle ownership, 1971/2*

	Average hectarage planted[2]	Average production kg.	Ownership of implements per cent
Cattle owners	4.5	3,500	81
Non-cattle owners	3.0	800	29

[1] Production of the three major crops, sorghum, maize, and millet, countrywide in the 1971/2 crop year.
[2] The data in this column strictly relate to cattle holders and non-cattle holders, rather than owners and non-owners, but as noted in the text the two are highly correlated. Because the area planted may include a small amount of other crops, notably peas and beans, it is not possible to calculate cereal yields from this table.

Source: Agricultural Survey for 1971/2 (MOA, 1973), various tables recalculated. For similar results see also FAO, 1972b:20.

In Table 5.5 data from the 1971/2 Agricultural Survey, the most comprehensive undertaken in Botswana, have been reworked to compare the arable production of cattle owners with that of non-cattle-owning farmers.[8] The Table strikingly demonstrates that, not only do non-cattle owners manage to plough only about two-thirds of the average hectarage of cattle owners, but that, even more significantly, their yields are smaller. Hence average production is very much lower, being in that year less than a quarter of that of cattle owners. Although great stress cannot be laid on the precise figures in Table 5.5, there is abundant evidence from other sources and other agricultural surveys that arable production among non-cattle owners is very low indeed. The most important cause of this lower production revolves around the difficulties experienced by these households in having their lands ploughed. Taking the 1971/2 season again as an example, it was estimated in that year that 56 per cent of all households ploughed with their own cattle, 11 per cent with 'mafisa'd' cattle, 15 per cent with hired cattle, and 37 per cent with borrowed or exchanged cattle (MOA, 1973: 63). These figures include some overlapping arrangements. Although the proportion of hired arrangements is rather small, Curtis (1972) has shown that the 'borrow' or 'exchange' arrangements, which are of most relevance to non-cattle owners, frequently involve the exchange of one factor of production for another, such as working in the cattle owner's field or lending him implements. Yet non-cattle owning households tend to be those which are also short of other factors of production. The fact that a high proportion are headed by women imply that they are short of labour,[9] and Table 5.5 further indicates that this group lacks implements. At the same time the traditional social obligation to plough for one's poorer relatives, if necessary without recompense, is slowly applying to a narrower and narrower circle (Curtis, 1972).

The overall effect of these cumulative disadvantages is not generally that the poorer households are unable to plough, rather that they are unable to plough an adequate area at the optimum time. Their ploughing tends to be left until the end when the rainy season is already advanced. Hectarages are lower and yields are lower. In short these households are faced with a whole range of constraints to arable production which they cannot readily overcome.

GOVERNMENT PROGRAMMES FOR ARABLE AGRICULTURE

After 1962, the approach to agricultural extension in Botswana was to concentrate on a few farmers who had sufficient cattle to plough and who were willing to adopt improved techniques such as planting in rows. Once a farmer was registered with the scheme then he received considerable support and advice from the local agricultural demonstrator. Lever, studying the service in 1968, found that there was one demonstrator for about 25 farmers in the scheme and that on average the registered farmers were visited nearly twice a month (Lever, 1970: 29, 34).

Lever concluded that the benefits of the scheme scarcely outweighed its costs. Certainly there was little evidence that the results were diffusing beyond the small group of registered farmers, so this approach was abandoned in 1973 in favour of a more widespread extension effort. The new approach, if it is to be successful, requires much better management and the co-ordination of various methods of extension, such as working with groups of farmers, farmer courses, radio programmes, and visual materials. So far this does not seem to have happened and it is probable that field staff still tend to concentrate on the easier and more satisfying work with a small number of successful and demanding farmers.[10] However, reorganization of the service is being undertaken.

There was very little research into cereal-crop production before independence but in 1967 a large research station was opened, and two years later, a more systematic programme of research into improved methods of arable farming under Botswana's 'dryland' conditions was started. By 1976, the results of the research were grouped together as a new farming system and began to be tested under field conditions.[11] Although the new method has several elements, which need not necessarily all be introduced together, the two most important are those which relate to water conservation. Instead of ploughing the land in preparation for planting, 'sweeps' are used to break up the surface and the stubble without turning the soil over. This reduces evaporation loss. Ideally, the first sweep of the ground is undertaken soon after harvest so that few weeds are left during the dry season which can later take up the moisture from the first rains. The other important water-conserving element is early and systematic weeding after germination, which in turn is facilitated by planting in rows rather than the more traditional method of broadcasting.

At the same time, a wheeled 'tool carrier' has been developed. This is locally called a Makgonatsotlhe, meaning the 'machine that does everything'. Various agricultural implements such as sweeps, planters, cultivators, or a scotch cart body can be attached to the basic frame of the machine. The Makgonatsotlhe is an important innovation in Botswana in two ways. First, because it is a wheeled vehicle and is not usually used for ploughing, the draught power required is very much reduced. It can in fact be drawn by four donkeys. Second, the total capital outlay for the machine and its associated draught power is much less than for the traditional ploughing system used in Botswana.

Preliminary results from the first farmer trials of the new system suggest that a major increase in yields can be achieved.[12] But it will not really have been tested until there have been some years of low rainfall. Whether farmers in general, outside the confines of the research and testing programmes, will come to see the new system as offering a better and less risky return to their labour has yet to be seen. Nor is it clear to what group of farmers it will appeal. Those who already have access to oxen for ploughing together with traditional implements may be rather slow to invest in new implements unless the benefits of the new system prove to be dramatically obvious. For those farmers who do not own cattle or the necessary implements, it might be expected that the combination of Makgonatsothle and donkeys would be attractive. But few such farmers could summon the wherewithal to purchase the new system, and it seems improbable that many being unaccustomed to producing a surplus would be willing to purchase on credit, even if they could offer the security usually requested by a credit institution.

This is not the place to make definitive judgements on one farming system or another; that is for the farmers themselves to do. But two general conclusions should be drawn. First, it is technically possible, using comparatively labour-intensive techniques, to attain much higher yields in Botswana's climatic circumstances, even in years of poor rainfall, than is now commonly achieved. It may be that Botswana will never be as productive as the maize regions of South Africa or Zimbabwe, but some improvements in arable agriculture can certainly be made which would enhance the well-being of many Batswana. The frequently experienced pessimism on this subject is misguided. Second, as the earlier discussion has shown, many poor farmers in Botswana lack adequate means of production. Technical change will merely pass them by unless some way is found of providing them with the tools to do the job. Whether this should be by a redistribution of cattle wealth, or by diverting some of the mineral revenues directly into providing agricultural capital for deprived farmers, or in some other way is a matter for political debate.

CROP CONSUMPTION AND MARKETING

Although various series of data for the import and export of cereal crops up to 1971 have been published, there are major discrepancies between them and we have not considered them sufficiently reliable to reproduce here. Data since 1971 are even more fragmentary. However, from a number of independent studies it can be estimated that the per capita consumption of cereals is around 120 kilograms a year (FAO, 1974: 85, FAO, 1972c: 8, Biggs, 1966: 9, BP, 1963: 9). From this it may be inferred that current consumption is approximately 80,000 tonnes a year. Comparing this figure with the production data in Table 5.4 and bearing in mind, on the one hand that that Table excludes production of millet, and on the other that allowance has to be made for the following season's seed, it may be tentatively concluded that Botswana is self-sufficient in cereal production in a good crop year, though there are always exports of maize and imports of maize meal. However, because the distribution of household production is so skew, national self-sufficiency is no indication of household self-sufficiency. In a good year, perhaps only just over half of farming households produce sufficient cereal for their own consumption. In a bad year, the situation is very much worse.

In general the association between crop production and annual rainfall is very clear from the data in Table 5.4. However, 1975 was an unusual year, in that although good rains were experienced crop production was down by nearly a half. This phenomenon is believed to be the result of many households not planting at all, or planting lower hectarages in the 1975 season because they were still carrying food surpluses from the previous exceptionally good year.

If this explanation is correct then it demonstrates the need to have adequate market and transport arrangements if farmers are to produce for a surplus rather than simply for their own subsistence needs. This has never been a major problem for the larger arable farmers who tend to be found in the south-east corner of the country and who could readily sell their surplus to the South African Maize Board. But until the establishment of the Botswana Agricultural Marketing Board (BAMB) in 1974 small farmers with a surplus to sell would take it in bags to the local trading store, where typically they would get a price much below the floor price in South Africa for that year.[13] Traders did not usually store crops from year to year but would sell the purchased grain to the South African Maize Board. In other years, households would wish to purchase grain from the trader, which in turn was imported from South Africa. Thus a household would find itself purchasing grain in a poor year at several times the price for which it sold grain in a surplus year. While some of the price margin may be attributed to local monopoly exploitation by traders, such an *ad hoc* marketing system involving large transport costs was inherently inefficient.

At the time of writing BAMB had only been in operation for four seasons and it was difficult to assess its impact in raising and stabilizing prices. Following the enactment of the enabling legislation early in 1974, BAMB came swiftly into operation for that year's exceptionally good harvest at a time when producer prices seemed to be plummeting. Although BAMB did not yet have any permanent facilities of its own an emergency sorghum-buying programme was launched. Rather late in the season, six buying depots were established which, together with two co-operatives acting as agents for the Board, purchased 5,800 tonnes of sorghum, most of which had to be stored outside. The purchase represented about 8 per cent of the crop for that year.

For the future BAMB estimates that a turnover of 10,000 tonnes of cereal and 5,000 tonnes of pulses and sunflower, which are increasingly grown as cash crops, will be necessary to achieve financial viability. In 1977, this was much higher than current turnover and there seemed to be a danger that the Government would give BAMB a monopoly on export sales, and thereby encourage the sort of legendary inefficiency to which parastatal marketing boards in Africa appear to be liable.

In the meantime, however, BAMB's purchasing and pricing policy seems to be exemplary and in some respects is more suited to the small farmer than that of the BMC. In 1976 BAMB purchased at four depots

and eleven co-ops, whereas BMC only purchases at Lobatse. BAMB
gives producers immediate cash payment; the BMC only pays after the
animal has been slaughtered. BAMB's minimum-purchase quantity was
just one bag, worth about six Pula; the usual minimum BMC quota is
twelve cattle which can be worth up to two thousand Pula. Even
during the 1974 emergency-buying programme BAMB records that
45 per cent of the grain purchased came from producers with less than
ten bags for sale (BAMB, 1975). While this obviously excludes the
many producers who had no surplus at all, it does illustrate BAMB's
potential to provide a market for the smaller farmer.

DROUGHT RELIEF

Traditionally, in times of drought, households depend for their food
and livelihood on either livestock or hunting or a broad network of
family relationships. Since the long drought of the 1960s, however,
international food aid, especially that provided by the World Food
Programme (WFP), has come to play a prominent role. WFP aid started
in the drought of 1965 and since independence food-for-work programmes have been operated every year in which there has been a
partial crop failure, that is following the harvests of 1966, 1968,
1969 which was continued into 1970 and 1973.[14] In 1970, there was
some government concern that this repeated food aid was acting as
a disincentive to arable production, and consequently the Food and
Agriculture Organization undertook a survey into the numbers and
social and economic characteristics of food-for-work participants
(FAO, 1974).

Table 5.6, based on that survey, indicates how households reported
that they obtained food when their own harvest was insufficient.
Fully two-thirds of the responses indicated some traditional mechanism, either selling stock or seeking help from others, while only 12
per cent of responses indicated food-for-work programmes. Interestingly,
the same survey estimated that fully 38 per cent of rural households
had in fact been involved in a food-for-work programme at some time
or other, which suggests that the breakdown of traditional mechanisms
may have gone further than people are willing to acknowledge to
themselves.

The same survey showed that food-for-work programmes had
benefited the poorer more vulnerable households more than the richer
households—one of the very few programmes in Botswana to do so.
Table 5.7 compares some of the features of households which had
participated in food-for-work programmes for more than six months
with those households which had never participated. Once again the
characteristics of lacking cattle, low arable production, and female

household head appear to be clustered together. Syson, working in one village only, found even more striking and direct evidence that food-for-work programmes benefited the poorer households. In that survey, 76 per cent of the poorest 24 per cent of households had participated in food-for-work schemes, compared with 42 per cent of the rest (FAO, 1972b: 56).

TABLE 5.6 *Methods of obtaining food when harvest is insufficient*

	Per cent of responses
Sell cattle or smallstock	25
Live with relatives	12
Ask for food from others	12
Family member sends money	11
Borrow money from kin	8
Reliance on traditional mechanisms – SUBTOTAL	68
Work in mines	6
Work for another farmer	7
Food-for-work programme	12
Other	7
TOTAL	100

Source: FAO, 1974: 50.

TABLE 5.7 *Characteristics of food-for-work participants*

Household characteristics	Households participating in food-for-work for more than six months	Households never participating in food-for-work
Percentage headed by women	39	27
Percentage holding cattle	43	58
Cereal production in previous year (kg.)	400	860

Source: FAO, 1974: 31, 32, 40.

Finally, the FAO survey found that six times as many women as men participated in food-for-work programmes, which indicates a great deal about customary attitudes towards manual labour in Botswana society. Yet the Government's labour-intensive road-building operation, which has been in existence since 1973, has never employed women, and in early 1977 was still resisting doing so. This supports the general thesis put forward by Boserup (1970) that in Africa, although women frequently undertake more subsistence labour than men, they tend to be excluded from similar work when cash pay is involved. With a large proportion of Botswana households effectively headed by women such discrimination is especially unfortunate.

AGRICULTURAL CREDIT

The commercial banks have been the main source of loans to the agricultural sector, and their operations have increased considerably in recent years. Bank advances to the sector at the end of 1976 amounted to P13 million. This was nearly four times greater than at the end of 1970, although they had remained a fairly constant proportion—at just less than 20 per cent—of all bank advances. However, as the banks usually require fixed assets for security, and as their loans are relatively short term, it is reasonable to conclude that most of these agricultural advances have gone to large cattle owners and freehold farmers, and that they have financed cattle trading rather than new investment.

For small and medium cattle owners the National Development Bank has been more important. Most loans have been either for the drilling of boreholes for cattle watering, or for agricultural implements and equipment. In the first eleven years of its existence the NDB made about 4,000 agricultural or water loans, so nearly one in ten cattle owners would have had a loan if none had had more than one. The average size of the loans was P1,300. The NDB undoubtably contributed to the overall increase in agricultural production since independence, a contribution which has been facilitated by its ability, under the Agricultural Charges Act of 1967, to accept cattle as security for its loans. But under rather conservative management, which has at least had the beneficial effect of maintaining viability and keeping bad debts extraordinarily low, the growth of the NDB's operations has been rather slow.

It is doubtful if the NDB has had much to offer to those households who own no cattle. Not only do they not have the necessary security to offer, but also NDB borrowers have to be recommended by the agricultural demonstrators who, for most of the period, have had effectively no contact with non-cattle-owning households.

THE FUTURE FOR AGRICULTURE

Fig. 5.3 summarizes the discussion so far for each group of farmers defined at the beginning of the chapter. The problems faced by each group, the solutions which are being proposed by the Government, together with some comments are also shown in the diagram. By now the logic for dividing farming households by cattle ownership should be apparent. Those who own no cattle are disadvantaged in a number of ways. They

(1) have lower arable production because of reduced access to draught power;

	Own no cattle (45% of rural households)	Own less than 50 cattle (40% of rural households) (25% of all cattle)	Own more than 50 cattle (15% of rural households) (75% of all cattle)
Arable farming	Problems: Poverty, shortage of capital Many households headed by women. shortage of labour Lack of draught power for ploughing Little access to credit Generally not reached by extension services Little security against drought. Prospects: Little prospect for improvement without major changes in policy Capital will have to be provided including access to cattle.	Problems: Low yields Seasonal labour shortages Marketing. Prospects: Research indicates that yields can be increased substantially Establishment of BAMB should improve marketing But diffusion and adoption of new methods may be slow and further research required.	Arable agriculture often only of secondary importance to owners of large cattle herds.
Cattle rearing		Problems: Overgrazing, especially around villages and communal watering points Low productivity and rates of offtake. Prospects: Government proposes introduction of communal ranches to improve the grazing and permit more efficient management But little popular enthusiasm for communal ranching, and this programme in practice likely to be given low priority.	Problems: Some overgrazing around boreholes *De facto* land grab during the early 1970s Inadequate slaughtering capacity in time of severe drought. Prospects: Establishment of leased commercial ranches in tribal areas should improve the grazing and permit modern management But in practice this is likely to increase the grazing demand in the already overgrazed communal areas Therefore some reduction in the national herd is required.

FIG. 5.3 *The agricultural sector*

(2) suffer from absolute labour shortages because of the link between a male head of household and cattle ownership;

(3) suffer from greater poverty, because cattle are an important source of income;

(4) have little access to rural credit because cattle or other fixed assets are required for security;

(5) are more vulnerable in times of drought because cattle and small-stock represent a reserve of food and wealth;

(6) have not benefited from agricultural extension which has been usually directed towards cattle owners.

With the exception of food-for-work no programme has been designed for or especially benefited those households who own no cattle, though some are now planned for the future. Yet the cluster of disadvantages experienced by this group makes it unlikely that many will be able to improve their standard of living by their own efforts. Nor can one pretend that this large minority of poorer households are poorer just because they are lazy, or have suffered misfortune, or were born stupid.

The full impact of these multiple disadvantages may not yet have been felt because the income of this group is still enhanced by traditional social ties and exchange customs. The very concept of household, which we have used freely, actually disguises the complex social arrangements for support which traditionally characterize Tswana society. Many of the households with no cattle, perhaps especially those headed by unmarried women, have close links with households that do own cattle, or else receive remittances from migrant workers. Indeed agriculture is just one, albeit fundamental, source of rural incomes, which also include hunting and gathering, fishing in some parts of the country, traditional manufacturing, as well as remittances. It is by no means easy to encapsulate all these activities and all the relationships between individuals and groups—whether or not these are called households—into a concise description of rural incomes. An attempt to do this, however, is made in Chapter 7. The point to stress here is that as development proceeds, and as the subsistence rural economy transforms into a cash economy, the concept of economically independent single-generation households will become more and more realistic. As it does so the problems of those who do not own cattle will become chronic, unless some remedial action can be taken.

We have advocated government intervention to furnish this group of households with the capital resources they now lack to engage independently in farming. Whether this should be in the context of the new 'dryland' farming system is more difficult to judge. Some observers would advocate more research, although this can easily become an excuse for inactivity. Others believe that the future development of agriculture in Botswana has to be based on irrigation. This subject is discussed briefly in Chapter 9, in the context of a discussion of the country's water resources. We have not given it more attention because it seems essentially a long-term solution, about which very little is yet known (although more should be found out), whereas other possibilities seem nearer to hand. Certainly, whatever judgements are made as to the means, without much greater capital investment in agriculture—made quickly and in a fashion which directly strengthens the hands of those who are now most deprived—rural distress and impoverishment will become very much more serious than it now is.

For owners of small herds of cattle the outlook for improving arable production appears to be bright as research results become available and the marketing of crop surpluses is made easier. Nevertheless, progress may be restrained by the customary attitudes of farmers, who tend to regard cattle rearing as their 'cash crop', with arable farming and smallstock as no more than a subsistence sideline. Paradoxically the immediate prospects for these farmers making a greater return from cattle rearing is rather limited. The recent considerable increases in output from the livestock sector have largely been fortuitous, the result of a period of good weather and of high beef prices on the European market. There is little reason to expect similar good fortune in the future. In the meantime, the bill for the social costs—the overgrazing and deterioration of the fragile ecology, which have accompanied the increased individual benefits—has yet to be paid. When it is, whether by destocking, fencing to control grazing, or worst of all desertification, the private returns to cattle ownership may appear much less attractive. The present approach to the problem does not seem very promising. But at least a start has been made; as long as the problem was merely debated, the eventual destruction of the range would have been greater, notwithstanding the temporary respite given by the recent years of exceptionally good rainfall.

CHAPTER 6

MINING, INDUSTRY, AND DEPENDENCE

The existence of several ancient iron workings shows that men, probably Sarwa, mined in Botswana long before the beginning of the recorded history of the territory. In 1866 gold was discovered in the north-east in what later became the Tati concession area. This caused an influx of white fortune-hunting prospectors, and a small settlement, Francistown, emerged which even today retains the atmosphere of a frontier pioneering town. But the prospect was not very good and the scale of mining was very small though it continued in a desultory way until 1964. The remains of no less than 45 mines are now scattered about the area (Smit, 1970: 202). Between 1950 and 1965 both asbestos and manganese were mined in south-east Botswana, but output was never considerable and in one year only, 1961, did their combined value exceed half a million Pula.[1]

Thus when the British Economic Survey Mission made its pre-independence report on future prospects for economic development in Botswana there was no mining at all in the territory, nor had the existence of any further payable mineral deposits been proven. This circumstance no doubt accounts for the report's pessimism, which was shown to be mistaken very soon after independence. Mining, especially the diamond mine at Orapa and the copper–nickel mine at Selebi-Phikwe, has in fact become a leading sector of the economy and has absorbed a great deal of governmental resources over the period. The impact of this rather unexpected turn of events on the economy has been described in some detail in Chapters 3 and 4. The present chapter looks at the mining sector itself, at how and why it came into existence and at some of the issues which this entailed. One important theme will be that of economic dependence: mining, and to a lesser extent manufacturing industry, has been promoted by the Government partly to reduce the nation's reliance on foreign aid, on a single export commodity, and on migrant labour. But as a result it now relies more heavily on transport routes through South Africa, on expatriate manpower, and on one or two multinational corporations.

The origins of modern mining date back to the late 1950s when Tshekedi Khama negotiated a prospecting agreement covering the Ngwato Tribal Reserve with the Rhodesian-based mining company RST.[2] The agreement was signed in June 1959, just three days before he died. A local prospecting company, Bamangwato Concessions

Limited, or BCL, was incorporated, in which RST and associated companies held the major interest. By 1966, BCL had identified three promising ore bodies, a copper deposit at Matsitama and two copper-nickel deposits almost adjacent to each other at Selebi and Phikwe. Two years later, in February 1967, it was announced that 33 million tonnes of ore had been proven at Selebi-Phikwe and that a mining feasibility study was to be started (BCL, 1967: 8).

At the same time De Beers was also prospecting in the territory for diamonds. In the early 1950s three small diamonds had been found in the Motloutse river-bed. In 1955 a painstaking search for the source of these stones was begun. Twelve years later, in April 1967, a major diamondiferous kimberlite pipe was discovered just below the Kgalagadi sand at Orapa, a small cattle post two hundred and fifty kilometres west of Francistown.

These discoveries breathed life into the Government's hopes for economic growth, and for balancing its budget without British grants-in-aid. After the agricultural setback of the years of drought, it was not surprising that the yet untried mineral sector should appear the most promising focus of emphasis. The Transitional Plan, published on independence day and before the mineral potential was fully known, already envisaged a multi-faceted regional project based around the water resources of the Shashe river. As yet the idea was rather sketchy:

The Shashe Complex is the one major development scheme at present envisaged capable of making a dramatic impact on the economy. The development of copper mining at Matsitama and possibly at Selebi, the industrial development at Francistown and Shashi Siding when ample power and water supplies are made available, the irrigation of a larger area of arid land, and the possibility in time of the production of salt and soda ash at Sowa (Sua), will transform an entire region of the country. It is for these reasons that such a large proportion of the development expenditure in this Plan is to be devoted to it. (RB, 1966a: 9)

Two years later the Shashe Project concept had grown to include copper-nickel mining at Selebi-Phikwe, copper mining at Matsitama, extraction of soda ash from the brines in Sowa Pan, diamond mining at Orapa, and a coal mine at Morupule, together with the necessary power, water, and transport requirements. But such a multifarious scheme was impossible to sustain. The Matsitama copper prospect was not as attractive as that of Selebi-Phikwe and BCL concentrated its efforts on the latter.[3] More analysis of the Sowa Pan brine deposits, also being prospected by an RST subsidiary, was required before an extraction scheme could be designed. The Orapa prospect was rather isolated and physically independent of the other proposals and was therefore developed separately. Thus by 1970 the Shashe Project had come to mean just the opening of the Selebi-Phikwe mine, a small colliery at Morupule to supply coal to Selebi-Phikwe, and the associated power, water, transport, and town.

In encouraging and promoting mineral development the Botswana Government, in common with governments elsewhere, was faced with three sets of issues. The first was to ensure that the infrastructure would, so far as possible, not just serve the mines themselves but would also confer benefits on the country as a whole. Second, the fiscal arrangements for the mines should maximize the financial flows to the Government itself, a consideration which was critically important for Botswana at that time. Third, the mineral development should not lead to regional imbalance within the country. The manner in which these issues were addressed for both Orapa and Selebi-Phikwe will be considered in the following pages. To them will be added a fourth issue, which it might have seemed luxurious to raise in the late 1960s but which has nevertheless become a prominent concern, that is the extent to which the mining development has led to greater economic dependence on the technology and resources of multinationals and on transport arrangements within southern Africa. In conclusion, consideration is given to the extent to which mineral development has fostered the growth of secondary linkage industries in Botswana, and more generally to the constraints on industrialization.

TRIBAL MINERAL RIGHTS

Regional imbalance as a result of mineral development, which in some African countries has led to civil war and attempted secession, has scarcely been controversial in Botswana. Nevertheless, at independence, mineral rights in the tribal areas were still vested in the individual tribes and not in the State. Both Orapa and Selebi-Phikwe are in the Ngwato tribal area and royalties from these mines would, under these arrangements, have accrued to the Ngwato tribal treasury. One of the first actions of the independent Government was to arrange for tribal mineral rights to be ceded to the State. The President set in motion a political debate on the issue, and together with his ministers toured the country, meeting with the chiefs and addressing kgotlas on the subject. He appealed to national sentiments and argued that the national Government was the body best able to encourage and control mining development. All of the chiefs and tribes in kgotla agreed to the President's proposals during the course of 1967, and on 29 September, just one year after independence, the Mineral Rights in Tribal Territories Act was passed by the National Assembly. This important and far-sighted legislation was an early assertion of the modern ideas of the new Government over traditional authority. But its passage was undoubtedly simplified by the limited knowledge of the mineral potential at the time, the ethnic homogeneity of the Batswana, and most importantly by the fact that Seretse Khama, the State President, also happened to be the traditional leader of the only tribe which at that time had any prospect of mineral wealth.

Apart from this legislation, and the mining companies' policy to recruit their employees nationally rather than locally, regional issues have not been important. Paradoxically, this reflects the paucity of secondary linkages associated with the mines, a matter which will be taken up later. Had Orapa and Selebi-Phikwe turned out to be industrial growth poles then regional imbalance might have now become a major political issue.

INFRASTRUCTURE

Because of the existence of a number of potential mining projects in the north-east, of which the Selebi-Phikwe mine was considered to be just the first, the Government was anxious that the power and water facilities, and transport arrangements for Selebi-Phikwe should be designed with the region as a whole in mind. It was equally insistent that the associated town should break away from the South African and Zambian Copperbelt tradition of barrack-like mining company towns, with rows of single-men's worker quarters on one side and ranch-style houses for the inevitably white management on the other. The Government wanted the new town to be an integrated local community. Accordingly, it decided at an early stage to make itself, rather than the mining company, responsible for providing the necessary infrastructure.

In 1967 it approached the United Nations Development Programme for technical assistance to prepare feasibility studies. The consulting engineers appointed to undertake this work presented their final report at the end of 1968. Two alternative schemes were proposed in which electric power would either be generated locally or imported from South Africa. In the first scheme a 60 MW thermal power station would be located at Selebi-Phikwe using coal from a mine to be developed about a hundred and fifty kilometres away at Morupule. The coal would be transported by rail and for this purpose branch lines would be required from the main railway line: 14 kilometres between Palapye and Morupule, and 65 kilometres between Serule and Selebi-Phikwe. A gravel road to serve the town would also be built parallel to the latter branch line.[4] Water, which the mine requires in abundance, was to be provided by throwing a dam across the large but ephemeral Shashe river. The best dam site was some 60 kilometres to the west of the mine at Tonota where it would impound 85 million cubic metres of water sufficient, if necessary, for several years' consumption. At Selebi-Phikwe itself a town would be established initially to accomodate about eight thousand people, comprising the mine workers and their families and others working in the town (Gibb, 1968a: 2-3). The alternative scheme depended on imported power from South Africa and involved the building of a power transmission line from Selebi-Phikwe to the South African border, together with a small emergency power station at the town itself. Under this scheme the Morupule colliery and the two railway branch lines would not be required, and the dam and water pipeline could be rather smaller. The first scheme was estimated to cost about P42 million, including nearly P10 million for the town itself, and was 75 per cent more expensive than the second scheme at an estimated total cost of P24 million (Gibb, 1968a: 4). In addition the cost of power under the first scheme was estimated to be 60 per cent more expensive than imported power.

The choice was of course between greater or lesser economic dependence on South Africa. It has been described here in some detail as an illustration of the magnitude of costs which may be associated with pursuing a policy of economic independence. The Government in fact did not hesitate to choose the more expensive scheme with independent generation of power. There is no doubt that in reaching this decision it was principally influenced by the general issue of economic independence, and the particular danger of sabotage to which a transmission line from South Africa would be susceptible. Other non-quantified economic and technical considerations favoured this choice, for example the additional local employment which would be created at the colliery and power station, but these alone could scarcely justify the extra financial cost involved.[5]

The World Bank, which had agreed to arrange a consortium of donor agencies to finance the infrastructure, was less concerned with the issue of economic dependence and favoured the second alternative. But when it was announced that Seretse Khama was to travel to Washington in March 1969 in order to discuss this and other matters with the President of the World Bank, opposition from that quarter melted away before his arrival.

The Canadian International Development Agency (CIDA) and the US Agency for International Development (USAID) were the two principal lenders for the infrastructure apart from the World Bank itself. Both these agencies required that the bulk of goods and services financed by their aid loans should be purchased in the donor country, a restriction which is not easy to accomodate in multi-donor infrastructure schemes which largely consist of integrated civil enginnering.

TABLE 6.1 *Initial investment in the Shashe Project*

Mine investment by BCL[1]	P millions	*Financing*[2]	P millions
Pre-production expenses and exploration	24.9	Equity	32.9
Mine development	12.7	Loan through BRST from Amax and AAC	8.9
Concentrator	5.8	8¾%–9½%, DM222 million	
Smelter	27.6	loan from German	
Services	10.0	bank consortium	51.7
Employee housing	4.9	6½%, R13, 5 million	
Management contractor	4.9	loan from Industrial	
Working capital	8.2	Development Corpor-	
Contingencies, and		ation of South Africa	13.5
escalation	8.0		
TOTAL	107.0	TOTAL	107.0

Infrastructure investment by government[3]	P millions	*Financing*	P millions
Power facilities	20.3	Interest-free, 50-year,	
Water facilities	12.3	$30 million loan	
Road and railway	4.0	from CIDA	20.3
Township	7.3	2%–3%, 40-year, $6, 7	
Engineering and		million loan from	
administration	5.5	USAID	4.5
Interest during		7¼%, 25-year, $32 million	
construction	3.0	loan from IBRD	23.1
Feasibility, design, and		Other grants and loans	3.4
temporary works	2.7	Shortfall[4]	3.8
TOTAL	55.1	TOTAL	55.1

[1] As estimated in January 1972; eventual investment to make the plant operational was much higher.
[2] All currency conversions at rates applicable at the time of the loan.
[3] As estimated in July 1973 and very close to final costs.
[4] Later financed by exchange gains as the Rand (Pula) devalued

Sources: BRST Preliminary Prospectus January 1972 (BRST, 1972b: 13, 39);
The Shashe Project in North East Botswana (MFDP, 1973b: 4–5).

In both cases it is likely that the costs were higher than if the same facilities had been purchased on the open market, though this was compensated for by the soft terms on which the finance was made available.[6] Altogether about P55 million, roughly equivalent to the total GDP at the time the project was being planned, was borrowed by the Government. The sources, terms, and allocation of these borrowings are shown in Table 6.1.

The approach adopted at Orapa was completely different. De Beers was concerned that security arrangements should be suitable for diamond mining. The location of the deposit was very isolated. The Selebi-Phikwe project was already stretching the Government's administrative and borrowing capacities to their limits. For all these reasons, the Government agreed to a suggestion from De Beers that the township at Orapa, and the power and water facilities should be financed, constructed, and managed entirely by the company.

Orapa town, which has a population about a fifth that of Selebi-Phikwe, is built entirely behind a security fence containing an area of some 160 square kilometres. Apart from a few government and bank officials the entire workforce of the town is employed by the mining company, either in the mine or in the company-run shops, hospital, schools, and farm. Only those with business in the town are permitted to enter, for which application has to be made in advance. The security argument for making Orapa a closed town—that it helps to control the illegal buying and selling of diamonds from which the nation loses as well as the mining company—is undoubtedly a strong one. But some, even if small, potential for economic linkages is lost as a result. In fact, since the mine was opened the balance of opinion on the matter has changed and steps are proposed to open up the town, while retaining or even tightening the security arrangements around the mine itself.

By contrast, the principal difficulty in establishing the 'open town' at Selebi-Phikwe has been controlling the population growth of the town. Although planned for an initial population of about eight thousand, it was estimated that in 1971, two years before the town was complete, the population was already ten thousand. By 1975 it had reached 21,000 (MFPD, 1977: 86). Most of these people moved to a nearby unplanned settlement known as Botshabelo, to benefit directly or indirectly from the jobs in the construction sector while the town and mine were being built. Construction employment declined just when mining employment grew and the population stayed on. Thus for each of the two thousand primary jobs in the mining sector there are now about ten people living in the town and being supported by the urban economy. In this respect at least the benefits of the open town have been wider than those of the closed town at Orapa.

Many of these people have benefited through 'informal' economic mechanisms, a phenomenon which is given closer examination in the next chapter. Formal economic linkages have been much slower to emerge. In the case of Orapa it is no exaggeration to say that there are virtually no formal links with the rest of the Botswana economy, other than the wages paid to the Botswana workers and the dividend, royalty, and taxation payments to the Government. Given the physical isolation of Orapa, the openness of the Botswana economy, and the minimal transport facilities required to move the diamond output, this absence of economic linkages is largely inevitable. Similarly, although the potential would appear to be greater, very few formal linkages have yet arisen out of the Shashe Project. The Shashe dam does not supply water to anywhere other than Selebi-Phikwe, though it may do so in the future. The power station transmits power to Francistown but to none of the villages which lie on the route of the transmission line. In the absence of a network of feeder roads into Selebi-Phikwe from the surrounding villages, the main road and rail spur into the town do not greatly benefit the region. Nor, as will be seen later, has there been much linked industrial growth.

There are two reasons for the limited impact of the infrastructure associated with the Shashe Project. First, when a large project, such as this, is being planned there is a natural tendency to minimize the initial investment, perhaps especially in this case where the project was much larger than anything which had previously been attempted in Botswana and was wholly financed from foreign borrowing. Thus, the series of marginal investments, necessary to spread the benefit of the infrastructure more widely, are deferred and may be expected to take several years, perhaps even decades, to complete.[7] In this respect, it is probably too early to reach a final judgement. Second, when specific proposals to use the basic infrastructure for other purposes are examined, it is frequently found that the technology is 'inappropriate'. For example, although a high-voltage transmission line from the power station at Selebi-Phikwe passes close to the small village of Mmadinare it is more economic to provide power for the village by building a new lower voltage line direct from the power station itself (Merz, 1975b: 82). Or it may prove more expensive to pipe a small volume of water to a village from the Shashe dam, than to provide a local supply by sinking boreholes. In short, the infrastructure required for the mining industry is on such a large scale that it is difficult to match up with the very small demands of the surrounding, largely agricultural, communities. It is far easier to develop linkages with other towns or mines within the region than with the traditional sector on the doorstep.

THE TWO MINES

The Government's primary objective for the mineral sector was that the fiscal arrangements should provide sufficient domestic revenue for it to achieve financial independence. By comparison infrastructure issues were secondary. But before discussing the rather different fiscal regimes which were applied to the two mines it is appropriate to give a brief account of their operation.

About thirty-two million tonnes of copper–nickel ore have been proven at Selebi-Phikwe. It was intended that this should be extracted at an initial rate of two million tonnes a year, firstly by opencast and underground workings at Phikwe and later by an underground mine at Selebi, which is a few kilometres distant. Taking into account probable as well as proven reserves, the life of the mine was expected to be twenty-three years. The ore is crushed, concentrated by separating it from unwanted material, and then dried. The concentrate is then smelted using a technically sophisticated 'flash smelter furnace' and two electric furnaces. The output is a matte which contains about 80 per cent copper and nickel and a small quantity of cobalt. One of the early sticking points in the negotiations for the project was the Government's insistence that the ore should be fully refined within Botswana in order to maximize the domestic benefits. But the company was unwilling to do this, and would have probably abandoned the project had the Government not given way. Instead the matte is railed to Maputo and shipped for refining to Port Nickel in Louisiana, where one of the project shareholders, Amax, had spare refining capacity. After refining, all of the copper output and two-thirds of the nickel are sold to Metallgesellschaft in West Germany. Annual output was initially expected to be 46,000 tonnes of matte, containing 18,000 tonnes of nickel and 17,000 tonnes of copper. In addition, and largely for environmental reasons, elemental sulphur was to be extracted from the smelter flue gases for sale in South Africa (MFDP, 1973b). In 1972 when construction was nearly half complete, the mining company estimated that its investment would be P107 million. Of this P33 million was to be equity capital. The financing plan, as envisaged at the time, is shown in Table 6.1.

Commissioning of the mine started at the end of 1973. The plant was run for a few days and then closed down (BCL, 1974: 3). It simply did not work.[8] A team representing the two principal investors visited the site in March 1974 and, amid much mutual recrimination, agreed on modifications. But it was not until two years later that the plant was beginning to operate even close to its original specification. By the end of 1976 total production of matte since the plant had been opened was only 56,000 tonnes, little more than planned output for one year. In the meantime, apart from the cost of the modifications themselves, all the fixed costs including a full staff and labour complement had to be financed. As a result the two major shareholders had to put up an additional P131 million of short-term loans between the end of 1973 and the end of 1976. A strike in July 1975, which caused a total shut down for several weeks, exacerbated the situation.

Table 6.2 summarizes the operations of BCL as these problems unfolded. The company did not begin to operate as a going concern

TABLE 6.2 *Operations of BCL*

	1969	1970	1971	1972	1973	1974	1975	1976
				P millions				
Fixed assets at year end[1]	7	14	32	76	124	183	193	201
Cumulative loss at year end							35	60
Financed by								
Equity at year end[2]	3	3	3	39	39	39	39	39
Long-term loans at year end			34	69	69	76	84	83
Short-term loans from Amax and AAC	4	10	27	2	13	69	124	144
				Thousands of tonnes				
Production of matte						7	17	33
Containing nickel						3	6	12
copper						3	6	13

[1] Fixed capital investment; working capital excluded. Up to 1973 the figures are net of depreciation. From 1973, following normal accounting practices for mines in southern Africa, no depreciation is included.

[2] From 1972, 15 per cent of the equity held by the Botswana Government.

Sources: Annual Reports of BCL and BRST and *BRST 1972 Prospectus* (BCL, 1970–1977; BRST, 1970–1977).

until the end of 1974, when the total investment had reached P185 million, all the costs up to this date having been capitalized. Two years later the investment exceeded P200 million and a loss of P60 million had been incurred. Production improved during 1977 and 1978, but losses were still being incurred because of the depressed prices for copper and nickel.

While the Selebi-Phikwe operation was proving so disastrous, that at Orapa was turning into a considerable success. This was a much simpler project in almost every respect. Operations started in July 1971, a year and a half earlier than in Selebi-Phikwe and, incredibly, only four years after the deposit had been discovered.

The Orapa diamond pipe is the second most extensive in the world, covering an area of more than a hundred hectares. Open-cast mining is used and nearly three million tonnes of earth and rock are shifted and sifted each year.[9] But the pit is so extensive that even in 1977 it was still only a few metres deep. The total depth of the pipe is not known but it is expected that production will continue for a very long time. The annual yield of diamonds in the early years was about 2.4 million carats, an output which was then worth about P20 million and which weighs about half a tonne. Production has since been increased to 4.5 million carats; a new mine nearby at Letlhakane has been opened, with a third one at Jwaneng planned; and diamond prices have risen by leaps and bounds, being in 1978 about three times what they were in 1971. From the beginning the mine itself has operated smoothly, though it is little more than a quarrying operation, and, apart from the fear of water shortage in 1973, there have been few problems. Mining has continued without interruption.

Table 6.3 summarizes the accounts of the mining company from 1971 to 1976. It can be seen that the original investment was covered out of gross profits in less than two years. Over the total six-year period gross profit has been P102 million, of which the Government has taken 52 per cent in taxes, dividends, and royalties. The DCF return to the company on its original investment over just the first six years was between 25 and 30 per cent.

FISCAL ARRANGEMENTS

In principle, in negotiating a mineral concession both parties are anxious to extract the maximum financial benefit for themselves from the project. But within this framework the values placed by the parties on other aspects of the project, such as the time preference for money or the technical details, may be quite different. What is a significant benefit to one side may be a minor concession to the other. Moreover the negotiating strength of the two parties generally is unbalanced and

TABLE 6.3   *Operations of De Beers Botswana*

	1971	1972	1973	1974	1975	1976
			P millions			
Undepreciated fixed mining assets at year end[1]	19.7	20.7	26.2	28.5	33.4	45.8
Financed by						
Shares[2]	9.1	9.5	9.5	9.5	10.5	14.8
Share premium	10.3	11.7	11.7	11.7	12.7	16.9
Cumulative retained profits	0.6	1.3	2.6	11.6	8.8	12.1
Loans						1.2
Sales revenue	n.a.	17.8	21.3	29.4	27.2	32.5
Operating costs	n.a.	3.3	3.5	5.9	6.9	8.4
Gross profit	1.5	14.5	17.8	23.5	20.3	24.1
Distribution of gross profits						
Tax			3.3	7.3	5.8	7.0
Royalty	0.1	0.9	1.1	1.5	1.4	3.4
Dividends	0.8	12.9	12.1	5.7	15.9	10.5
Retained profits	0.6	0.7	1.3	9.0	−2.8	3.3
Of gross profit less retained profit						
Accruals to Botswana Government	0.2	2.8	6.2	9.7	18.2	15.6
Accruals to De Beers	0.7	11.0	10.3	4.8	4.9	5.2

[1] Excludes value of diamond samples at approximately P0.5 million.
[2] The Botswana Government held 15 per cent of equity up to 1975 and 50 per cent thereafter.

Sources: Annual Reports of De Beers Botswana Mining Company (Proprietary) Limited (Debswana, 1972–1977); *Annual Statements of Accounts* (RB, 1972–1977).

changes with time. Initially the mining company, which has the necessary detailed knowledge and access to technology and finance and which can, in theory at least, pick and choose between potential projects in various countries, is likely to have the commanding position. But as more and more of the investment in the project is undertaken so this position is steadily eroded, while that of the government is enhanced. This tends to cause instability in mining arrangements to a much greater extent than in the manufacturing sector. It largely explains the now classic pattern, experienced in so many countries, of initially generous mining concessions followed by their renegotiation on terms more favourable to the host governement. As the following paragraphs show, events in Botswana have conformed to this pattern.

From the late 1960s until the attempted commissioning of the plant, the Selebi-Phikwe mine was expected to be sufficiently profitable to satisfy both the Government and the investors.[10] But not all potentially profitable projects are implemented. This one was impelled by events to the north. Following the breakup of the Central African Federation, and apparently for exchange-control reasons, RST transferred its interests in BCL from Rhodesian- to Zambian-based companies within the group. A few years later, however, UDI had occurred in Southern Rhodesia and there was a real prospect of nationalization of the Zambian copper mines which caused considerable uncertainty about the future of the mining companies in that country (Faber and Potter, 1971: 62-5). As a result, RST showed much greater interest in its BCL property in Botswana than it might otherwise have done. Accordingly, towards the end of the 1960s BCL expenditures on investigations and feasibility studies grew considerably. By the end of 1969, before agreement had been reached on the fiscal arrangements, more than seven million Pula had been invested by the company (Table 6.2). Though the essential principles were agreed in 1970 the detailed negotiations actually took more than two years to complete, between early 1970 and early 1972, and during this period its ever increasing sunk costs gave the mining company as much incentive as the government to see the project come to fruition. Eventually, no less than 42 interrelated agreements were negotiated covering every aspect of the Shashe Project. They were all signed on 7 March 1972 in Gaborne.

The impetus behind the Orapa negotiations was much more basic; the project was simply expected to be extremely profitable, though this was probably better understood by De Beers than by the Government, which was largely dependent on the company side for financial forecasts. An agreement was negotiated and ratified by the National Assembly in 1970. It was notable for its simplicity. It set out the royalty and taxation provisions; it provided for the Government to have a 15 per cent free equity share in the project, and incorporated a clause which provided for renegotiation in 'abnormal circumstances'. Later the Government began to realize just how profitable the Orapa mine was, so when De Beers approached the Government in 1974 for a lease to mine the two further diamond pipes which had been discovered near Letlhakane, the Government used the 'abnormal circumstances' clause to reopen the original agreement. The second round of negotiations was much tougher and was characterized by hard and acrimonious bargaining. Encouraged by international trends in the negotiation of mineral concessions, the Government expected that a greater proportion of the financial benefits of mining should flow to the public sector rather than to private capital. Further prospecting had also shown that the Orapa mine was not an isolated deposit, rather that Botswana was an important diamond province. The De Beers group is both the largest diamond mining organization in the world, and also through the Central Selling Organization handles 80 to 90 per cent of the world diamond production which reaches the open market. As such it could not risk simply withdrawing from Botswana. This would have invited Botswana to find other partners for its diamond mining, thereby posing a potential threat to the De Beers monopoly. On the other hand, De Beers was also in a strong negotiating position. Its monopoly position not only stabilizes diamond prices, which have not fallen over several decades, but by limiting production and stock-piling manages to maintain prices at a monopoly level. In addition, the company has acquired unrivalled expertise in diamond prospecting and mining. Thus Botswana, like other diamond-producing countries (including the USSR), has an interest in co-operating with De Beers and in preserving its monopoly on sales. In these circumstances there were great potential benefits for both sides in the event of a mutually satisfactory outcome to the negotiations and considerable losses for both parties if they had broken down.

The negotiations were concerned with four principal issues: the shareholding of the company and in particular what equity the Govern-ment should have; the royalty payable; the tax structure; and what would happen in the event of the project being more or less profitable than anticipated. To some degree, equity holding, royalty, and tax arrangements are substitutable, in so far as each provides a financial flow to the Government. This substitutability was fully recognized in the negotiations leading up to the 1975 De Beers agreement. Much of the discussion revolved around what was a reasonable DCF rate of return on the company capital, irrespective of what particular com-bination of dividends, royalty, and taxation would achieve that rate of return. However, having noted this, it is useful to consider each of these aspects in turn.

Much of the literature on investment in developing countries has concentrated on the issue of nationalization – that is, whether the government of the country concerned should seek to have a majority of the equity in a particular company. Apart from the political kudos which nationalization confers, there has been a tendency to exaggerate the value of both 51 per cent participation by a government or com-plete nationalization. As Penrose (1976) points out, unless a country is well endowed with its own managers and engineers, and has access to technical and marketing information, it is doubtful if nationalization brings much actual control. Modern corporations tend to be run by those who have access to information, rather than by those who own shares.[11] In Botswana, nationalization has not been a political issue. There is no history of exploitation by multinationals in the territory, and when the Orapa and Shashe projects were being conceived, the country had neither the financial resources nor any of the necessary expertise to contemplate a nationalized mineral sector. But the original prospecting agreement with RST negotiated by Tshekedi Khama provided that the owner of the mineral rights, originally the tribe and later the state, should receive 15 per cent of the equity of the eventual mining company free of any consideration. A similar provision was made in the original 1970 agreement with De Beers. Apart from the right to dividends which this confers, it also provides the Government with a seat on the boards of the two corporations, which can give useful access to information on the projects and some limited responsibility for their operation. Reciprocal advantages can flow to the mining companies, which often consider their problems are misunderstood by the government, but which can exploit government participation to influence the formulation of policy more favourable to the mining sector. In the 1975 De Beers agreement, this concept of co-operation was taken a stage further. As a result of that agreement the Government now has 50 per cent of the equity of the local company, again free of consideration, the other half being owned by De Beers. The theory behind this rather unusual arrangement is that the mining venture should be seen as a partnership in which both the Government and the company have an equal interest. The theory may not work well in practice. The unnecessarily acrimonious negotiations had already soured the relationship between the two parties. The Government will have difficulty in finding people of sufficient calibre to represent it on the board, who also have the time to give full consideration to the mining company's affairs.[12] Equally, the De Beers board members, belonging to a larger, secretive diamond world, will no doubt carefully control the flow of information concerning the project to the government members.

Royalty payments, whether or not based upon a percentage of production or sales, may be formally regarded as the price the mining company pays for the ore to the holder of the mineral rights, in this case the Government. But they serve an additional fiscal function by providing a floor to financial flows to the government, so long as the project continues in operation. On the other hand, precisely because royalties reduce the risks to the government they increase them to the company, which may therefore be less willing to invest. Moreover, fixed royalties can have the effect of rendering marginal prospects completely unviable and thereby reduce both the scale, and consequently the total economic benefits, of the mining sector. Thus there are dangers in a government trying to assure its revenue flow by setting royalties too high. In the case of the Shashe Project the Government was particularly concerned to minimize its risk, and a minimum annual royalty of P750,000 was written into the agreements irrespective of whether or not there was any production in the year in question. With the operational failure of the mine, the royalty seemed likely to be, for some years to come, the only direct net financial flow to the Government. In the circumstances, it was not surprising that the Government insisted on an increase in royalty payments as a condition of agreeing to the capital restructuring of the project which took place early in 1978. It was able to do this, of course, because the two major shareholders were committed to the project, having by that stage made their investment. In the 1975 De Beers agreement the rate of royalty was not specified, because the Government considered this the most suitable instrument to share in any excess profit, above the target rate of return, which the company might make.

In negotiating a tax arrangement, the company side generally has two particular concerns, apart from the actual rate of taxation itself. First, it is anxious to write off its investment against taxes as quickly as possible. Multinational corporations investing in developing countries are concerned about political stability and the risk that once the investment has been made the government might change the rules of the game. This implies that the investor often has a much shorter time preference for his share of the total profitability of the project than the government, and rapid write-off is a good example of a small concession by a government which can be seen as a major benefit by the investor. Second, the investor is frequently concerned that the rates of taxation initially in force may be increased in the future, and therefore seeks to negotiate a special tax agreement ratified as appropriate by the national assembly or legislative body. Government have equally good reasons for trying to avoid the rigidity which special tax agreements impose, as there may be future occasions when, for perfectly legitimate reasons, it is necessary or desirable to raise the general level of taxation. But in circumstances such as those of newly independent Botswana, it is very difficult to avoid being forced into special tax agreements, and both the Shashe Project agreements and the original De Beers agreement included special taxation provisions which were ratified by the National Assembly. In the 1975 renegotiations with De Beers the Government used its negotiating strength to avoid any special tax arrangement at all, and De Beers is currently subject in Botswana to normal tax legislation as it applies from time to time. No doubt the Government would wish to negotiate future mineral concessions on this same basis. But it is unlikely to be in a sufficiently strong bargaining position with any other company to succeed.

By now it will be clear that the Shashe Project agreements are as precise as the 1975 De Beers agreement is vague. In the former case, the precision extends to changed circumstances. For example, if profitability increases above what was expected the fiscal regime also changes in a carefully defined way. More importantly, as it turned out, the Shashe Project agreements were contrived, largely by the World Bank, to give complete downside protection to the Government's infrastructure investment. Much of the detail and the bulk of the set of 42 agreements are concerned with these matters. The financial flows between the company, the Botswana Power Corporation, the Water Utilities Corporation, the Selebi-Phikwe Township Authority, and the Government itself are all precisely defined in ways which were intended to protect, and have protected, the Government, and ultimately its lenders, against financial loss.[13]

By contrast, the flexibility and simplicity of the 1975 De Beers agreement was achieved partly because neither the Government nor any of its agencies had any direct investment in the project. But in addition, the Government regarded flexibility as a paradigm for future agreements. It considered that if a target rate of return for the investor's capital could be agreed, then the details of royalty or taxation rates should be adjustable from time to time, if the operation actually turned out to be significantly more or less profitable than the original target. It was argued that if future governments did not have their hands tied by rigid and precise agreements, they would be less tempted to take precipitate action such as penal taxation or expropriation. This line of argument was not convincing to De Beers which felt that the flexibility would all too likely be used to cream off excess profits in good times, but not to make corresponding adjustments in bad. In addition the approach did not offer any very positive rewards for greater efficiency.

Nevertheless agreement was reached. The target rate of return has not been disclosed, but it is believed to be handsome, even though the Government will receive 65-70 per cent of the gross profits of the Orapa and Letlhakane mines through the combination of royalty, dividends, and taxation (RB, 1975c). The Government and the company have now settled down somewhat uneasily to run the mines on the new 50:50 basis, and by 1978 agreement had been reached to open a third, very large diamond mine at Jwaneng in the south of the country.

The fact that the 1975 De Beers agreement left so much discretion to future governments aroused some critical comment among mining companies, and may well have discouraged other potential mining investors away from Botswana. Certainly, no other new mining projects, apart from Jwaneng, seem likely in the near future, though this lack of interest may in part be the result of a general uncertainty about the future of southern Africa.

Whether the Government was right or wrong to insist on flexibility in the 1975 De Beers agreement appears to us to depend very much on its objectives for the mining sector and the future role it will play in the economy. If mining is to continue to be the engine for economic growth, then the Government could have made Botswana a more attractive investment environment without laying itself open to exploitation. But there is a good case to be made for setting aside further mineral projects for the time being, for the sake of concentrating resources on the neglected agricultural and rural sectors. Unfortunately, present government policy appears to fall between two stools. A great deal of administrative resources will be devoted to the development of the new diamond mine at Jwaneng. There is every expectation that this will be extremely profitable, but, as with Orapa, the economic linkages will be small and the country will become more dependent on one multinational corporation and upon one commodity.

DEPENDENCE ON MULTINATIONALS

Botswana had no alternative but to involve multinational corporations in the provisions of the finance and technology for its mining development. Nevertheless, whilst investment by multinationals may be inevitable—and sometimes desirable—for such large projects, it is also possible to pursue a strategy of diversification which would limit or neutralize the degree of dependence on foreign investors. The greater the diversity of investing companies, of their home countries, and of their activities within the developing country, the smaller will be the relative effect of each one of them upon that country's economy. This general principle has been recognized in Botswana and has been applied to sources of foreign aid with some success. There has been less success in diversifying sources of private investment, and in particular in reducing the role of South African capital.

In order to illustrate this point it is necessary to analyse the ownership of BCL and how this has changed since the project was first contemplated. BCL was originally controlled by Rhodesian- and Zambian-based companies in the RST group. In 1967, when RST's Zambian interests appeared to be threatened by nationalization, a local company, Botswana RST, or BRST, was established. BRST acquired the 61 per cent of BCL equity which had hitherto been held by Zambian RST and associated companies. BRST was in turn a subsidiary of RST itself, based in London, and which at this time was partly owned by the American company Amax. Thus when a P4.1 million rights issue capitalized BRST early in 1968, Amax took up its full entitlement and later emerged as the major shareholder of BRST with 43 per cent of the equity. One of the smaller shareholders was the Anglo-American Corporation/Charter Consolidated group of South Africa, or AAC.

In 1969 it became apparent that the World Bank would insist on BRST shareholders guaranteeing the loan which it was to make to the Botswana Government for the infrastructure. Many of the smaller shareholders were unable or unwilling to offer such a guarantee, and this gave AAC, which was willing, an opportunity to enlarge its holding in BRST by easing out some of the other minority holders. In 1970, AAC and Amax agreed jointly to provide the required guarantees both on their own behalf and on behalf of the other shareholders, eventually to equalize their own holdings in BRST, and in the meantime to put up short-term finance for the project (BRST, 1972b: 5). The minority shareholders in BCL were as yet unaffected by these deals. But in March 1972, following the signing of all the project agreements, they exchanged their BCL shares for equivalent holdings in BRST, and 15 per cent equity was ceded to the Botswana Government. At the same time there was a further rights issue in BRST, which AAC and Amax used in order to effect the agreed equalization of their holdings at about 30 per cent each. The end result is that BCL is owned 85 per cent by BRST and 15 per cent by the Government, and BRST, a publicly quoted company in which the Government has no share, is owned 60 per cent by AAC and Amax and 40 per cent by private investors.

Thus the Selebi-Phikwe investment is jointly controlled by the South African Company, AAC, in which there are also considerable British interests, and the rather different American company, Amax. For a long time it was not clearly worked out which of these two major shareholders should take operational and technical responsibility for BRST and BCL. There were frequent changes of local management, while, in the meantime, much of the design was being undertaken by what remained of the original RST team in London. This combination of factors, against the background of an unclearly defined division of responsibility, largely accounts for the subsequent technical failure of the plant.

More germane to the present discussion is that AAC and De Beers are interrelated companies, both under the control of the South African industrial magnate, Sir Harry Oppenheimer. Thus Botswana's mining investment to date is dominated not only by South African capital, but also by one corporate group. Botswana has not yet succeeded in attracting non-South African investment into the mining sector, other than Amax's stake in BRST, even though several companies are prospecting there. It is not difficult to hypothesize an explanation for this. The further away an investment opportunity is from a multinational's home base, the greater will be the ignorance of the political and economic environment of the potential investment, and accordingly the greater will be the perception of risk. Thus an opportunity in Botswana is likely to appear far less risky to a company based in Johannesburg than it would be to a company based in, say, Houston. Similarly, a corporation which has already invested in Botswana with some success is likely to be far more receptive to other investment opportunities within the country than would an outsider. In this connection, the difficult renegotiations with De Beers appear to have discouraged new mining investors rather more than De Beers itself, as demonstrated by its decision to open a third mine at Jwaneng.

TRANSPORT DEPENDENCE

The modernization of the economy, of which mining is the most prominent aspect, brought with it greater dependence on the Rhodesian operated railway through Botswana, and on transport routes to the sea. Botswana's copper-nickel and meat exports, together with the bulk of its imports, are all moved by rail. In addition there is now a significant amount of internal railway traffic, notably cattle being taken to the abattoir and coal moving from the Morupule colliery to the mine and power station at Selebi-Phikwe. As the southern African region has become more unstable, concern for the security of these arrangements has come to occupy considerable time and energy of Botswana politicians and civil servants.

The railway, which runs from south to north through the eastern side of Botswana, was built and run by Cecil Rhodes's British South Africa Company at the end of the nineteenth century. It formed part of his ambitious plan for a route from the Cape to Cairo. There were various changes in its operation during the first half of the present century, but from 1959 operational responsibility was divided at Mahalapye, the centre of the Botswana stretch of line. South of there it was operated by South African Railways, and to the north by Rhodesia Railways. In 1966, Rhodesia Railways took over operation of the entire line as far south as Mafeking, just over the border in South Africa. The line is owned by Rhodesia Railways, and an annual 'wayleave' payment is made to the Botswana Government.

The line has probably been of greater relative importance to the Botswana economy than to that of Zimbabwe. In 1900, only a few years after it was completed, Southern Rhodesia acquired a much shorter route to the sea with the opening of the Salisbury-Beira line. Later another link was built between Bulawayo and the port of Maputo, then called Lourenço Marques. But the Botswana line retained some secondary importance as trade developed between Northern and Southern Rhodesia and South Africa, although the route taken is a rather roundabout way to the Johannesburg industrial area. When a

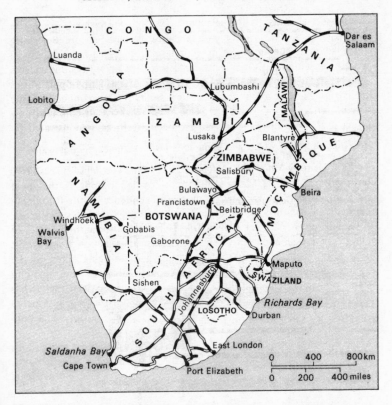

Fig. 6.1 Main railway system of southern Africa

more direct route between there and Bulawayo, through Beitbridge, was proposed in the late 1960s, the Botswana Government began to fear the line would cease to be economic and would be abandoned. This possibility, which was never very probable, disappeared altogether in 1976 as a result of the closure of the Beira and Maputo lines to Southern Rhodesia by the independent Government in Mozambique. By that time, the Beitbridge link had been completed, and it began to handle the bulk of the diverted traffic. Since then there appears to have been little increase of Rhodesian traffic moving through Botswana (Table 6.4). Ironically, the opening of the Beitbridge link made it easier for Botswana to resist international pressure to increase sanctions against Southern Rhodesia by closing the line, as this would clearly not now have a decisive effect on the Rhodesian economy (Fig. 6.1).

By contrast the line through Botswana has been of steadily growing

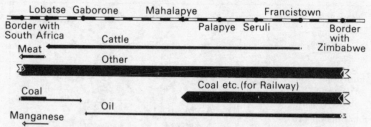

Note: Through traffic, which was approximately three times the Botswana-generated traffic, is excluded (Table 6.4)

Sources: Principally *National Development Plan 1973–78* (MFDP 1973 *a* :254) and *Statistical Abstract 1973* (CSO 1973 a: Table 38)

Fig. 6.2 Botswana-Generated traffic on the railway, 1968

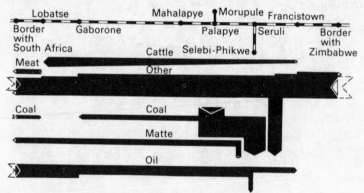

Note: Through traffic, which was approximately double the Botswana-generated traffic, is excluded (Table 6.4)

Sources: Ministry of Works and Communications and *Annual Reports* of Botswana Meat Commission (BMC 1977), Botswana Power Corporation (BPC 1976) and Bamangwato Concessions Ltd. (BCL. 1977).

Fig. 6.3 Botswana-Generated traffic on the railway, 1976

importance to the economy of Botswana itself: the tonnage, with either its origin or its destination within the country, has more than doubled since independence (Table 6.4). This is amplified in Figs. 6.2 and 6.3 which show the nature and volume of Botswana freight moved in 1968 and 1976 respectively. While the data behind these two diagrams are somewhat fragmentary, having been derived from a number of sources, they clearly demonstrate the increasing importance of the railway line to the economy. Copper–nickel matte is now exported southwards, and an even greater tonnage, especially of coal, is moved

TABLE 6.4 *Railway operations*

	1967	1968[1]	1969	1974/5	1975/6	1976/7[2]
			Freight carried in thousands of tonnes			
To Botswana from						
The north	141	207	225	225	234	140
South Africa	97	112	145	222	254	222
From Botswana to						
The north	41	52	74	20	16	6
South Africa				45	79	94
Internal traffic	33	35	46	213	300	406
TOTAL Botswana traffic	312	406	490	725	883	868
Transit traffic	n.a.	1,243	n.a.	1,363	1,565	1,656
TOTAL all traffic		1,649		2,088	2,448	2,524

[1] Various sources show small discrepancies in the statistics for 1968.
[2] Estimate based on six months' tonnage from July to December 1976.

Sources: Statistical Abstracts (CSO, 1968-1970); *National Development Plan 1973-78* (MFDP, 1973a: 254); *Statistical Bulletin, March 1977* (CSO, 1977: 22); Ministry of Works and Communications.

inwards to Selebi-Phikwe. The numbers of cattle and the tonnage of meat transported by rail have more than doubled, corresponding to the growth of the livestock sector. The residual category of 'other goods' has also doubled, reflecting the growth of imports as the economy has grown.

In spite of the railway's importance to Botswana, there has been virtually no railway expertise within the country. Most of the eight hundred Batswana workers employed on the railway are unskilled, and are engaged on track maintenance. Only in 1974 did Rhodesia Railways, in response to government pressure, begin to train Batswana for skilled or supervisory positions. The administration, the maintenance of locomotives and rolling stock, and the train crews continued to be based in Bulawayo. Botswana's main transport artery was thus potentially vulnerable to the turmoil and upheaval of the transition from Southern Rhodesia to Zimbabwe.

To counteract this vulnerability, Seretse Khama announced in September 1974 that it was his Government's intention that the line should eventually be operated by Botswana. But progress towards this objective has since been slow because of the daunting financial and economic costs involved. Not only is considerable capital investment required but also, if Botswana Railways is to cover its costs, its tariffs will have to be much higher than those of Rhodesia Railways because of the smaller scale of its operations and because the latter generally ran the Botswana line at a loss.

The establishment of Botswana Railways will eventually reduce an important aspect of international dependence over which Botswana does have some control. It has far less control over transport arrangements between the border and the sea. In theory, imports and exports can take either the northern route via Zimbabwe and Mozambique, or the southern route through South Africa. But the northern route has been closed during the observance of sanctions against the Rhodesian economy by Mozambique, while the southern route is increasingly vulnerable to the threat of unrest in South Africa or to further estrangement of South Africa-Botswana relations. One of the greatest dangers to the Botswana economy is that for a period of time both routes might be closed simultaneously.

In the long term, one possibility for reducing this risk, which has been raised from time to time, is the construction of a third railway route westwards across the Kgalagadi desert from Francistown to Gobabis in Namibia, whence there is already a railway to the Atlantic port of Walvis Bay.[14] Despite the size of such an enterprise it could be viable if linked with a mining project, perhaps for coal, and would change the whole transport pattern of the region. This is one of the most enticing and exciting proposals for the future.

The vulnerability of Botswana's transport arrangements was underlined by events at the end of 1973. When the OPEC countries increased oil prices in that year, the Arab oil producers also imposed an embargo on the sale of oil to South Africa. In reality the ban was ineffective. It was widely ignored by the oil companies, and Iran never participated. Since Botswana imports its petroleum products from South African refineries, the Government quickly realized what the economic consequences of a successful embargo against South Africa would be for Botswana. In such circumstances the rail-link with South Africa could be useless. It was therefore decided, early in 1974, to establish a bitumen road link with Zambia, and the Lifeline Programme was launched for this purpose. The road was to run from Gaborone, northwards along the line of the existing road to Francistown and Nata. From there a new road would be built to Kazungula, where there is a tiny border with Zambia at the confluence of the Zambezi and Chobe rivers. The total length of the road is about a thousand kilometres, and although the southern half had been planned to be bitumenized before 1980, at the time less than a hundred kilometres had already been completed. An attempt, which in the event was unsuccessful, was made to accelerate donor project appraisal for the construction of the southern half as far as Francistown,[15] and new finance was sought to bitumenize the two northern sections from Francistown to Nata and from Nata to Kazungula. The programme should be completed in the early 1980s, by which time there will be a continuous all-weather road between Zambia and the principal towns of Botswana.

Although the completion of the Lifeline Programme will reduce Botswana's dependence on rail transport, directing all trade through Zambia would be extremely expensive and hazardous, and could only be contemplated by Botswana as a short-term emergency measure. But the new road system will improve internal communications, and there may be some small growth of trade between Zambia and Botswana. In the past beef from Botswana has been airfreighted to Zambia from time to time, and the new road could restimulate these exports. Zambia for its part produces a range of manufactures which are not produced in Botswana. However, while Botswana remains behind the protective tariffs of the Southern African Customs Union, manufactured imports from Zambia are unlikely to be competitive, notwithstanding the improved communications between the two countries. Ironically, the most apparent early outcome of the road improvement was the facilitation of trade between Zambia and South Africa. Botswana has not benefited from this exchange. On the contrary, road maintenance costs have considerably increased, and little or no compensatory benefits have been received.[16]

MANUFACTURING INDUSTRY

The manufacturing sector represents about seven per cent of total domestic output. This is a small proportion, even by African standards, although its growth has kept pace with that of the economy as a whole. During the 1960s the BMC accounted for almost the entire production of the sector, and still accounts for nearly half. A few other establishments also process domestic resources. These include a maize mill at Lobatse and a tannery in Francistown which produces game skins, trophies, and similar tourist artefacts. An additional manufacturing activity is that of the smelter at Selebi-Phikwe which concentrates copper-nickel ore into a matte containing nearly 80 per cent metal. This operation, however, is conventionally included in the mining sector. Apart from some engineering workshops attached to the mines there are vitually no other manufacturing linkages to the mining sector.

If these resource-based industries are excluded, the rest of the sector is very small indeed and consists largely of import-substituting activities. The enterprises concerned generally produce goods which, by virtue of high transportation costs, enjoy a measure of natural protection—such as furniture or building materials—or are the final packing or bottling stage of a process substantially carried out in South Africa. A few of these enterprises have been fostered by the Government-owned Botswana Development Corporation (BDC) or by the Botswana Enterprises Development Unit (BEDU) which is a government department. But, apart from the free managerial and technical assistance which BEDU renders to its clients, there is very little artificial protection or subsidy. In particular, Article 6 of the Customs Union Agreement, which permits tariff protection of infant industries in the three BLS countries for up to eight years, has been used only once by Botswana, to protect a BDC-sponsored brewery.

The Customs Union offers unrestricted access to the southern African regional market. But the number of establishments which exploit this opportunity, apart from the resource-based industries referred to above, could probably be counted on one hand and their output is extremely small. Selwyn (1975) argues that the main cause of this situation is that the attractions of the core of the region outweigh any advantages which the periphery has to offer for industries which are not tied to a particular location. Such industries will tend to become established in the main urban centres of South Africa rather than in BLS. Industries located close to the core of the region enjoy distinct advantages, including those of being close to the main market, the proximity of linked industries and services, and lower utility costs. The main advantage that the peripheral areas might be expected to offer is lower wage costs. But even where such a differential exists—and it might not in the cases of BLS and South Africa—it is often not sufficient to draw industries away from the centre, where commercial risks are perceived to be lower.

Political factors have also favoured industrial concentration. South Africa has, on occasion, discouraged industries from locating in the three BLS countries by hinting or threatening that it would refuse entry to the resulting imports. Although it may never have gone so far as actually to violate the free-trade provisions of the Customs Union Agreement, a hint or threat of protection can be just as effective if it causes the abandonment of the project.[17] Moreover, foreign investors have been inclined to regard BLS as being potentially more unstable than South Africa, despite the growing potential for internal conflict in the latter. If multinational corporations have recently begun to attach greater risk to investment in South Africa, and to show greater distaste for doing so, the outcome may simply be a reduction of investment in the region as a whole, rather than its diversion to one of the three peripheral countries.

The implication of this analysis is that so long as Botswana remains a member of the Customs Union, and continues to eschew special measures to attract foreign investment, manufacturing industry will continue to play a very small role in the economy. Should the country therefore introduce industrial incentives or withdraw from the customs area in order to establish protective domestic tariffs? Either course would be fraught with dangers.

The arguments against offering tax concessions or subsidies to attract industry are threefold. First, there is a risk of conceding more than is necessary. Some industries, benefiting from tax concessions or subsidies, might locate in Botswana even without the incentives, and in practice it is difficult to distinguish these from other industries where the incentives offered genuinely affect the location decision. Second, when subsidies are paid to foreign investors, the net benefit to the domestic economy as a result of the new industry may be very small. If profits and dividends are exported, exemption is given on company taxes, the managers are expatriate, and imported materials are used, then the only benefit accruing to the domestic economy to offset the cost of the subsidy is the wage bill for the employees. In Botswana, as in Lesotho and Swaziland, there is a third argument against such a policy. The South African Government already offers extremely generous subsidies and incentives to industrialists to locate near the bantustans, apparently with only limited success (Selwyn, 1975: 30). It is doubtful if subsidies offered by the BLS countries would be any more successful, especially as they would be in competition with those offered by South Africa.

The more extreme course of opting out of the Customs Union altogether and encouraging the growth of domestic industries behind protective tariffs is hard to analyse. In simple terms the issue is whether the probable increase in the cost of living, the possible loss of the South African export market, and the certainty of reduced government revenues from customs and excise duties would be outweighed by the value-added flowing from the new industries which could be established as a result. The question has been examined in an interesting paper by Mosley (1978), who concluded that, on optimistic assumptions, a marginal advantage would flow to Botswana if it withdrew from the Union. But this conclusion is extremely sensitive to the assumptions used in his analysis. In particular, it assumes that the theoretical economic viability of an industry is a sufficient condition for its establishment and satisfactory operation. One does not have to look far in Africa for industrial opportunities which are not being exploited or for enterprises which are grossly inefficient. In short while the political arguments for leaving the Customs Union may be considerable and eventually overwhelming, the economic case is by no means established.

Under any conceivable set of policies or system of trading relations the potential for modern manufacturing in Botswana will remain rather small. On the other hand, more explicit recognition and encouragement could be given to the considerable amount of traditional manufacturing activity which already takes place in the economy. Many people through-out the villages and towns of Botswana are engaged in brewing traditional beer, sewing, producing simple traditional furniture, tanning and preparing skins, making donkey carts, repairing bicycles, metal-working, and so on. Their output scarcely registers in national statistics, and it is all too easy for outside observers to underestimate the importance of such activity and the contribution which it makes to the well-being of the people, simply because it cannot easily be measured. One recent study suggests that in 1974 as many as 61 per cent of all rural house-holds had some income from 'manufacturing' and that the mean household income from this source was P42 per year (CSO, 1976f: vi).

Moreover, modern manufacturing production, whether local or imported, frequently forces out informal village production. For example, the traditionally produced pig-fat soap or 'kgotla' stools have to compete in the market with mass-produced toilet soap or furniture. Such competition is not solely on the basis of price and quality. Local taste often appears to favour the modern mass-produced article. A striking and important instance of this type of competition in Botswana is the production of traditional beer, the brewing and sale of which furnishes thousands of rural women with a small cash income. The same type of beer is also brewed on a large scale in Gaborone and Francistown by a local affiliate of a South African company. Pro-duction is then distributed throughout the country in paper cartons. The employment and income generated by this method of production is spread very narrowly. Such competition makes it logically impossible to promote both the modern manufacturing sector and the informal village sector at the same time, at least where the same or substitutable goods are concerned. Unfortunately government policy, as well as the activities of BEDU and the BDC, generally tend to favour the modern sector.

FUTURE PROSPECTS AND CONCLUSION

The discussion of this chapter has come a long way from the initial optimism and euphoria which surrounded the Orapa and Selebi-Phikwe prospects. It is now necessary to bring some of the various themes to a conclusion.

The implementation of the two major mining projects has provided a considerable impetus to economic growth since independence, and the revenue earned by the Orapa mine has helped to alleviate the country's reliance on foreign aid. But the operation of the two mines has deepened other manifestations of economic dependence, of which the most urgent has been the insecurity of transport arrangements. Accordingly, in order to protect the mineral sector investments, the

Government embarked on two expensive programmes—the construction of the north-south road through Botswana to Zambia, and the establishment of Botswana Railways which will in due course operate the existing railway line through the country. By the time they are complete, these two schemes will have absorbed considerably more than a hundred million Pula of capital investment, an amount which is comparable with the flows of government revenue from the mines up to the late 1970s, and which is equivalent to nearly half the value of the annual GDP. It is true that this investment in transport infrastructure is being financed mainly from foreign aid, some of which might not have been available for other projects. It is also true that the southern section of the north-south road will have other, more tangible economic benefits, and that the whole economy—not just the mining sector—will derive some protection from the programme. Be that as it may, a portion of the cost of these schemes should be weighed in the balance when the overall benefits to the economy of the mineral projects are assessed.

Mining in Botswana has as yet created few economic linkages with the rest of the economy. On the other hand, future mining projects with much broader linkages are perfectly conceivable. For example, the country has enormous reserves of low-grade coal which, if exploited on a large enough scale, might justify the construction of a railway link to Namibia. Equally, the extraction of soda ash from the brines of Sowa Pan, together with the copper deposits which are being prospected in the north-west, could perhaps be turned to the same end. Furthermore, some of these projects could justify the transfer of a fraction of the vast water resources of the Okavango Delta to the east of the country and thereby permit irrigated agriculture *en route*. Sketching out such vast schemes is an exercise in which Botswana's planners like to indulge from time to time, but few of these projects have yet been shown to be sufficiently viable to attract the serious interest of technical partners.

In fact the further development of the mineral sector will be problematic over the next few years. As a new order emerges in Zimbabwe, Botswana's transport difficulties can be expected to be reduced. But the forces of the liberation struggle will then focus upon South Africa itself, and as long as the political situation in that country remains unsettled, projects in neighbouring countries may fail to draw new investors, especially from outside the region. Perhaps only the Anglo-American De Beers group, which is heavily and irrevocably committed in southern Africa, will be willing to invest further in Botswana. If the Government wishes to promote the continued expansion of the mining sector, it may have no other choice than to accept this situation, as indeed it seems to have done in agreeing to the new mine at Jwaneng.

But this will bring deepening dependence on one mining house and greater reliance on diamonds for both foreign exchange and public revenue. The danger is not yet serious: beef exports remain relatively important, the prices for nickel and copper must one day improve, while diamond prices—thanks, admittedly, to the De Beers monopoly—have been extremely stable. Yet the spectacle of other African economies being dislocated by wide fluctuations in the prices of one or two export commodities warns that a decision to rely on diamonds should not be taken lightly.

CHAPTER 7

MIGRATION, EMPLOYMENT, AND INCOME DISTRIBUTION

This chapter is concerned with the central issue of income distribution in the country as a whole and with how Botswana's development pattern has affected it. The primary concern is to analyse the changes in economic activity practised by the Batswana, and the incomes that accrue from these to different groups of households. Complex patterns of labour and family flows between rural and urban, rural and rural, and domestic and foreign locations of economic activity have become established. The effects of these migratory movements on family structure and stability are considered in this chapter, and some assessment is made not only of the levels of income earned but also of the very different costs for different families in earning them.

The Batswana have always been migrants—much more so than the populations of other central and southern African countries (Kuper, 1975). This has been a function of their classic settlement pattern whereby most Batswana live in or around a few large tribal capitals, which are often many miles from the places where they grow crops or graze cattle.

In addition to keeping their main home in the village,[1] families often maintain another dwelling at their land areas to which they move during the rainy season, leaving the village populated mainly by children and the elderly. Furthermore, for frequent and sometimes long periods during the year, the men and older boys are absent at the cattle post, where the owners of larger herds sometimes maintain a third dwelling. This kind of circular, seasonal migration which has been characteristic of Batswana society for many hundreds of years remains an important feature of life in the rural areas even today. But it is possible to identify two major changes which have occurred during the course of the last century and which have fundamentally affected patterns of labour use in the rural areas, the migration of people both within the country and abroad, and the distribution of income in the country as a whole.

The first of these changes is the growth of the institutionalized system of foreign labour recruitment by the South African mines. As shown in Chapter 1, the Batswana began to seek work in South Africa from the end of the nineteenth century onwards, in part as a means of earning the money needed to pay the taxes imposed by the protectorate administration. However, the gradual disintegration of the traditional economy, caused in part by the penetration of mass-produced, mainly South African, consumer goods additionally strengthened the need to earn cash incomes. The migrant labour system provided a ready source of cash to the young men, and labour flows to South Africa continued to increase in scale and importance until independence and beyond. Botswana's heavy dependence upon the migrant labour system has had important consequences for income distribution, particularly amongst the poorer families.

The second development which has had an even greater impact upon settlement, migratory, and income patterns has been the growth of the towns since the early 1960s. As a result, formal urban employment has been growing rapidly, and, since most job opportunities have occurred in these urban centres, rural–urban migration has become established on a large scale. A primary effect of this urban development has been the creation of new ways for Batswana to earn cash incomes. This has not been limited to those who have been lucky enough to find jobs in the formal sector—the pattern of transfer incomes and of informal sector earnings have significantly changed for many rural dwellers. At the same time the structure of earnings from formal employment has changed. The colonial salary scales inherited by the Government have been modified considerably. Wage differentials in both the public and private sectors have been much reduced, and greater equality of incomes from formal employment has thus been promoted. The Government's experience with incomes policy was initially very encouraging. Since 1974/5, however, the growing power of urban labour, and particularly of élite groups employed in the state sector, has brought pressures that threaten to stifle further attempts at redistribution via the wage and salary structure. Meanwhile, as elsewhere in Africa, the amount of open unemployment, and of petty employment for poverty-level wages continues to increase. In the following sections each of these developments are analysed, and the combined effects of Government policies on the overall distribution of incomes and employment opportunities are assessed.

INTERNATIONAL MIGRATION

In the early days the migrant labour system was the only means whereby the poorest Batswana—those without cattle—could earn money incomes, which were needed by all households as the cash economy became more established. Workers were rarely in the position of choosing between alternative employment opportunities at home and abroad. Wages in South Africa were not much different from those that were paid locally, and the key to the early growth of migrancy is the lack of cash-earning opportunities at home, rather than the attractiveness of work abroad.[2] During the 1930s the level of migration was still fairly modest, comprising about 10,000 workers. However, it became much more significant after the Second World War. The number of absentees from Botswana had increased to about 50,000 by the mid-1960s, and had reached about 70,000 ten years later. Although the data are not entirely reliable, approximately one-third of Botswana's male labour force typically work in South Africa. Up to half of these men find work in the South African mines.[3]

The most important explanation for this recent trend is the increase in the level of wages paid in the South African mining sector. Between 1964 and 1976 minimum wages paid by the gold mines increased much more quickly than those paid in Botswana. Whereas minimum cash wages in the South African mining sector in 1969 were only half the minimum wages paid by the Botswana Government, by 1976 they had moved ahead of those paid both by the Government and by BCL, the copper-nickel mining company at Selebi-Phikwe (see Table 7.1).[4] The fact that the gold mines also provide workers with board and lodging meant that by the end of the period the total benefits of working in the South African mining sector were much greater than those obtainable from similar work within Botswana. As a result the number of Batswana recruited by the Mine Labour Organization—the largest official recruitment agency in Botswana—increased by more than one-third, from about 19,000 to 26,000 workers between 1975 and 1976. In the same year the total number of Batswana in the South African mining sector as a whole increased to about 32,000 workers.[5]

These trends suggest that the supply of migrant workers to South Africa is highly responsive to changes in wage rates. People prefer to work in Botswana if they have the chance of doing so. But the recent increases in mine wages have radically altered the relative attractions of seeking work at home and abroad. This can best be appreciated by considering the effects of the recent wage changes upon the savings behaviour of migrant mineworkers. Almost all Batswana working for employers associated with the South African Chamber of Mines participate in the system of 'voluntary deferred pay', whereby a proportion of their earnings is deducted at source, and subsequently paid to the workers upon their return to Botswana. In addition most workers send some money home, either during or at the end of their contracts. We estimate that transfers from all these sources by the average mineworker increased from about P200 to P360 between 1974 and 1976 (see Appendix 2), apart from 'in-kind' transfers of other goods bought in South Africa. Such cash savings were equal to about 40 per cent of the annual earnings of an unskilled manual worker employed by the Botswana Government in 1974, and about 55 per cent two years later.

TABLE 7.1 *Minimum daily wages in Pula for unskilled work in Botswana and in the Sourth African mines, 1969–1976*

	1969	1972	1974	1976
Botswana Government[1]	0.63	0.80	2.00	2.40
Bamangwato Concessions Ltd.[2]	([3])	1.08	1.54	2.00
South African Chamber of Mines employers[4]	0.34	0.72	1.60	2.50

[1] No additional allowances given.
[2] This is the copper-nickel mining company at Selebi-Phikwe. Employees also received subsidized housing and free water, electricity, and medical services.
[3] The company was not operating in 1969.
[4] Employees also received free housing, food, water, electricity, and medical services.

Sources: RB, 1970d; DP, 1974a; DP, 1976; and data provided by the Ministry of Finance and Development Planning.

Such high rates of saving would be quite impossible to achieve from a manual worker's salary in Botswana, given the cost of living in the urban areas, and this explains a large part of the attraction of the migrant labour system to rural Batswana.[6]

The recent increases in mine and other wages in South Africa have thus had a major impact upon the inflow of cash to Botswana brought by returning migrants. Estimates suggest that the inflow from mineworkers alone has increased from about P2 million per year in the late 1960s, to about P10 million in 1976.[7] Most of this increase is a result of escalation of wages over the period rather than from the increased magnitude of labour flows. Although there are no data on cash transfers by workers in other sectors, it is almost certain that these have also increased—even if less markedly so than those made by miners—over the same period. Since between a quarter and a third of rural households have at least one absentee member working in South Africa, one important question concerns the extent to which the changing pattern of earnings and of cash transfers has affected rural household incomes over the decade.

Direct evidence is patchy. Early studies tended to throw doubt upon the significance of the income benefits of the migrant labour system to rural households. For example, a survey conducted in the village of Manyana, in south-eastern Botswana, in 1971, found that cash transfers from migrants provided a very small part of total village incomes, in spite of a very high rate of absenteeism.[8] In the same year, studies in Shoshong also suggested that the income benefits of the migrant labour system were very small. Although almost one-third of households in that village had at least one absentee worker in South Africa, the average annual cash remittance received by these households was less than P7 per worker. Remittances from absentees, which, including those working elswhere in Botswana, comprised half of the village labour force, contributed only 4.5 per cent of total household incomes in Shoshong (FAO, 1973: 9, and 1972b: 26). However, these data refer only to cash received by households during the period of absence of the migrant worker. They therefore seriously underestimated the total incomes generated by migrants, since transfers of both cash and goods occur mainly at the end of a worker's contract, when he or she returns home to rejoin the household.

More recent evidence, which takes account of total transfers in cash and kind from mine earnings, comes from a rural-incomes survey covering over 1,000 rural households in Botswana over the twelve months from March 1974 to February 1975 (CSO, 1976f). That survey estimated that the median household income in cash and kind from 'deferred pay', for those households with absentee mineworkers, was P60.[9] However, this sum is only about one-third of the value of the average deferred payment paid to mineworkers in 1974 (Appendix 2). This suggests that a fairly substantial part of the savings made by migrant labourers may not find their way back to the workers' families. The explanation for this is said to be that miners typically spend a large part of their deferred pay on non-durable consumption items in Botswana before returning to their homes.[10] One can imagine many possible reasons for this phenomenon. Miners have cause to celebrate at this time: the tensions of work and life in the mining compounds are over; after collecting their deferred pay, miners feel rich, and they are on their way home. Aside from that, however, it is also possible that the size of typical payments under the deferred-pay system are so high, relative to monthly cash earnings received, that workers tend to treat them as 'windfall gains', and exhibit consumption behaviour that is atypical of their normal pattern.

In addition to these transfers of about P60 from deferred pay, the rural-incomes survey found that returning mineworkers sent about P40 in cash and about the same amount in durable goods bought in South Africa, to their families, during or at the end of their contract. Thus, the typical total income transfer by migrant mineworkers to rural households in 1974 is estimated to have been about P140 in cash and kind. This was equal to about one-third of average cash earnings by migrant mineworkers in that year,[11] and to approximately one-fifth of the median rural household income, as estimated by the rural-incomes survey. Appendix 2 shows that since that date average wages paid by the mines have more than doubled, and this has probably had an even greater proportional impact upon transfers. Incomes from agriculture, in comparison, barely increased in real terms.[12] Accordingly, transfers from mineworkers have almost certainly become a larger component of the total income of rural households, and a more important source of their growth between 1974 and 1977 than previously.

Though this may be so, income transfers of the size mentioned above would be totally inadequate if they were the only source of income for a family. It has been estimated that in 1974 an adult woman and her small child needed an income in cash or kind of P215 per annum to live at a basic minimum level of subsistence in the rural areas of Botswana. The typical transfer income from minework of P140 in that year fell well short of providing for these basic needs of even the smallest family. Remittances would need to rise substantially before they could be said to be capable of supporting an average family of five or six persons.

What of the longer term costs and benefits of migrant work? Some recent studies have found cattle ownership to be strongly associated with those who have been migrant labourers at some time in the past (though inversely related to current patterns of absenteeism).[13] These results tend to confirm the view that, for families with no cattle—particularly those in the smaller villages—the migrant labour system has been the only means of accumulating enough capital to buy cattle and to start farming. Even in such cases, savings have often had to be accumulated over many years. These circumstances may involve great hardship for household members left behind. As explained in Chapter 5, not only do they not have cattle with which to plough, so that they have to hire a team of oxen, but they are often without male labour to do the ploughing. Sometimes labour can be hired. But, because of the general shortage of men in the villages many women are forced to rely on the help of older children or neighbours. This almost invariably means that acreage ploughed and crop yields are much lower than they would be if the absentees were available to help. For such families the migrant labour system carries a cost in terms of lower agricultural income. But it remains for many families the only way of accumulating enough capital to generate a viable future income from the land.

The most serious costs of the migrant labour system, however, relate not to its negative short-term effects upon agricultural output,[14] but to its impact upon the structure and stability of the family. Although some women do find temporary work in the agricultural sector in South Africa, absenteeism is overwhelmingly a male phenomenon. For most rural districts, between 20 and 30 per cent of the males in the working age-group are in South Africa at any one time, and in the south-east of the country the proportion of male absentees is even higher than this.[15] The absence of so many males has, over the years, raised the average age of marriage, and may have tended to keep the birthrate lower than it might otherwise have been.

It is not surprising however, that the system has also made sexual relationships more impermanent than they might otherwise be. The evidence suggests that the increasing rates of absenteeism have been associated with an increase in the number of children born out of wedlock and in the number of women bearing children by more than one man.[16] For those who have married, it appears that long absences in the mines act more to increase marital discord and infidelity than harmony, which in turn tends to increase the rates of desertion and divorce (Schapera, 1971: 251).

This is now a more serious problem than it was fifty years ago, in that other types of family support mechanisms are also breaking down. As elsewhere in Africa, the urban centres have attracted younger members of the labour force away from the rural areas, many of whom become permanent urban residents. Equally, within the rural areas, the traditional seasonal migration to the lands appears to be giving way to more permanent migration away from the tribal capitals. Moreover, the increasing monetization of the rural economy has substantially reduced the role of the household as a self-sufficient economic unit. In these, and other ways, the patterns of economic dependence within Batswana families are changing. These changes are tending to erode traditional household structures which typically included several generations living together.

As the nuclear family becomes more widespread, women are becoming more isolated both socially and economically as a result of the migrant-labour system. Several recent studies point to the seriousness of this problem. Syson's surveys in Shoshong, for example, revealed that in that village almost 30 per cent of the women over the age of 15 years were unmarried mothers. One-third of all households were effectively headed by women. Of these, three-quarters were headed by single women or widows, most of whom had children, and in the remainder the male household head was absent, usually at the mines.[17] Thus, a large number of women have to fend for themselves without the benefit of remittance incomes. The increase in labour flows to South Africa in recent years is of considerable importance to this group. Although it is true that the higher incomes which are now being generated as a result of the increases in mine wages will have brought relief to many families, there are many others that have become casualties of the migrant-labour system. The increasing number of families headed by women where there are no (present or absent) male members of working age is evidence for the fact that the growing number of mineworkers has led to an increase in the number of seriously poor or destitute people.

There are those who believe that the recent increases in wage rates paid to Africans in South Africa have brought clear net benefits to the surrounding countries through greater cash remittances. Though it is true that remittances have increased substantially, an emphasis upon the aggregate income benefits alone hides the wider costs of the migrant-labour system both to society as a whole, and to particular population groups within it. Viewed from the perspective of the very poorest households in Botswana which may not receive any remittances at all, the recent growth in the number of absentees give cause for concern: the enhanced labour flows abroad will have increased the number of women who are unsupported and economically isolated as a result of the absence of males, and the problem of absolute poverty in Botswana is likely to have increased rather than diminished as a result of these trends.

DOMESTIC EMPLOYMENT AND INTERNAL MIGRATION

The high levels of industrial investment and output growth since independence brought big increases in formal[18] sector employment within Botswana. The number of such workers increased from about 20,000 in 1964 to about 62,000 in 1977, representing an average growth of almost ten per cent per year over the period.

As might be expected from the pattern of events analysed in Chapter 3, employment growth was particularly marked between 1968 and 1974. The construction phase of the two major mining projects at Selebi-Phikwe and Orapa, together with the burgeoning needs for physical infrastructure in the capital boosted employment considerably. It can be seen from Table 7.2 that the main increases occurred in trade, in central government and in the construction industry, and that the latter increased its share from six to sixteen per cent of total formal-sector jobs over these years.

More recently, however, employment growth slowed down some-what, as a result of the changing structure of output and lower overall rates of economic growth. Employment in the construction manu-facturing, transport, trade, and finance sectors fell in 1977, and the small growth in total employment at that time was almost entirely due to the continued expansion of the public sector. This poor progress was mainly a reflection of the economic recession that began in 1974/5 (see Chapter 3). There is evidence, however, that the large increase in legal minimum wages introduced in July 1977 (q.v.) had strongly negative effects upon employment in some sectors, which aggravated those of the underlying economic trend (MFDP, 1978).

In spite of these sectoral set-backs at the end of the period, Bots-wana's record of job-creation after independence was a notable one.

TABLE 7.2 *Estimated formal-sector employment by economic sector, 1968-1977*[1]

Sector	1968	1972	1973	1974	1975	1976	1977
Freehold agriculture	4,150	4,825	4,625	4,450	4,250	4,025	4,250
Mining and quarrying	825	1,675	3,525	4,100	4,525	5,450	5,500
Manufacturing	1,700	2,650	3,000	3,400	3,850	4,275	4,150
Electricity & water	[2]	[2]	325	525	650	750	975
Construction	1,575	6,475	7,225	8,075	9,000	6,125	6,950
Trade and hotels	4,000	7,850	8,600	9,400	10,250	10,500	10,000
Transport & communications	1,125	1,125	1,350	1,650	1,975	2,025	1,850
Finance	}2,550	}3,150	}3,150	}3,300	2,000	2,675	2,425
Community services					1,575	1,875	2,100
Education	1,850	3,350	3,350	3,800	4,375	5,000	5,300[3]
Central government	6,000	9,175	10,075	11,175	12,200	13,600	15,150
Local government	975	1,025	1,750	1,700	2,675	3,075	3,350[3]
Total	24,750	41,300	46,975	51,575	57,325	59,375	62,000

[1] All figures are rounded to the nearest '25'. Small differences appear between data in this table and in the earlier published sources owing to improvements in the methods used for grossing up the survey data.
[2] Estimates not separately available: included under manufacturing.
[3] Provisional estimates.

Sources: CSO, 1968 and 1978a.

The proportions of the labour force and of the population employed in formal-sector jobs doubled between 1964 and 1975 (Table 7.3). Admittedly the country was starting from a very low base; but, even so, annual growth rates of employment of ten per cent are most unusual, and it is almost unprecedented for these to be sustained for more than a decade. This, then, represents extremely rapid progress by standards elsewhere in Africa and the Third World. Nevertheless, the picture painted by these aggregate data needs to be qualified in a number of respects.

First, although employment creation in the formal sector averaged about 3,000 jobs per year over the period, the active domestic labour force has been increasing by between 5,000 and 6,000 per year.[19] Thus, the labour force outside the formal sector continued to increase by over 2,000 persons annually—almost as many as those who were able to find formal jobs. These data point to the harsh fact that in most poor countries the formal sector cannot hope to absorb even the annual increment to the domestic labour force. By implication, unless other policies are pursued, those in the subsistence sector—including the number of people who are seriously poor and destitute—will continue to increase.

TABLE 7.3. *Population and employment, excluding self-employment in agriculture, in urban areas, and in the country as a whole, 1964-75.*

	March 1964	August 1971	August 1975
Total population (*de jure*)	550,000	635,000[1]	700,000[2]
(*de facto*)	503,000	579,000[1]	640,000[3]
De facto rate of growth p.a. (%)		1.92	
Rate of natural increase p.a. (%)		3.08	
Urban population	21,400	59,500[1]	93,300
Rate of growth p.a. (%)		15	12
As % of total *de facto*	4	10	15
Total formal employment	20,000	37,000[4]	57,300[5]
As % of *de facto* population	4	6.4	9.0
Rate of growth p.a. (%)		9	11
Urban employment: Formal	8,000[6]	19,000[7]	28,600[8]
Informal	250[9]	n.a.	5,000
Domestic service	1,500	4,000	5,400
Total	9,750	n.a.	39,000
Rate of growth of urban formal p.a. (%)		12	11
Rate of growth of urban total p.a. (%)		n.a.	14
Urban formal as % of total formal	40	51	50
% of urban pop. in formal employment	37	32	30
Activity rate in urban areas (%)	45	n.a.	42
Rural employment: Formal	1,200	1,800	28,600
Domestic	2,500	4,000	5,400
Informal[9]	1,500	n.a.	4,000
Seasonal	6,000	n.a.	8,000
Total	22,000	n.a.	46,000
% of rural population in employment	4.6		8.0

[1] Allows for an under-enumeration of the population of Selebe-Phikwe by an estimated 5,000 persons in the 1971 population census. See RB, 1977a:86. Includes an expatriate population of 11,000, together with an estimated 10,000 nomads who were not enumerated.

[2] Assumes constant fertility, declining mortality, and no permanent emigration (CSO, 1972c:A96).

[3] Assumes temporary migration has remained a constant proportion of the *de jure* population.

[4] Comprises non-agricultural cash employment excluding domestic servants as given by the census, plus an estimate for formal employment in agriculture based upon the manpower survey of the following year.

[5] From Table 7.2.

[6] Employment data in the 1964 census are given only for "urban districts". Census estimates have been reduced on the assumption that the rural areas around the towns had the same ratio to population as the national average outside the "urban districts". Domestic servants excluded.

[7] Reported cash employment in urban areas as given by census, less domestic servants plus a proportional increase to allow for under-enumeration at Selebi-Phikwe.

[8] Employment survey over estimates employment in Gaborone, since urban–rural breakdown based upon postal address of establishments. Gaborone employment revised on basis of migration survey. Other urban employment taken from employ-

Second, the geographical distribution of new job opportunities has been heavily weighted towards the urban areas. Until 1971 about two-thirds of the new jobs were in the urban centres, and since that date rural and urban job-creation appear to have been running at about the same rates (Table 7.3). This, of course, is a direct result of the urban bias of the pattern of investment: during the 1970s half of all new formal jobs occurred in the five urban centres which included only between ten and fifteen per cent of the population. Over the period 1964–71 the degree of urban bias was even more extreme.[20]

Third, as a consequence of this pattern of investment, there has been an enormous increase in the urban population of the country. In 1964 the urban population comprised some four per cent of the resident population.[21] It can be seen from Table 7.3 that over the following eleven years the urban population more than quadrupled, with fifteen per cent of the population living in urban areas by 1975. Overall, the growth of Botswana's urban population was about fourteen per cent per year between 1964 and 1975. This was from small beginnings, but was exceptional by any standards. Although urban growth has been a characteristic feature of African development over the past ten or twenty years, Botswana has had a faster rate of urbanization than any other country in sub-Saharan Africa (Todaro, 1973: 44). The major growth centres have been Gaborone and Selebi-Phikwe, where annual rates of population growth of 17 and 20 per cent respectively were sustained until 1975. The diamond centre of Orapa, on the other hand, was built as a closed township, surrounded by a high security fence, and migration there has been so far closely restricted to those who have jobs in the mine together with their immediate dependents.[22] In the older trading and manufacturing centres of Lobatse and Francistown urban investment has been more limited, and growth rates of around four and six per cent respectively have occurred over the period.[23]

It is clear then, that rural–urban migration in Botswana, as elsewhere, has been strongly associated with the pattern of urban investment and job-creation since independence. Nevertheless, it is significant that the population of the towns has been growing at a consistently faster rate than the growth of jobs in the urban formal sector. Thus the proportion of the population with formal jobs has fallen from about 37 per cent in 1964 to an estimated 30 per cent in 1975. This, in turn, implies either an increase in the average number of people

ment survey, after excluding reported farm workers, and including an estimated 1,200 jobs in Orapa.
[9] Rough estimates. See text.

Sources: BP, 1964a; CSO, 1972c; MFDP, 1973c; CSO, 1976h; RB, 1977a; and Stephens, 1976.

supported by each worker by almost one-third, or alternatively some increase in both the number and proportion of alternative ways of earning a living in the towns.

Other opportunities in the urban informal sector have in fact grown rapidly from insignificant proportions before independence. The 1964 census found about 2,000 persons in non-agricultural self-employment, most of whom were craft or other types of production workers. Although the regional distribution of this employment is not known, the great majority of such persons were probably working in the villages— particularly in Serowe and the other tribal capitals, which had much larger populations at that time than either Gaborone or Lobatse. Francistown was the largest and oldest of the 'modern' towns, and it undoubtedly supported a certain amount of informal work prior to independence. But the number involved was probably not more than a few hundred persons. By 1974, however, the informal sector was much in evidence. In the market areas close to the stations in the urban centres beer, vegetables, firewood, curios, furniture, tinware, and other craft items were sold, whilst in the peri-urban areas small-scale un-registered traders, builders, taxi services, tailors, hairdressers, vehicle repair services, and a wide range of other enterprises could be found. A survey conducted in that year showed that informal wage and self-employment in the four main towns involved about 4,500 persons— equal to almost 10 per cent of formal employment in the country as a whole, and almost 20 per cent of urban formal employment at that time (CSO, 1974: 49). Thus, although the proportion of the urban population with *formal*-sector jobs has decreased, the urban *informal* sector has increased at a faster rate than formal employment. Accordingly, the evidence suggests that the proportion of the urban population that is economically active has declined only slightly—if at all—since independence, if work in both the formal and informal sectors is included.[24]

In the rural areas, on the other hand, the proportions of the population and labour force in cash employment are very much less than in the towns. Such employment accounts for only about 8 per cent of the rural population, and even this includes a large number of workers who are employed only on a seasonal basis. The increase in the rural population between 1964 and 1975 was probably more than twice as large as the increase in rural jobs—excluding self-employment in agriculture—over the period.

Thus the main direct beneficiaries of economic growth in terms of new job opportunities have been the residents of the urban areas, which is why more than ten per cent of the population have moved from villages to the towns since 1964. On the other hand, the recent nature of urban growth means that rural–urban links in Botswana are still very strong indeed. Many of the migrants retain a permanent home in their village of origin, where several of their family members still live, and to whom they make frequent visits and gifts. It is important to realize, therefore, that the urban bias in the distribution of job opportunities does not necessarily mean that the wage benefits of these opportunities are entirely confined to the urban centres. Urban-rural transfers are substantial, and these considerably complicate any assessment of the impact of urban investment on the overall distribution of family incomes in Botswana.[25] This is a theme which will be returned to later. First, however, it will be useful to consider the changing distribution of income from the point of view of changes to the structure of earnings over time in different jobs and economic sectors.

INCOMES POLICY AND THE DISTRIBUTION OF EARNINGS

The distribution of incomes in Botswana has changed very significantly over the past twenty years. Major climatic changes have affected crop and cattle production and these events have affected the incomes of almost all rural families. In addition, increased opportunities to find urban work, both in Botswana and abroad, have altered the structure of household incomes in both rural and urban areas. The cost of living increased rapidly, particularly after 1973. Although earnings too have increased quickly, there have been changes in the relative returns from wage and self-employment, from skilled and unskilled work, and from employment in the agricultural sector as compared with other economic activities. In what follows, an attempt is made to assess the impact of these different pressures and events upon the alleviation of poverty and inequality in Botswana, distinguishing particularly between the consequences of government actions, the consequences of other interest groups, and the effects of natural events.

Wages and salaries in the public sector

One of the most direct influences upon the structure of earnings has been the Government's own wages and salary structure. The public sector has always been the largest employer in the country, and has accounted for more than 20 per cent of total formal employment. Until recently the Government employed about half of the expatriates working in the country, and an even higher proportion of skilled and educated workers—both local and expatriate—have been in government service.

Until the end of the Second World War, Europeans employed by the protectorate government, most of whom were recruited from South Africa, were working in occupations for which Africans were not then eligible. In response to growing pressures for African advancement, however, the promotion of Africans into the European grades was increasingly recognized by the administration as being inevitable. In 1948, following the report (BP, 1948) of a British Salaries Commissioner, T. Fitzgerald a dual salary scale for all the higher posts which had previously been reserved for Europeans was introduced. Fitzgerald argued that Europeans would be required in government service for many years and their pay would have to be determined in the light of levels needed to attract such workers from abroad, including Britain. On the other hand, a lower rate for Africans was appropriate—not only because 'inducement' was not needed for such workers, but also because there was a danger of creating an expensive local élite, which might in future raise the cost of government services to prohibitive levels. In the light of these considerations it was decided that the pay of an African occupant of a high post would be restricted to three-quarters of that payable to a European.[26]

Although it might appear that these inducement arrangements were similar to those adopted subsequently in most African countries, there was a critical difference in the circumstances of southern Africa. The existence of a large settler population in South Africa meant that many of the Europeans employed in the administrative headquarters in Mafeking were recruited locally. Only a minority of such officers came from Britain. The argument that all European officers needed an inducement to serve in Mafeking therefore seems rather implausible.[27] In fact, the need to pay different salaries to African and European employees arose mainly because of the growing differentials in the earnings of white and blacks doing the same work in South Africa. The adoption of this differential meant that rates of pay in the Protectorate Government also were based upon ethnic discrimination in the same way as those in South Africa.

Nevertheless, before the mid-1950s the issue of equal pay for equal work seems not to have been of major importance. Although the 'three-quarters' rule, as it became known, was always unpopular among African staff, the number of individuals affected by it was small enough for their opposition to be contained by the administration. By the end of the decade, however, the numbers of Africans being recruited into the clerical, executive, and secretarial grades of the public service grew, and opposition to their receiving lower salaries than locally recruited whites increased accordingly. The report of an independent salaries commissioner, Sir Rex Surridge, rejected these African claims in 1959 (BP, 1959). The grounds for so doing echoed the arguments put by Fitzgerald ten years earlier: some differential was needed on financial grounds, and there was also a need to prevent any widening of the gap between the peasant and the African bureaucrat.

As a result of Surridge's proposals the racial elements in the salary structure became more entrenched. The three-quarters rule was to be kept. In addition, the civil service was to be divided into three Divisions. Divisions I and II were to include all posts in the service at and above senior clerical levels, together with all other European personnel in more junior positions. The Division III was to comprise all other posts and personnel. Not surprisingly, there was loud protest from African civil servants,[28] so that less than two years later another commissioner, Sir Richard Ramage, was appointed to review the difficulties arising from Surridge's recommendations, and to report on desirable changes in the structure of the public services in the High Commission Territories.[29] His report accepted the charges that the existing arrangements were discriminatory, and argued that urgent action was required if 'wide repercussions' were to be avoided. Accordingly, he abolished the Divisions created by Surridge, and introduced four main classes of the public service: administrative and professional, technical and executive, clerical and equivalent, and subordinate (daily paid) staff. The most important change was that, henceforth, no inducements were to be given to any officers, irrespective of race, recruited in southern Africa. Foreign-recruited personnel would probably have to receive supplementary allowances, but where necessary these would be paid by the British Government not by the local administration.

These changes, which were introduced in 1961, created the basic structure of the civil service in Botswana which remained unchanged until 1978.[30] They also augured a recruitment policy which, for the first time, did not discriminate between people on the basis of race. It is significant that this was the same year in which South Africa was expelled from the Commonwealth, and when the question of the eventual political independence of Botswana, Lesotho, and Swaziland was finally settled. The implementation of Ramage's proposals in the three High Commission Territories represented a clear rejection of the labour policies followed by South Africa.

The principles used by Ramage in framing his recommendations were undoubtedly correct, and they were an important step towards removing discrimination from the hiring practices of the administration. However, the assumption was made that the bulk of expatriate officers recruited to the protectorate administration would continue to come from South Africa. It followed that if common scales for locally recruited white and black officers were to be introduced, they would have to be governed by the wages paid to whites in South Africa. In order to ensure that this competitiveness was maintained, Ramage introduced increases of 20 to 30 per cent in the senior scales with much lower increases for junior posts. Thus the salary scales were lengthened and differentials were widened. As a result the salaries of the most senior officers in Government were up to 40 times more than the wages earned in the most junior unskilled grades.

Even with hindsight, it is difficult to see how this salary structure could have been avoided. At that time over 300 of the white civil servants were South African, and it was not possible to replace most of these in the short term by contract officers from Britain. Moreover, the fact that Bechuanaland was administered from Mafeking implied that the concept of inducements for South African nationals (white or black) could not at that stage be introduced, as happened later, after the move of the capital to Gaborone. Thus the salary scales inherited by Botswana at independence were explicitly based upon South African wages and salaries. The unskilled grades were mainly influenced by black wages, and remuneration in the more senior positions was designed to be competitive with professional and technical salaries paid to South African whites.[31] The unfortunate consequence was that Botswana inherited a civil-service salary structure at independence which at that time was amongst the most unequal in Africa.[32]

At an early stage the new Government committed itself to three basic principles of incomes policy: first, that all employees should be paid a wage which would allow them to clothe, feed, and house their families; second, that average rural incomes should not lag behind minimum urban wages; third, that existing differentials between the highest and least well-paid formal-sector jobs were inequitable, and would be reduced (RB, 1968b: 9). Given the nature of the salary structure inherited at independence, together with the widespread and increasing extent of rural poverty as a consequence of the drought, these were ambitious goals. Nevertheless, Table 7.4 shows that at least in the area of government salary policy, some of these aims have been translated into action—albeit with important shifts in emphasis over the years since independence.

It can be seen that there was no change in the pre-independence salary structure until 1970. The salaries review commission of that year (RB, 1970d) framed its recommendations explicitly on the basis of the urgent need to reduce inequalities in pay. As a result of this review the salaries in senior posts were cut by up to 7 per cent. Although increases were granted in the lower grades, these were generally less than the increase in the cost of living since 1964. The only group to receive an increase greater than the rise in the cost of living over the period were unskilled labourers.

This new salary structure which remained unchanged for the following three years represented a very significant move towards greater equality in pay. By 1973, the salaries for most senior professional and

TABLE 7.4 Changes in government salary scales[1] (Pula), 1964-1978

	1964	Increase '64-70 %	1970	Increase '70-4 %	1974	Increase '74-6 %	1976	Increase '76-8 %	1978
Unskilled labourer[2]	166	27	211	150	528	20	634	12	713
Skilled labourer[2]	317	17	370	97	729	20	871	12	977
Junior clerical	318	17	372	42	528	20	636	8	684
Senior clerical	576	2	528	45	768	20	924	26	1,164
Technical	1,488	—7	1,380	32	1,824	21	2,208	10	2,424
Admin./professional	2,172	—1	2,160	25	2,700	21	3,264	31	4,288
Departmental head	5,790	—7	5,400	18	6,360	20	7,644	33	10,176
Permanent secretary	6,030	—7	5,580	23	6,864	20	8,244	45	11,976
Ratio									
Perm. sec./unskilled	36/1		26/1		13/1		13/1		17/1
Admin./unskilled	13/1		10/1		5/1		5/1		6/1
Admin./junior clerical	7/1		6/1		5/1		5/1		6/1
Urban cost-of-living index	63.2		74.6		100		125		156
% increase in index		18		34		25		25	

[1] All salaries shown are net of housing allowances. Such allowances were granted as a tax-free supplement to the staff grades (junior clerical and above) until 1978, in which year they were incorporated in basic salaries and became subject to income tax. These allowances therefore increased the actual differentials in incomes between workers in the skilled and unskilled labour grades and those in more senior posts to levels above those shown in the Table. Emoluments for all posts in the junior clerical grades and above were typically 20 to 25 per cent higher than the rates shown, although differentials within the staff grades were unaffected by the payments. Starting salaries are used for the above comparisons, except with Admin./Professional. Here, the third notch of the scales is shown, owing to anomalies which prevent a comparison of starting salaries in 1964 and 1970. Salaries in the Table remained unchanged between each of the years shown.
[2] These annual rates are calculated on the basis of 22 working days per month.

Sources: Salaries Commission Reports: BP, 1964c; RB, 1970d; DP, 1974a; DP, 1976, and RB, 1978a.
Cost-of-living-index: 1970-8: Central Statistics Office, Gaborone, 1964-70: estimate, based upon South African indices.

administrative posts in Government had not been increased since 1964, and many officers within these grades were actually paid less than they would have received ten years previously. Given the inflation of almost 60 per cent over these years, this represented a substantial drop in real terms, and the differentials in pay were reduced significantly at all levels of the service (Table 7.4).

During the early 1970s, however, there was growing disaffection within the civil service over the salary policy pursued by the Government. The real-income losses had in the past been concentrated at the higher end of the service, where expatriates tended to be in the majority, many of whom received at least compensatory increases in inducement and other allowances. As more local officers were promoted into these posts, opposition to the freezing of salary scales mounted. Accordingly, the Government appointed a new salaries review commission in 1974. Three factors were important in shaping the increases granted at that time. First, the country's financial position was much improved: the Government was no longer dependent upon Britain for recurrent support, and revenues from customs duties and diamonds were growing rapidly. Second, the general election of September 1974 was drawing near and the politicians were anxious to give some tangible evidence for the success of their earlier policies. Third, the international inflation brought substantial price increases for Botswana from 1973 onwards, and the rising level of urban costs—accentuated by the Government's pricing policies for services provided by the parastatals[33]—began to cause real hardship for the poorer families.

As a result, a political decision was made to grant substantial increases in wages for the poorest groups in the public service. Increases of up to 150 per cent were granted to the lowest paid workers (Table 7.4). This effectively doubled the real value of their earnings as compared to their position in 1964. Those in skilled manual and junior clerical/secretarial grades were also made considerably better off in real terms than they had ever been before. The increases were less marked at higher levels, such that officers in the technical grades and above were not fully compensated for increases in the cost of living that had occurred since 1970. These employees, therefore, continued to experience a decline in their standards of living. The effect upon differentials was dramatic. The ratio of salaries at the top and bottom of the service was halved as a result of the 1974 review. Unskilled labourers henceforth received the same wages as school leavers starting work in the junior clerical grades, and the differential between their earnings and those of professional officers was much reduced. In terms of restructuring the wages and salaries paid by Government the commitments to reduce differentials and to ensure a basic minimum standard of living for the lowest paid employees were being honoured.

Viewed from the perspective of the distribution of income from Government employment these changes were very progressive.[34] On the other hand there was some conflict between the results of the 1974 salaries review, and the spirit of the white paper on incomes policy published two years earlier. It had been argued there that a major principle of policy would be to ensure restraint in granting general wage increases as a means both of encouraging a faster growth of formal employment by protecting labour-cost advantages, and of preventing growing inequalities in the distribution of urban and rural incomes. However, it could not be pretended that the increases granted in 1974 were an exercise in restraint. On the contrary, they increased the government salary bill by between 60 and 70 per cent, which resulted in some redirection of resources away from investment towards consumption expenditure. They also indirectly stimulated the upward movement of private-sector formal wages in 1974 and 1975. Accordingly, at least in the short term, some amount of formal-employment growth was sacrificed,[35] and there was undoubtedly some widening of the rural–urban income gap.

The timing and magnitude of the increases in 1974 were probably more influenced by the fact of a forthcoming general election than by anything else. In this connection it is important to note the apparent reversal of policy that has taken place since that date. The two more recent salaries review commissions of 1976 and 1978—both of which were free of electoral pressures—have resulted in some increases in salary differentials within the public service (Table 7.4). In 1976, equal percentage increases were given throughout the service, which had the effect of maintaining existing differentials. Two years later, however, much higher increases were granted to those in senior posts than to unskilled groups. The reasons given for this pattern of increases were that the erosion of differentials had reduced incentives and productivity, and that there was an increasing danger of losing the more skilled and experienced Batswana to the international labour market. By 1978, therefore, the interests of the more powerful and articulate groups within the civil service were beginning to win out. Earlier efforts to reduce differentials were reversed, and the further reduction of inequality was no longer the main criterion used by the Government in determining its own salary structure.

Policy towards private-sector wages and salaries

The Government's involvement in direct wage-setting in the private sector during the early years of independence was minimal. The salaries inherited from the colonial period by the public sector were much higher than those generally paid in the private sector at that time, and the Government was content to leave wage determination to the normal market process. Whilst Government wages were held to be a guide to non-government employers (RB, 1968b: 9), minimum-wage legislation was not at that stage introduced.

However, during the long period between 1964 and 1973, when middle and senior salaries in Government remained frozen, private-sector wages increased considerably and many employers began to pay more than the typical government rates. Cases of public officers resigning to take jobs at much higher salaries in the mining and commercial sectors became increasingly common after 1970. In order to avoid inflationary competitive bidding for scarce local manpower—which could not, at least in the short term, do anything to increase the overall supply of such workers[36]—the Government had to take a more direct role in wage-setting outside the public sector. These circumstances led to the incomes policy white paper of 1972 (RB, 1972b).

The main tenet of incomes policy thus became that basic local wage and salary levels in the private and parastatal sectors should not exceed those received by comparable grades of government employees, taking into account differences in conditions of service and other non-monetary benefits. A National Employment, Manpower and Incomes Council (NEMIC), chaired by the Assistant Minister of Finance and Development Planning, was given responsibility for ensuring the implementation of this policy. Although the Council initially met regularly, and discussed a wide range of issues, it remained an advisory rather than an executive body. Equally, the incomes policy itself was not supported by legislation. By 1974 it had become clear that the policy was not being heeded: the employees of the larger companies were continuing to receive increases in earnings to levels that were much greater than those paid by the Government.

The government salaries review of 1974, however, marked the beginning of a much tighter period of enforcement. In July a central Government Wages Policy Committee was formed, which, by authority of the President but still not by law, was given the job of evaluating all wage and salary revisions proposed for the larger employers in the private and parastatal sectors before their introduction. Between 1974 and 1976 this Committee directly regulated the wages and salaries paid by most of the big firms, including the mines, railways, banks, and the parastatals in addition to many smaller establishments in the commercial and manufacturing sectors. Negotiations were concluded with firms which accounted for about one-quarter of formal employment outside the public sector. But since the larger firms tended to be the wage-leaders, the proportion of employees in establishments that were offending the government guidelines which were brought back into line as a result of the Committee's work was much higher than that figure suggests.

There were, however, some problems. In cases where real grievances were felt by the workers they had few alternatives to taking strike action.[37] This, indeed, happened in the case of both of the mines and the commerical banks during 1974 and 1975, although the Government in each case refused to compromise, and the strikers returned to work without their demands being met. In the light of these experiences however, it would have been desirable to involve the unions during all the discussions of the Committee, thereby enabling them to express their opinions prior to the determination of wage ceilings for their establishments. The atmosphere of secrecy that surrounded the work of the Wages Policy Committee tended to make industrial relations worse than might otherwise have been the case.

Since 1976 the Committee has been much less active. The meetings became more infrequent, and the evidence suggests that private-sector wages again began to move ahead of government rates at this time.

On balance—over the decade 1966 to 1976—Botswana's experience with this aspect of incomes policy was relatively successful. Its main aims were to reduce differentials within the formal sector, and to reduce the real incomes of the higher-paid workers. Owing in part to the fact that the period of strict enforcement of the policy coincided with a time of rapid inflation, these objectives were promoted. In addition, by 1976 some measure of homogeneity in salary structures as between different sectors and industries in the economy had been achieved, and labour turnover was probably lower than it had been in the early 1970s, with consequent benefits for productivity. More recent changes have reversed these trends, although data are not yet available with which to assess their full extent and impact.

The other main aspect of direct government involvement in private-sector wage determination has been in the area of minimum wages. As already noted, minimum national or urban wages were not introduced in the early years of independence, and the 1972 policy paper on incomes made a virtue of this fact. The position taken by the Government was that minimum unskilled wage rates in the urban areas were adequate, and that the specification of such rates could easily over-estimate the capacities of small employers to pay higher wages. This not merely ran the risk of reducing the growth of formal employment, but carried the additional danger of placing informal-sector employers outside the law in yet another way.

Opinion within Government, however, was divided on these points, and pressures from both the Labour Department and the Office of the

President led to the establishment of five Wages Councils in 1973 under enabling legislation which had been enacted in 1969. These bodies promulgated Regulation of Wages orders for the construction, transport, manufacturing, wholesale and retail, and hotel and catering industries which became effective from 15 July 1974. The rates adopted ranged from an annual equivalent of P211 for workers in the wholesale and retail trades, to P222 in hotel and catering, and P296 in the other sectors (BGG, 1974a). These were between 40 and 56 per cent of the minimum government rates (Table 4). By comparison, typical cash wages for domestic servants in the towns were about P180 per year at that time, and wages in the urban informal sector were often much less.

In 1977 the official minimum rates were raised to an annual equivalent of P422 in all industries. This represented a considerable increase in real terms,[38] and the ratio between the new minimum wages and the lowest wages paid by Government increased to 67 per cent. The unusual aspect of these changes was that they represented a move towards a single national minimum wage below which no-one would be paid. The only exclusions from the regulations were the Government and the mining sectors, where rates much higher than these minima were already paid, and agriculture, where the minimum-wage concept could not be readily applied.

The Government's main concern, in promulgating minimum-wage legislation, has been to prevent the exploitation of unskilled workers by employers. Wages Councils therefore attempted to take account of what was believed to be a wage that would provide a minimum acceptable standard of living for a worker and his family on the basis of available poverty-datum-line (PDL) studies. There are, however, a number of problems with using PDL criteria for minimum wage setting. First, the acceptable minimum level of income obviously varies with the age–sex composition and overall size of the family. Second, the income needed by a given family varies in different parts of the country, particularly as between urban and rural areas owing to much higher urban costs. Third, there is a danger of biasing the calculation of a PDL by the over-specification of items to be obtained through cash transactions as opposed to exchange or even non-market channels.[39] These problems, therefore, raise questions about which sort of PDL should be used as a guide to setting the minimum wage.

The main difficulty with the new minimum wage, however, was not so much the level at which the new rate was set, as the fact that it was to be applied uniformly throughout Botswana. For households of identical composition official studies suggest that the urban PDL is about twice the level required in the rural areas. Although this differential appears to be exaggerated,[40] it is nevertheless unlikely that a minimum wage, based upon rural costs and which could be afforded by all rural establishments, could possibly protect urban workers, who face much higher costs, from suffering extreme poverty. Similarly a national minimum wage which was strongly influenced by urban conditions would be quite beyond the pocket of many small employers in the rural areas. It is clear that PDL criteria, carefully used, should continue to be the most important influence upon minimum-wage legislation. But there are good grounds for moving to the more conventional idea of separate rural and urban rates in future, if serious distortions in the labour market are to be avoided.

In spite of these caveats, the net results of these policies have been generally supportive of some of the major principles of incomes policy espoused by the Government in 1968. Since independence the Government successfully narrowed the differentials in earnings from formal employment very considerably: in most sectors of the economy the incomes of professional and other senior employees had been reduced to between two-thirds and three-quarters of their real value in 1964, whilst those of unskilled employees doubled in real terms between 1964 and 1977. This has been achieved by progressively reducing the linkages between local and international salary structures: salaries paid in senior posts are no longer governed by South African rates and there has been a real effort to determine the lower wages and salaries on the basis of local prices and costs.

These structural changes in the pattern of earnings from wages and salaries, however, provide only partial evidence for whether or not the Government's objectives of creating a better overall distribution of incomes are being achieved. Most of the labour force do not receive regular cash wages, and the income increases to the lowest-paid workers may have turned the terms of trade against the self-employed including rural farmers. Here the critical issues are how the distribution of other incomes has changed, and how quickly these have been increasing relative to incomes from wage employment; whether the poorest rural dwellers are now better or worse off than they were; and how their incomes compare with those received by some of the poorest urban groups. It is to these questions that we now turn.

CHANGES IN RURAL INCOME DISTRIBUTION

Household incomes in the rural areas are very unequally distributed: it is estimated that the poorest 40 per cent of households receive 12 per cent of total rural incomes, whilst the richest 20 per cent control some 58 per cent of income. The Gini coefficient of income distribution in the rural areas is put at 52 per cent, which indicates a high degree of income inequality by international standards.[41]

TABLE 7.5 Income profiles[1] for the rural population, 1974/5

Percentile income groupings	Crops	Animals	Wages	Manufacturing	Trading	Services	Hunting	Gathering	Housing	Transfers	Other	TOTAL
Poorest 10	9	14	9	10	—	2	9	22	11	19	−5	100
10–30	10	13	17	6	1	3	1	16	10	19	4	100
30–50	10	19	21	5	2	2	1	12	9	14	5	100
50–70	11	31	17	6	1	2	1	7	6	11	7	100
70–90	8	39	20	4	1	1	3	5	5	8	6	100
Richest 10	5	40	38	1	1	2	4	3	2	5	−1	100

[1] The decile rankings are calculated by dividing total household income by the poverty-datum-line for each household separately. In effect, the PDL is a 'consumption-needs index' which takes account of differences in both family size and age–sex composition between households.

Source: Computer analysis of data from the Rural Income Distribution Survey held in Botswana in 1974/5. For further analysis of these relationships, and explanation of the methodology used, see Colclough and Fallon, 1979.

An analysis of the pattern of income distribution which takes households as the basic unit, however, is to some extent misleading. Larger households also tend to have larger incomes, in part because they have more labour available to them than smaller households. Owing to these differences in family size, therefore, the distribution of household incomes will be more unequal than the distribution of per capita incomes. Table 7.5 shows the main sources of income for 90,000 rural households in Botswana, ranked according to total income expressed as a proportion of the PDL for each household. Since the PDL takes account of both sex and age structure this produces a more refined measure of the characteristics of various poverty groups than would a ranking based upon either household or per capita incomes alone.

The fundamental feature of the structure of household incomes shown is the extent to which it is influenced by patterns of cattle ownership. There is a strong positive relationship between the size of the family herd and annual household income; this variable is the single most important determinant of rural incomes, and much of the inequality of rural income distribution stems from an even more unequal distribution of cattle ownership: whereas livestock provide only about thirteen per cent of the income of the poorest third of the rural population, it is the source of forty per cent of the incomes of the richest third.

It is clear, then, that changes in the distribution of cattle ownership over time will have had a greater impact upon the overall distribution of incomes in the rural areas than any other factor. The evidence suggests that this pattern of ownership has been becoming more unequal since the early 1960s, and, in particular, that the proportion of rural households owning no cattle has increased from around 30 to about 45 per cent since independence. This trend was mainly a result of the drought which particularly affected families owning only a few cattle, though it may also be the result of modernizing social forces which have caused the fragmentation of households but not of cattle herds. Stock losses at that time resulted in perhaps 12,000 to 15,000 middle-income rural families being relegated to the ranks of the poorest groups.[42]

This trend will also have worsened the distribution of incomes from arable agriculture, as explained in Chapter 5. In spite of the series of good rainfall seasons since the late 1960s and the significant increase in crop production in consequence, the output gains have accrued mainly to the larger farmers, and, more generally, to cattle-owners rather than to those who have had to hire or borrow draught-power for ploughing purposes. Thus, because of the increase in the number and proportion of households with no, or restricted, access to oxen, the distribution of crop incomes is also likely to have become worse over the period.

The effects of changes in employment opportunities and of wage incomes are more difficult to assess. Formal employment has, as we have seen, increased faster than the labour force, and the proportion of the rural population with regular jobs has doubled from about 2.5 per cent in 1964 to about 5 per cent in 1975.[43] The distributional effects of this, however, depend upon whether these jobs have been taken by persons from the poor or from the richer households. There are some indications that here too the main benefits have been captured by the richer groups. First, the very poorest rural households often comprise single women with children without males of working age. Such families are unable to benefit from employment opportunities, even if they were available. Second, the incidence of job-creation in the rural areas has been mainly concentrated in the larger villages, which are the main centres for local government and district trading activities. It is the richer rural households who can afford to maintain additional dwellings at their lands or cattle posts who live in these centres,[44] and they are therefore likely to have had more favoured access to new jobs than those not living so close at hand.[45]

Table 7.5 provides evidence for these relationships. It can be seen that even after allowing for differences in family size and in the age-sex structure of families, the richer households have much higher incomes from livestock and from employment than poorer households. The main reason for this is that employees in the two groups are generally holding different types of jobs. The employment incomes of the poorest households are usually from informal or seasonal work in agriculture, including cattle herding, where wages paid are very low.[46] The growth of the national cattle herd, at a rate of some 10 per cent per year since the late 1960s, will have increased the number of such jobs. On the other hand, the increasing concentration of ownership will also have brought negative employment effects through scale economies. It is probable that the overall impact of this on job-creation has been much less than that of the growth of formal employment, to which the richer groups have more privileged access. On balance, then, it is likely that the distributional implications of increases in wage-employment opportunities have been neutral or even negative in the rural areas, and that they have done little or nothing to alleviate directly the poverty of the poorest groups.

The only item of rural incomes which has increased in such a way as to bring greater proportional benefits to the poorer than to the richer families is transfer incomes. It can be seen from Table 7.5 that transfers represent about one-fifth of household incomes for the poorest third of the rural population. Indeed, these tend to be the most important income source for this group, except in the case of the very poorest households, for whom gathering activities provide the largest single source of income. These transfer incomes come mainly from migrant mineworkers, but also include transfers from family members in the urban areas of Botswana. We have seen that the real value of the earnings of Batswana mineworkers in South Africa more than doubled between 1972 and 1976, and that earnings from unskilled work within Botswana almost doubled over the same period. If the assumption is made that remittances were maintained as a constant share of the incomes of those workers sending them over this period,[47] this would have increased the real incomes of the poorest third of rural households by about 20 per cent, assuming that the real value of other items of their income were maintained over those years.

Thus, changes in rural income distribution were probably greatest during the immediate post-independence years. Between 1965 and 1973/4 the average real growth of agricultural output was close to 16 per cent per annum.[48] These increases, however, were mainly captured by cattle owners—the richest half of the rural population. Over these years real wages for unskilled workers increased only slightly in real terms, both in Botswana and South Africa, which probably meant that the real value of transfers to the rural areas remained approximately unchanged. During this period, therefore, the distribution of rural incomes deteriorated sharply. Since that date, however, the situation has been reversed. Real output in agriculture has made slow progress whilst transfers have increased at a much faster rate. As a result, the growth of household incomes of the poorer families between 1973/4 and 1977 was probably slightly faster than that of the richer groups.

These recent trends, however, are not very significant, particularly in view of the apparent changes in government salaries policy since 1976. The fundamental fact is that, because of the highly inegalitarian ownership of capital in the rural areas, the poorer households have not received much benefit from the agricultural recovery that has occurred since independence because such households have very limited access to cattle. The distribution of formal employment opportunities appears, if anything, to have exacerbated this bias against the poorest groups. Over the whole period the distribution of income in the rural areas has deteriorated, and, as Chapter 5 has shown, unless something is done to change access to or ownership of capital amongst the poorest 40 per cent of rural households, it is probable that rural income distribution will continue to become more unequal in the future. Special action is required if the plight of the poorest is to be eased.

RURAL–URBAN CONTRASTS

As in the rural areas, household incomes in the towns are also derived from a wide range of sources. The main difference is that a much smaller proportion of urban household incomes come from agricultural activities, and a much higher proportion are from wage employment. Though it may be generally true that the better-off members of the urban formal sector have a restricted range of income sources—usually one or two wage or salary incomes per household—this is not true of all such families: many Batswana in senior posts in both the public and private sectors hold substantial numbers of cattle, and their farming interests in some cases supply the major part of their annual income. Poorer urban households also have many different sources of income. Apart from wage employment in the formal or informal sectors, such families may receive irregular incomes from manufacturing, trading, or service activities in the informal sector, from transfers from the rural areas, from directly productive work in agriculture, particularly at ploughing time when they may leave the town for several weeks, and from a range of other sources such as house construction and the making of clothes or utensils. Comparisons between rural and urban household incomes therefore have to take account of all these income sources if they are to present a valid picture. Equally, however, they have to take account of the much higher cost of living in the towns: owing to much higher rentals and the cost of urban services, most rural families moving to the urban areas would have to be able to increase their incomes substantially in order merely to preserve their standard of living.

The reality of migration, however, is that whole families generally do not move together. People go to the towns singly, or in pairs, leaving the other members of their household behind in their village. Thus the typical household composition in the towns is rather different from that in the rural areas. Urban households are smaller, older, more educated, and include more males of working age than either the rural or national average (CSO, 1974: 27). For these three reasons—the complexity of income sources, the higher urban costs, and the differences in household structure—the problem of comparing rural and urban incomes even in principle is extremely difficult.

In practice, the data necessary to describe urban income distribution in detail do not exist. However, a survey of three peri-urban areas undertaken in 1974 gives some indication of household incomes amongst the poorest members of the urban community, which provides some details about the tail-end of that distribution. Since this is the most relevant sector with regard to rural–urban migration, it provides a means of focusing upon some of the contrasts mentioned above.

Table 7.6 shows that the median household income in the peri-urban areas in 1974 was substantially less than that for the rural areas, but that because of much smaller households, incomes on a per capita basis were slightly higher in the peri-urban areas at that time.[49] This, however, does not take account of the considerably higher costs of living in the peri-urban areas. Even though there are reasons to suspect that the peri-urban survey underestimated incomes on an annual basis, it seems clear that, in real terms, these were significantly less than average rural incomes in 1974.

TABLE 7.6 *Household incomes in rural and peri-urban areas, 1974*
Pula per annum

	Rural	*Peri-Urban*
Median household income	630	438
Average family size	6.5	4.25
Median per capita income	97	103

Sources: CSO, 1974; CSO, 1976f.

Most workers living in these areas had found regular jobs in the modern part of town. Such employees comprised one-quarter of the population of the peri-urban areas in 1974. A further 8 per cent were working in wage or self-employment in informal jobs within the peri-urban communities themselves. Although the implied activity rate of one-third was less than for the urban areas as a whole (Table 7.3), there was on average more than one employee per household, and average household income from wages or salaries in the peri-urban areas was about 20 times the average incomes from the same source received by the lowest decile of the rural population in 1974 (P438 per household, compared with about P24 for the poorest 10 per cent of rural households). Even with unemployment rates for men of around 18 per cent, and, therefore, a probability of finding a job of about four-fifths, the move to town remained an attractive prospect for the poorer rural dwellers—particularly when most members of the rural household could stay behind, at least initially, until a steady urban income source had been secured. Thus, in spite of higher urban costs, it is likely that, for poorer households at the fifth or tenth percentile of the rural income distribution, the move to town would result in considerable income benefits irrespective of whether the work found was in the formal or informal sectors, together with a much better chance of finding a regular job than in the rural areas.

There have been no surveys conducted which give a reliable indication of the distribution or levels of household incomes for the richer parts or the urban centres. Given that for the majority of urban residents most household income comes from employment, our earlier analysis

TABLE 7.7 Comparison of distribution of urban-employment income with that of rural household income

Category of worker	URBAN WORKERS				RURAL HOUSEHOLDS 1974
	Number of workers[1] (1)	Av. monthly earnings (Pula) (2)	Cumulative % of income (3)	Cumulative % of workers (4)	Cumulative % of rural families with % of income shown in Col. (3)
Urban informal	2,000	10	2.6	8.3	14.0
Urban domestic	4,500	15	11.4	26.9	39.0
Unskilled formal	13,164	28	59.7	81.2	90.0
Skilled, junior secondary	3,209	56	83.2	94.4	98.0
Skilled, senior secondary	932	75	92.4	98.2	99.7
Skilled, post-secondary	356	110	97.5	99.7	99.95
Skilled, university	74	254	100.0	100.0	100.0

[1] The number of workers in each category are rough estimates, based upon surveys conducted between 1971 and 1974. The assumption is made that formal employees in each category are divided as between rural and urban areas in the same ratio as for total formal employment.

Sources: MFDP, 1973c; CSO, 1974; CSO, 1976f: 84.

of the movement of wage differentials over time might suggest that household-income distribution in the urban centres has been improving since independence. It is clear that the distribution of incomes from employment on a per-worker basis *have* been improving, and Table 7.7 shows that, even with the inclusion of workers in the urban informal and household sectors, the distribution of urban incomes from wages and salaries in 1972 was better than the rural household income distribution for 1974/5. Subsequent changes in the distribution of earnings from employment will have further strengthened this trend. Thus, if the estimated urban incomes shown in Table 7.7 were randomly distributed among all urban households, one could confidently claim both that urban-household-income distribution was more equal than that in the rural areas, and that it has been improving over time.

But the distribution of urban-employment income is not random among all urban households. First, as discussed earlier in this chapter, the proportion of the urban population in formal-sector jobs has declined by about 20 per cent since the early 1960s. Since there is no evidence to suggest an increase in the average size of urban households over the period, this implies a considerable increase in the proportion of households without wage support from the formal sector. Second, the overall activity rate has also declined over these years, although it has been supported to some extent by an increase in the proportion of informal-sector workers. Third, although there is no hard evidence on this point, it is almost certain that the proportion of the urban labour force that is unemployed has increased significantly since 1970.[50] Finally, the cluster of characteristics needed for eligibility for the more skilled and remunerative jobs in the formal sector (fluency in English, middle or higher levels of education, urban contacts or influence, etc.) themselves tend to be correlated with levels of household income or wealth; thus there is a tendency for the higher wage incomes to flow to households with other significant sources of income, whereas the opposite is the case for incomes from unskilled or informal employment. For these reasons, the assumption that the distribution of employment incomes is random across urban households is probably incorrect. On the contrary, relationships in the urban labour market, together with the fact that migration from the rural areas continues at a higher level than the rate of formal job-creation, suggest that the proportion of very poor urban households has considerably increased since independence.

The net effects of recent changes in earnings from employment upon the overall distribution of income in the urban areas are, therefore, difficult to assess.[51] The Government's wage and salary strategy until the mid-1970s achieved more equality in the distribution of incomes amongst the formally employed. It resulted in a significant redistribution of employment income from richer (technical and professional) to poorer (unskilled, semi-skilled, and clerical) households. At the same time, however, the income gap between the latter group and those households which are dependent upon earnings from informal or domestic service work widened. Because the number of such households increased absolutely and as a proportion of the urban population, it is possible that overall income distribution in the urban areas has been getting worse. Whether this is tue or not, urban poverty is now a more serious problem than it was in the mid-1960s. Minimum-wage legislation can protect some of the lowest-paid urban workers, but not all of them, and it is clear that a broader policy of encouraging income growth in the informal sector is required if some of the very poorest groups in the urban areas are to benefit from redistributive policies.

INCOME TAXATION AND THE DISTRIBUTION OF POST–TAX INCOMES

The analysis of changes in income distribution has so far been exclusively concerned with household or factor incomes gross of taxes. Income taxation, however, is one of the most powerful means whereby governments can directly modify the distribution of incomes. It is therefore appropriate to end this chapter with some evaluation of the extent to which this instrument has been used by the Botswana authorities in general support, or otherwise, of their stated redistributive aims and policies.

Prior to 1973 the taxing legislation in Botswana dated from colonial times and was based mainly on South African taxing principles and provisions.[52] The basic rates of personal income tax that held throughout the period 1962–72 were the same as the South African rates in the early 1960s,[53] although they became subject to a surcharge of 20 per cent in 1962, and 30 per cent for the period 1967–72.[54] In 1973, a new Tax Act was introduced which raised the tax thresholds for all persons, but which also significantly increased the marginal rates of tax payable on annual incomes in excess of P3,000. These changes were expected to improve the distribution of income by reducing the burden upon the poorer people, and by increasing the tax bills of higher income earners (RB, 1973: para. 27).

In addition to income tax, all residents of Botswana over the age of 18 years, with the exception of married women and dependents, have to pay a local government tax. Introduced in 1965 (BGG, 1965) as a means of financing local services, it replaced earlier flat-rate taxes that had been levied by the colonial administration.[55] The amount of local tax payable was a fixed amount for each of five broad income bands, varying between a minimum of P3 for those earning less than P85 per year and a maximum of P48 for those earning more than P660 per year. Thus, although the new tax was an improvement on those it replaced, its operation within each of the income bands was regressive: richer people in each group paid a lower proportion of their income in local tax than the poorer people.

During 1976/7, changes to both local government and income tax were introduced. The local rates were increased and the relevant income bands were widened, with a new maximum of P84 being payable by those persons earning more than P960 per year. In addition a major reduction in the marginal rates of income tax was introduced which for most income levels reduced these rates to below those that had been operative prior to 1973 (RBSL, 1977).

Fig. 7.1 shows the combined effects of all these changes.[56] It can be seen, first, that throughout the period, taxation, as it has affected most families, has been regressive: those earning between P750 and P1,500 per year have paid a lower proportion of their income in tax than the very poorest people. In this connection, it should be remembered that over 90 per cent of rural families had a household income of less than P1,500 in 1974 (CSO, 1976f: 84). These regressive tendencies have therefore affected the major part of the population, not just the tail-end of the distribution.

Second, and contrary to the claims of the Government, it can be seen that the redistributive effects of the 1973 Act were limited. Married persons earning up to P1,000 per year continued to pay taxes to the local authorities at the same rates as before.[57] The raising of the threshold mainly affected the middle- and high-income earners—in particular, married persons earning between P1,500 and P9,000 per year now payed significantly less tax than previously. The increased marginal rates implied a higher tax rate only for those earning more than about P9,000 per year.[58] In 1972 these persons comprised less than five per cent of the tax-paying public (CSO, 1973a: Table 65).

Any redistributive effects that this legislation might have had, however, were completely undermined by the amendments made in 1976/7. It can be seen that the combined revisions to local and income tax rates at that time resulted in an increase in the tax bill for those earning less than about P5,000 per year, and a decrease for persons earning more than that amount. The reductions for the richest people were very considerable, with a decrease of up to ten percentage points in the proportion of income paid in tax by those earning in excess of P10,000 per year. This group, though a tiny proportion of the total population, control a large proportion of the nation's agricultural capital, and are in receipt of perhaps 20 per cent of personal income. It is difficult to avoid the conclusions that the 1976/7 tax changes

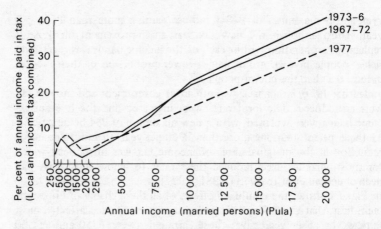

Fig. 7.1 The effects of successive revisions in local government tax and income tax legislation upon the proportion of incomes paid in tax by married persons, 1966–77

were heavily weighted in favour of this group, to the cost of the poorer people, and that the income-tax instruments were no longer being used in pursuit of income redistribution from the rich to the poor.

This picture is made even worse by widespread evasion of taxes amongst farmers and other self-employed persons. In 1972/3, for example, only 338 farmers were assessed individually for income-tax purposes (MFDP, 1974: 7). Even including the additional 500 or so farms that are registered as companies, this still accounts for less than 1,000 full-time farmers paying tax in that year—less than one per cent of rural households in Botswana. On the other hand, the rural-income-distribution survey found that about 4,500 rural households had incomes exceeding the married persons' tax threshold of P3,000 in 1974. Even on the basis of generous assumptions, it is almost certain that over half of the farmers who are liable for tax manage to avoid doing so. This high incidence of evasion amongst the richer rural families significantly increases the regressive tendencies inherent in Botswana's tax system. Their combined effects promote growing inequalities in the distribution of income over time.

CONCLUSION

Income distribution during the 1960s and early 1970s in Botswana became more unequal. Although income differentials from formal employment narrowed—mainly as a result of the declining real incomes of the more highly paid employees—in the rural sector the larger farmers quickly increased their incomes after the long years of drought. Small farmers, on the other hand, did not benefit from the changes in the weather cycle, because the pattern of cattle ownership remained unchanged, or worsened. There were, however, several important changes during 1973/4. The large increase in minimum government wages combined with continuing downward pressure on the real incomes of those in senior posts, the introduction of minimum-wage legislation, the period of strong enforcement of the incomes policy, and the rapid increase in mine wages in South Africa brought considerable direct benefits to lower-middle income groups. Similarly, as a result of wage restraint, sluggish progress in agriculture, and a slightly progressive Tax Act, the incomes of the rich were held back. Meanwhile some of the very poorest rural households benefited from increased transfer incomes from the urban employed, both in Botswana and South Africa.

However, after two or three years during which the major influences seemed to be working towards increasing income equality in all sectors, there was some reversion to earlier trends. The increase in the proportion of poorer urban households, associated mainly with declining urban activity rates and downward pressure upon the real earnings from informal and domestic employment, has probably arrested the redistributive influences in favour of the poorest urban groups. Perhaps more fundamentally, recent policies of the Government seem to be less clearly promoting the interests of such workers. The government salaries reviews of 1976 and 1978 which went some way towards restoring earlier differentials, the signs of some weakening in the political commitment to the incomes policy, and the taxation changes of 1976/7 which favoured the richer groups to the cost of the poor, all seem to signal some departure from earlier policies and objectives. However, these changes are perhaps too recent to signify, as yet, a fundamental redirection of Government's strategy. Changes in the balance of short-term political pressures are undoubtedly partly the cause of these recent developments: the 1974 election was comfortably won by the BDP, and the focus of articulate opposition, where it existed, shifted to the urban sector, and was located among the ranks of the employed workers, rather than those without jobs; civil servants increased their pressures for substantial wage increases, supported by the knowledge of healthier government finances; the unions outside Government became more sophisticated—though the strikes in 1974/5 were abortive, workers' organizations were, if anything, stronger as a result. All of these pressures have been important, and have caused the Government to react differently at different times.

Finally, however, and by way of introduction to issues discussed in the next chapter, it is certain that the growing expatriate presence in

Botswana has tended to become increasingly destabilizing from the point of view of policies aimed at promoting greater equality. It is painfully clear to most Batswana that a local professional worker receives an after-tax income that is small compared to those received by expatriate employees doing the same jobs. Inducement allowances and gratuities, which are not taxed, often triple the after-tax local salary for the job in question. The comparisons that are inevitably made between the conditions enjoyed by local and expatriate workers enhance the incentives for Batswana to accumulate personal wealth. Such contrasts are also an important ingredient in local pressures to reduce the tax burden and to increase local salaries at middle and higher levels of the income structure. These pressures have had some effect upon both the taxation and the incomes policies of the last few years that we have described, and the high degree of penetration of the Botswana economy by international economic influences is undoubtedly part of the reason for the changing policies that are being pursued.

CHAPTER 8

SCHOOLS, SKILLS, AND SOCIAL POLICY

Earlier chapters have shown that incomes from production in Botswana have increased very rapidly since independence, but that these increases have been unequally distributed among the population. Judgements about the extent to which people's welfare is changing, however, particularly of those in the poorest groups, must take account of their access to publicly provided services and, indeed, of changes in the quality of the services themselves. Expenditures upon education and health facilities by Government and other agencies have a particularly important impact upon the standard of living of the population. Providing everyone with at least the means of acquiring numeracy and literacy, and access to basic health care, are generally taken to be primary goals. Movement toward these goals is not only desirable in itself, but is also a crucial part of any investment strategy: the development of cognitive and manual skills in the population and the reduction and prevention of disease are critical to the improvement of productivity at work and of satisfaction in leisure. Any evaluation of development strategy would therefore be seriously incomplete without an assessment of these aspects of social policy.

EDUCATIONAL DEVELOPMENTS DURING THE COLONIAL PERIOD

Although the origins of formal schooling in Botswana stretch back to the middle of the nineteenth century, when Livingstone began his missionary work at Kolobeng in the Kweneng District,[1] its development over the following hundred years was slow, and was initially dependent entirely upon work by the missions. Foremost among these was the London Missionary Society, but other societies including the Hermansburg Mission, the Dutch Reformed Church, the Roman Catholic and Anglican Churches, and others came to Bechuanaland from about 1875 onwards. Their activities had resulted in twenty primary schools being established in the territory by the turn of the century, with an enrolment of about 1,000 pupils.

The first moves towards a system of local administration were made in 1910, when the London Missionary Society, being concerned about the danger of educational disputes among missions of different denominations, proposed the establishment of school committees which would supervise the work of schools within each of the tribal areas. Over the next few years such committees, which included representatives of the tribal authorities, the district administrations, and the missions themselves, were established in the Ngwaketse, Tawana, and Kgatla areas. This system of management involving local participation proved extremely popular, and was formally ratified for all the tribal areas by proclamation in 1938. Tribal school committees continued to function until 1966 when they were replaced by Local Education Authorities.

Complementary to this method of local control was a system of local financing. Though the Government initially had made small grants to the missionary societies that established schools in the territory, most of the resources for the early educational initiatives came from the missions themselves.

In 1903, however, two of the Tswana chiefs—Bathoen I of the Ngwaketse and Setshele I of the Kwena—decided that additional resources were required if the expansion of schooling in the protectorate was to proceed. They instituted in that year a levy of two shillings payable annually by every taxpayer, to meet the costs of maintaining schools and paying the salaries of the teachers. This system remained unchanged until 1919, when the levy was increased and extended by the Government to cover the whole territory. Thenceforth each African male was required to pay a sum of three shillings per year in addition to the hut tax. This Native Fund, as it was called, became the sole source of educational finance, with the exception of a small amount of grants-in-aid during the depression, until 1938. In that year, Tribal Treasuries were established for the payment of teachers' salaries, the purchase of school books and equipment, and the provision and maintenance of school buildings. To enable them to carry out these and other functions, each Treasury received 20 per cent of the local taxes—now increased to incorporate the education levy—collected in its area. The rebate of tax was later increased to 50 per cent. This method of financing primary education continued until independence.

Thus the growth of the primary school system depended not only upon local initiatives but also upon local resources. Tax revenues varied greatly between different areas, as did the share that each Tribal Administration was willing or able to devote to education. Consequently there was considerable variation in school enrolment ratios, in the quality of buildings, and in the provision of teachers and equipment between different parts of the country.

Primary school enrolments expanded rapidly during the 1950s, after an earlier period of decline (Table 8.1). As a result, about half of the school-age population was enrolled in primary schools at independence. But resources in the school system were inadequate to cope with this number of children. By 1965 the pupil–teacher ratio had deteriorated to over 40:1, and from a total of 1,345 primary classes, 231

TABLE 8.1 *Enrolments in the school system, 1946-1976*[1]

	Primary schools			Secondary[2] schools			
	Standard 1	Standard 7[3]	Total enrolled	Form 1	Form 3	Form 5	Total enrolled
1946	7,478	428	21,174	n.a.	n.a.	–	50
1950	5,812	383	16,293	n.a.	n.a.	–	132
1955	6,793	448	20,475	129	35	4	242
1960	11,541	684	36,287	278	107	18	561
1964	17,633	3,985	62,839	429	222	39	1,036
1966	20,616	4,614	71,546	530	316	80	1,531
1968	17,825	5,021	78,963	885	465	161	2,299
1970	12,721	6,913	83,002	1,336	826	252	3,905
1972	13,506	9,749	81,662	1,854	1,230	386	5,538
1974	20,756	13,811	103,711	2,362	1,650	531	7,055
1976	23,833	13,602	125,588	2,861	2,206	867	9,558

[1] Prior to 1960 the data cover African children only.
[2] Excludes private, unaided schools started after independence. Enrolments in such schools were insignificant prior to 1970, but since that date have increased to about 4,500. The majority of such students are enrolled in evening classes, and almost all leave after completing Form 3.
[3] The primary course was changed from eight to seven years in duration as from January 1964. Earlier enrolment figures are for the eighth year of school studies.
Sources: BP, 1946-1967; CSO, 1968-1977.

comprised 80 pupils or more. Overcrowding would have been even worse had it not been for the high degree of wastage within the school system: only about 40 per cent of pupils completed the full primary course, and the majority left school before completing the fourth year. Many of the schools were single-room buildings, which had to accommodate up to six classes. Thus it was common for classes to be held out of doors, and pupils would be sent home when the weather was bad. In addition to the shortage of resources of all kinds, qualitative deficiencies within the teaching profession also posed fundamental problems. Almost half of the primary school teachers were untrained prior to independence, and of those who had attended one of the teacher training colleges at Lobatse or Serowe,[2] most did not themselves possess more than an indifferent primary education. As is to be expected from the system of financing primary education employed by the Government, these difficulties were more extreme in the rural areas and small population centres than in the towns.

The colonial administration also left the provision of secondary education to voluntary initiative and its development has consequently been of relatively recent origin. The first school to introduce junior secondary classes was St Joseph's Mission, Khale, in 1944. A second school was founded from a levy imposed on the Ngwato people in

1948. This levy, initiated by the then acting Chief Tshekedi Khama, raised over £100,000 for a Ngwato Tribal College at Moeng. Although it was initially envisaged that the Ngwato Tribal Treasury would pay for the running of this school, there were some delays in the completion of the project owing to cost overruns and to dissensions within the tribe. In 1956 the College was reconstituted as a territorial institution, and the Government assumed responsibility for meeting the recurrent and future capital costs of Moeng College, as it was then renamed. Tribal levies led to the establishment of three other secondary schools during the early 1950s for the Kwena, Kgatla, and Ngwaketse tribes. These schools were run by the tribal authorities until after independence, and suffered from an acute shortage of school equipment and of boarding accommodation for pupils and teachers. Consequently teaching standards were low, and pupil wastage was high. Of the four other secondary schools in the territory that were operating at independence, two were mission schools, and one had been established as a private venture with neither mission nor government assistance.[3] Only one secondary school, located in Gaborone, was conceived and built as a government school prior to independence, and that was not opened until 1965. Apart from the two small teacher training colleges and a government training centre in Gaborone, no other post-primary education or training facilities were publicly provided prior to independence.

This neglect of formal education on the part of the administration had serious consequences. First, it forced a continued dependence upon education facilities available in surrounding countries—particularly South Africa—long after this was desirable. It was cheaper and more expedient to encourage qualified students from the protectorate to attend secondary schools and universities in South Africa than to foster local development of such institutions. Indeed annual grants were paid by the Bechuanaland Education Department to the Tiger Kloof School at Vryburg, run by the London Missionary Society and to the University College of Fort Hare, as a contribution to the costs of educating the small number of Africans from the protectorate who succeeded in gaining admission.[4] This was partly, no doubt, a reflection of the official view at the time that the territory would eventually become part of South Africa. If South Africa had not ceased to accept non-European foreign pupils to its schools and universities from 1954 and 1958 respectively, it is clear that educational development in Bechuanaland would have been even further neglected.[5]

Second, as a result of the Colonial Government's policies, Botswana was less well equipped for independence, in terms of the availability of local skills, than any other ex-British territory in Africa. Fourth- and fifth-year studies at secondary schools were not introduced until

1955. Even by 1964, only four of the eight secondary schools in the protectorate offered a five-year course, and the number of students in the higher forms was still pitifully small. In that year only 39 students were enrolled in fifth-form studies, of whom 27 passed the Cambridge Overseas School Certificate examination, 13 of them doing well enough to qualify for entrance to the university in Basutoland.[6] Yet at that time only 24 of the 184 administrative posts in the Protectorate Government were held by Batswana; furthermore, even at lower levels, only 275 out of 613 posts in the technical, executive, and secretarial grades were held by local officers. All of the former jobs were said to require a university degree, whilst many of the latter formally required five years of secondary schooling. Thus, the staffing requirements of the public service alone implied that the capacity of the school system was completely inadequate to provide for the needs of the newly independent Botswana.

THE GROWING IMPORTANCE OF LOCALIZATION AND ITS IMPACT UPON EDUCATION POLICY

Although there was mounting pressure from African staff during the 1950s, no clear policy on localization was initiated by the Protectorate Government until 1961. In that year, as a result of the review of the public service by Sir Richard Ramage (BP, 1961), the racial elements in the salary structure were removed, and the way was opened for Africans to be promoted on to the scales previously reserved for European staff.[7] In October 1961, as a result of local pressure, a Standing Advisory Committee of officials was appointed to recommend ways of facilitating localization over the following decade. Although most of the Committee's recommendations were not taken up, this initiative did lead to the building of the first government secondary school to be opened in the territory, in Gaborone. Three years later, further recommendations to the Legislative Council (BP, 1964d) led to the establishment of a government centre for the purpose of training artisan, clerical, executive, and secretarial staff for the public sector.[8]

In spite of these measures, the scale of the localization problem became steadily worse. The number of expatriates employed by the administration increased by over 70 per cent between 1959 and 1964, and at the time of independence, they occupied almost one-third of all established posts in the public sector (Table 8.2). After independence expatriate employment in the government service stabilized, but those in the private and parastatal sectors continued to increase. By 1972 expatriate employment in the formal sector was 65 per cent higher than in 1964. Most of these persons were skilled workers, and a further 13 per cent of all skilled jobs in the economy at that time were reported to be vacant (MFDP, 1973c: Table 2.2).

TABLE 8.2 *Progress with localization in the central government establishment and in the rest of the formal sector, 1959–1975*

	1959	1964	1968/9	1972	1975
Central govt. establishment					
Expatriate	401	683	684	669	584
Local	1,453	1,492	2,925	4,484	5,733
Total	1,854	2,175	3,609	5,153	6,317
% of expatriates	22	31	19	13	9
Other employment					
Expatriate	n.a.	1,400[1]	2,158	2,750	3,158
Local	n.a.	19,000[1]	18,954	32,267	45,030
Total	n.a.	20,400[1]	21,112	35,017	48,188
% of expatriates	n.a.	7	10	8	7

[1] Estimates only. Census did not provide a breakdown of the labour force by race or citizenship.

Sources: BP, 1959; BP, 1964a; BP, 1966: 17; CSO, 1968; RB, 1970d: Appendix IV; MFDP, 1973c; CSO, 1976h; Colclough and Chambers, 1977.

There were two main causes of these trends. The first was that an excessive emphasis has been placed upon the school system to provide the main route to skilled employment. During the colonial period—in Bechuanaland, as elsewhere—entry into the staff grades of the public service had been conditional upon possession of the requisite educational qualifications. These hiring standards for public appointments were also adopted by the independent Government (BP, 1966). The second reason was that the number of jobs in the formal sector increased very rapidly after independence—much more so than was initially forecast by the Government. In 1966, for example, it was expected that employment in the public sector would increase by only about one per cent per year over the period to 1970 (RB, 1966b: 80, 122). In fact, however, the government establishment expanded at an annual rate of about 11 per cent between 1964 and 1972, and formal employment in other sectors grew by about 7 per cent annually over the same years. The increases in demand for skilled workers matched the growth of total employment, causing frequent and substantial upward revisions in the Government's plans for the expansion of the school system.[9] As a result, secondary school and university development became the dominant concerns for educational policy.

There were other reasons, however, why these parts of the education sector were of pressing political importance. The fact that senior posts carried much higher salaries than more junior ones meant, in view of the recruitment policies described above, that a very strong relationship existed between the amount of schooling a person had had and their expected earnings. Although income differentials within the formal sector were reduced over the first decade of independence (Chapter 7), the salary benefits of undertaking higher education have remained substantial. These financial returns have brought strong political pressures on the Government to increase access to the top echelons of the school system, and have provided an additional reason for secondary school and university development becoming the major educational priorities of the post-independence period.

This emphasis upon increasing the capacity of the school system would in any case have been difficult to avoid, in view of the earlier neglect of education by the colonial authorities. But, in retrospect, it is also true that an over-cautious localization policy was adopted by the Botswana Government. The main concern after independence was to protect existing standards of efficiency by avoiding the premature promotion of poorly educated junior workers to more senior positions. In consequence, however, the possibilities of introducing accelerated training and up-grading schemes for capable Batswana who had not had the opportunity of more than a few years of schooling were not fully exploited.

The costs of these policies were felt particularly strongly in the private and parastatal sectors. Facilities for artisan and technical training at the Botswana Training Centre were rudimentary, and were barely adequate to meet the public sector's needs. Moreover, owing to its control of bursaries and to the high status attached to jobs in the civil service, the Government itself was able to recruit most of the leavers from the higher forms of the secondary schools and the university. By 1972, although Batswana comprised about nine-tenths of the skilled employees in central and local government, the proportion in other sectors of the economy was much lower than that. Following the preparation of a manpower plan,[10] based upon an extensive survey of the manpower and employment situation in 1972, the Government attempted to remedy this situation. Localization agreements requiring an increased commitment to on-the-job training schemes were individually negotiated with some of the larger employers in the private sector. In turn, the Government increased the supply of educated recruits to the private sector, and provided places at a new National Centre for Vocational Training for employees needing artisan and technical training in private and parastatal enterprises.

At the same time, the emphasis upon post-primary educational expansion was maintained. This was a period of very rapid economic growth and after 1970 formal employment increased at rates of 10 per cent or more per year. The skilled employment projections of the manpower plan suggested that the demand for workers with senior-secondary schooling or university degrees would double between 1972 and 1978, and the requirements for such workers were expected to triple by 1988. In order to meet these requirements, together with the additional need to replace expatriates working in the country, a major expansion of secondary schools—sufficient to double their capacity between 1973 and the end of the decade—was begun. Facilities for artisan and technician training and for university education were expanded even more rapidly.

THE RESULTS OF POST-INDEPENDENCE EDUCATIONAL POLICIES

The quantitative impact of these plans and policies is illustrated in Table 8.3. The first decade of independence can be characterized as one of rapid and unprecedented expansion of education and training. Whilst primary enrolments almost doubled, those at secondary and tertiary levels increased sevenfold over the ten years. In spite of this expansion, however, even by 1975 Botswana's school system was still small by the standards of other countries. In that year, for example, the secondary-enrolment ratio in Botswana was only about equal to the average secondary-enrolment ratio in 1970 for the 52 poorest countries with per capita incomes of less than $250. And at tertiary levels, Botswana's ratio of one per cent of the age group enrolled was less than one-quarter of the average tertiary enrolment ratio of those same countries in 1970.[11]

Nevertheless, the emphasis placed upon the expansion of secondary and tertiary levels of education had some unfortunate results. A major effect of this emphasis was a sharp increase in the real costs of schooling per student. Government expenditure on education increased from around 10 per cent of the recurrent budget in the late 1960s to over 20 per cent between 1974 and 1977.[12] Total recurrent expenditures increased from less than P1 million to over P16 million per year over the same period. But about half of these annual expenditures were absorbed by the comparitively small secondary and tertiary sectors (Table 8.4), even though there were more than fourteen times as many students in the primary schools than in publicly provided places in the post-primary system.

By the mid-1970s the annual costs per secondary-school student were about ten times as much as those for pupils in primary schools. Even more startling was that about 80 primary-school pupils could be educated for the cost of one university place.[13] These cost ratios, which are not very different from those found in many other African countries,

TABLE 8.3 *The growth of enrolments in the education and training system, 1965–1975*

	1965	1975
Primary education		
Population aged 5–14	140,000[1]	185,000
Primary enrolment	66,061	116,293
% of age group	47.2	62.9
Secondary education and post-primary training		
Population aged 15–19	54,000[1]	67,000
Secondary enrolments:		
Government and aided schools	1,172	8,434
Private schools[2]	135	1,483
Total	1,307	9,917
Technical training	50[3]	1,276
Teacher training	276	489
Agricultural training	–	138
Nursing training	50[3]	327
Total enrolled	1,683	12,147
% of age group	3.1	18.1
Higher education and post-secondary training		
Population aged 20–4	46,000[1]	55,000
Degree	44	314
Diploma	38	129
Teacher training[4]	–	42
Nursing training	1	58
Total enrolled	83	543
% of age group	0.2	1.0

[1] Resident population projections based on revised 1964 Census figures.
[2] Full-time students only.
[3] Authors' estimates. Excludes part-time or short-course training.
[4] Graduates studying for teacher's diploma included under degree.

Sources: RB, 1966c; Colclough, 1976b.

are the product of much smaller pupil–teacher ratios and much higher teachers' salaries at secondary and university levels than in the primary schools. Consequently, the rate of growth of educational expenditures has far exceeded the overall growth of enrolments.

Equally, the priority given to expansion of the higher levels of the system led to a neglect of primary education. The development of primary schooling remained the financial responsibility of the district and town councils, which devoted over half of their recurrent expenditures to education in most years after independence (see Table 2.1). These funds were raised in part from school fees,[14] but mostly from central government grants and local tax revenues. In spite of the very limited capital resources allocated to primary education prior to 1974 (Table 8.4), enrolments in primary schools continued to build up

TABLE 8.4 *Public expenditures on education, 1968-1975*[1]
P million

	1968	1970	1972	1973	1974	1975
Primary						
Capital	0.09	0.13	0.06	0.41	3.12	3.65
Recurrent	1.19	1.46	1.81	2.08	2.99	4.04
	1.28	1.59	1.87	2.49	6.11	7.69
All other						
Capital	0.21	0.34	0.46	1.65	2.47	3.59
Recurrent	0.71	0.99	1.82	2.09	3.17	4.64
	0.92	1.33	2.28	3.74	5.64	8.23
Total	2.20	2.92	4.15	6.23	11.75	15.92

[1] Calendar years except for capital expenditures in 1974 and 1975, which refer to financial years.

Source: CSO, 1968-1977.

rapidly. Between 1968 and 1974 an additional 25,000 places were created which represented an increase of total enrolments by about one-third. In addition to construction work by councils, local communities themselves built a considerable number of class-rooms but these self-help activities were insufficient to accommodate such a large increase in the school population. As a result, the shortage of class-rooms in primary schools increased from 30 per cent to 40 per cent between 1968 and 1972. Although after 1973 the Government considerably increased its capital expenditures in the primary sector, enrolments—spurred on by the cut in school fees in 1974—increased still faster, and the shortage of accommodation became worse. At the same time, the demand for additional teachers imposed by the expansion of enrolments had to be met by a big increase in the number of untrained teachers employed in the primary schools. Their number almost doubled between 1972 and 1976, and by the latter date the proportion of trained teachers employed was—at 62 per cent—no better than in 1968. All of this implies that although access to primary schooling was much increased by the mid-1970s, with about 90 per cent of the eligible age group enrolled,[15] the quality of education provided was on average little better than it had been at independence.

The quality of primary schooling is also subject to considerable regional variation the effects of which have been scarcely mitigated by recent expansion. The main reason is that there has been a strong and abiding urban and large-village bias in the provision of resources in primary education, even amongst schools run by the local authorities. The least qualified teachers, the highest ratios of students to trained teachers and the lowest ratios of physical equipment per pupil are found in the rural areas. Furthermore, the smaller rural settlements tend to be worse off in these respects than the larger centres.[16] In part as a result of these deficiencies, the rural 'success' rate in the primary-school leaving examination is approximately half of the urban rate.

Access to schooling—at least to the base of the system—is now much wider than it was at the end of the colonial period. To that extent, a larger proportion of the population have at least a chance of benefiting from the upward social and economic mobility which post-primary education brings. But less than 20 per cent of primary leavers gain access to Government secondary schools, and the benefits of primary education for those pupils for whom it is at present terminal are, to say the least, unclear.[17] Given the very low quality of education in the great majority of rural primary schools, and the unlikelihood of pupils from these schools getting a place at secondary level, the view that increased access to schools of very low quality represents progress is open to question.

In the light of the large differentials between average household incomes in town and country and of those between incomes in the larger and smaller villages (Chapter 7), the circumstances described above imply that educational opportunity increases with the wealth of households. Since schooling itself also greatly enhances the earnings potential of those who seek employment, the expansion of the system since independence has done little to break down existing patterns of inequality within the community.

MOVEMENTS TOWARDS EDUCATIONAL REFORM

Governments rarely pursue objectives with single-mindedness. Although it is true that the quantitative aspects of educational policy have had a dominant influence on the evolution of the education system in Botswana, the problems of escalating costs, of inequalities of access to schools and from schools to jobs, and of the quality of education provided by the schools, have never remained out of sight for long. Over the years since independence there have been strong pressures from both within and outside the Government to change the nature of education in a way which would allow some of these problems to be addressed. No account of the development of education in Botswana would be complete without some consideration of the lessons of experiments that have been tried.

The most significant and enduring attempts at reform in fact grew out of a series of educational ventures in Serowe, where a private secondary school had been established in 1963, using funds that had been mainly raised from overseas charities. The founder of this school

—Patrick Van Rensburg, who was at that time a political refugee from South Africa—felt that the other secondary schools in the country were producing an élite group who would find well-paid jobs in the towns, and who would soon become alienated from the real needs of rural Botswana. If Swaneng Hill, as the new school was called, offered a different kind of education to that given elsewhere, it was hoped that this elitism might be replaced by a commitment amongst the pupils to work more selflessly for the community.[18]

The three main aims of Swaneng Hill School thus became: to inculcate a commitment to social justice among the educated minority and to equip them with the knowledge and skills needed for development; to make secondary education less costly by requiring students to contribute in kind rather than in monetary fees; and to make the school a focal point for development in the community. In line with these aims, there were a number of features which distinguished education at Swaneng from that given in other secondary schools.

First, the curriculum was more diversified, and the subjects of metalwork, woodwork, building science, technical drawing, commerce, agriculture, and development studies were introduced. Second, the students were given a greater measure of responsibility in running their affairs than was the case in other schools. They cooked their own morning and evening meals. A co-operative was formed in the school and work was shared on a rota basis. An elected student council participated in the discussion of all important policy matters with regard to the running and management of the school. These developments were intended to encourage initiative, reliability, self-reliance, and a greater sense of responsibility—qualities that were recognized by the staff of the school as being important in future leaders of society.

Third, attempts were made to involve the school in the development of the local community. Pupils participated in the management of local consumer co-operatives; they helped with community development and training, with the building of primary school class-rooms in neighbouring villages, and organized an income and expenditure survey in Serowe on behalf of the Government. Discussion of plans for the development of the village were integrated within the development-studies curriculum. In addition, productive work was an important part of the school activities for all pupils and staff. Many of the school buildings and sports facilities were constructed using pupil labour on a voluntary basis in order to reduce costs and to improve pupils' motivations.

Between 1963 and 1969 these experiments progressed well. Van Rensburg was ably served by a highly motivated, though mainly expatriate, volunteer staff, who adopted his overall aims. The commitment of the staff to these principles was undoubtedly a major ingredient in the degree of success enjoyed by the school during these early years. As the school was a private rather than a government-sponsored organization, it was possible to show that the construction work undertaken by staff and pupils alike resulted in a much faster expansion of school facilities than would otherwise have been possible. In part, therefore, the acceptance by the pupils of approximately one-fifth of their time being spent in manual labour was due to the realization that their education depended upon this kind of commitment.

Nevertheless, the manual labour was always unpopular, and an increasing number of pupils did not make themselves available for voluntary labour on school projects. Eventually, it was decided to make participation in manual work compulsory for all the pupils, but opposition to it then took on a new force. Following demonstrations in 1970, a compromise was reached whereby compulsory manual work was retained only within the school, and participation in community projects was put on a voluntary basis.

An important reason for these difficulties was that the more congenial conditions prevalent in other schools acted as a paradigm for the students at Swaneng Hill School. In spite of devoted and charismatic leadership, the message of self-reliance and selfless work for the good of others was becoming very difficult to sustain when students at other schools in Botswana were not obliged to make such sacrifice. This was all the more true after 1970 when financial assistance was provided by Government, thereby putting Swaneng Hill School on the same footing as other aided schools elsewhere in Botswana. This further undermined the argument for productive work and self-reliance and hastened the move towards orthodoxy. The complaints about unfair treatment put forward by the pupils were no longer resisted by the Board of Governors. By 1973 the style of education given at Swaneng had changed, and it was no longer significantly different from that of the rest of the secondary school system.

The lessons of all this relate mainly to the difficulties of achieving reforms in one school, or a group of them, whilst leaving the rest of the school system unchanged. In Botswana, as elsewhere, the economic functions of schooling have overwhelming importance in the minds of both pupils and parents. The diversified curriculum, the practical activities, and manual work were seen by students at Swaneng to be a digression from the main functions of the school and a threat to their own performance in the Cambridge Overseas School Certificate examinations, on which their future job prospects depended. Comparisons with other schools in which such opportunities appeared to be better led to the collapse of the experiment. Similar events have occurred in other countries which have attempted to introduce reforms in this way

(Colclough, 1976a) and the Swaneng experience strongly supports the view that dual systems of education, whether at primary or secondary level will eventually fail owing to a lack of popular support.

Whatever the success expected of the attempts to reform secondary education, it was obvious that it would continue to involve only a small minority of young people. In an attempt to cater for the needs of at least some of those who could not secure entrance to the secondary school, Van Rensburg started a Builders Brigade at Serowe in 1965, which offered to some 40 young primary-school leavers an on-the-job apprenticeship-type training, in which trainees would work productively while they learnt to build. Since they were not paid salaries they could undertake building contracts for public and semi-public authorities at relatively low costs. Arising from these early experiences, a model of cost-covering vocational training has emerged which has since been replicated both in Serowe and elsewhere. By 1978, there were 13 brigade centres in Botswana, the smallest having 2 brigades, and the largest, at Serowe, having 25. Between 1969 and 1975 enrolments increased from 490 to 930 trainees; in addition, over 500 ex-trainees and other workers were employed directly by the movement in the rural areas in that year. The programmes embraced more than fifteen different trades and crafts, the main ones being building, carpentry, welding, farming, electrical trades, dress-making, textiles, and mechanics.

All of these brigades have aimed to cover their production, training, overhead, and depreciation costs within five years of starting up their operations. Five of the older established brigades in Serowe have achieved this, as have several others in other centres. Some brigades—mainly those involved in engineering, textiles, pottery, and farming activities—have transformed themselves into production rather than training units. Profits from these enterprises are used to cross-subsidize the capital and recurrent costs of other brigades. This has been a considerable help to new ventures during the early years of their operation.

There is also a conscious attempt to minimize the degree of capitalization. It is recognized that if brigades are to be widely replicable in the rural areas, capital will remain a constraint, and the training technology used must minimize the capital costs of extra student places. Though this reduces mechanization and productivity, thereby making competition with larger scale establishments more difficult, the total cost of running most brigades in the mid-1970s was about P250 per student per year. This was only about one-quarter of the cost of providing formal training for similar trades in government training establishments. The emphasis on minimizing the degree of capitalization is not based only upon cost considerations. There is also the need to impart skills which will be usable on leaving the brigades. If this kind of training is to promote rural-employment generation on a wide scale, skills that do not require a great outlay of capital for their use, either by the trainee in setting up his business or by the customer in payment for work completed, need to be the primary goal.

In the above ways, the brigades have been attempting to provide a model which could be widely replicable in Botswana and in other countries to facilitate employment creation, particularly for primary-school leavers who would be otherwise unemployed or employed in subsistence agricultural pursuits. They have nevertheless encountered considerable difficulties.[19] First, the brigades have had to compete with the formal sector of the economy. On the one hand, the high wages and consumption levels in the towns have acted as a magnet for the brigade leavers, and many of the carpenters, bricklayers, and mechanics have found jobs in the construction industry. Equally, the products of the bridgades have had to compete directly with cheap, imported consumption goods produced by much more sophisticated technologies. This had led to the dilemma of either increasing the degree of capital-ization and the sophistication of technology used, thereby sacrificing the principle of replicability, or, on the other hand, reducing the prices of the brigade products and thereby running the risk of decreasing the incomes of trainees to levels which remove the incentives to remain in production.

Second, if costs in the brigade movement are to be covered through production, markets have to be found for the goods and services produced. To some extent, this requirement can be met in the early stages by producing goods which are consumed by employees in the formal sector of the economy. In a small economy, however, such opportunities are limited, and this strategy inevitably limits the possi-bilities of employment creation in the rural areas to the rate of growth of wage employment in the formal sector. Wider and more rapid development as with other approaches to rural industrialization depends upon the growth of incomes and of exchange amongst participants in the rural economy.

The above factors will hinder the future development of the brigades, but it remains the case that their activities over the last ten years represents a very significant success in both national and international terms. This experience has shown that, at least under certain circum-stances, cost-covering vocational training can work in the rural areas. Those who work in the movement, however, would be the first to stress that continued success is entirely contingent on the economic possibilities that confront them. The diversification of local production opportunities is therefore the critical factor, and the main variables that can influence this are in the hands of the Government rather than in the control of the brigades themselves. Giving the brigades preferential access to public-contract work would undoubtedly be a help, as recent experience with school-desk manufacture has shown. But so long as competition from the formal sector—both domestic and foreign—remains unfettered, scale economies will prevent the brigade system from becoming a mass movement for rural training and production.

The reform initiatives discussed above originated outside the public sector, and until the early 1970s they received little more than moral support from the Government. More recently, however, the Government has become aware of the deficiencies and costliness of the existing school system. In 1975 a National Education Commission was appointed, which analysed the major educational problems confronting the nation. The many recommendations of the Commission, which have been broadly accepted by the Government,[20] imply a shift in the focus of educational policy away from the top towards the base of the school system.

The proposed changes include, at primary level, a much greater emphasis upon effective Setswana teaching, some shift away from an exclusive dependence upon examinations towards continuous assessment of students' performance, together with a quota system whereby the top 5 per cent of primary leavers in each school would secure a place in secondary schools, irrespective of performance. Although secondary schooling will initially remain selective junior secondary education would be gradually expanded, with the aim of creating a basic nine-year education cycle for all children by the 1990s.

These changes are desirable, but it is almost certain that most of them will not be implemented. The move towards universalizing junior secondary schooling would have enormous budgetary implications at existing cost levels. Although proposals have been made to reduce the salaries for junior secondary teachers, this would not be possible without more general changes in the salary structure in teaching and other professions. Equally, the acceleration in the number of pupils leaving the junior secondary schools would almost certainly result in the emergence of unemployment at this level comparatively quickly. This would lead to some increase in the qualifications required by employers for a whole range of clerical and sub-professional jobs, which, in turn, would cause the strong pressures on the Government to continue expanding higher levels of education to become even more intense.[21] For both of these sets of reasons, too early a shift in the direction of universal junior secondary schooling is likely to generate pressures that will undermine the new education strategy and entrench the tendency for a large proportion of the budget to be allocated to the top end of the system.

More fundamentally, however, significant changes in the relative earnings opportunities for Batswana at different levels of education are a *sine qua non* for effective educational reform. As long as they exist, these unequal opportunities will continue to have a dominant influence over what goes on in the schools. The process of job-search in Botswana is highly competitive and the 'length of stay' in formal education has—as in other poor countries—come to have a legitimizing role in the selection of those people who are to get the jobs with the highest rewards. Other clear routes to skilled employment are unlikely to emerge without strong government support, even though formal and informal training programmes provide an attractive and, often, cheaper alternative to schools, at least for technical skills (Colclough, 1974). However, if earnings differentials were much less (or the private costs of undertaking senior schooling much more) the need for this economic and social function played by the schools would be less strong. The fact that people stood to lose much less than at present if they failed to get through school or university could at once reduce the pressures on the selection process, allow other processes of skill-formation (or talent-spotting) to be given their due importance, and bring attendant opportunities for changing what goes on in the schools into more of an educative experience, rather than a predominantly certificate-seeking one.

The proposed changes to the structure and content of schooling which were adopted in 1977 are important. Nevertheless, because differences of personal incomes are very large, the single most important constraint on achieving real educational reform is the set of institutional relationships which link the school system to the labour market. Unless the earnings potential of persons with different amounts of education were made much more equal over the coming years, it is unlikely that the proposed education policies, standing alone, could secure significant benefits for the majority of those who attend school.[22]

HEALTH POLICY

Problems of rapidly rising costs, of too much emphasis upon the top rather than the base of the system, and the consequent irrelevance of expenditures to rural people are as common in the health sector of poor countries as they are in education. However, because 'being healthy', unlike 'being educated', does not lead directly into determining rank in a highly stratified socio-economic order, there are fewer problems in making sure that the health services are useful to those who receive them. Accordingly, there is less controversy over the question as to what kind of health service will most benefit the poor than there is about what type of school system would be best for that purpose.

That being said, the number of countries in which the health-care system does reflect the health needs of the majority of the population are few. The typical pattern is one of over-concentration upon curative rather than preventive medicine, and upon expensive urban hospitals which are used mainly by urban dwellers, rather than more modest rural facilities that can promote better health for more people at much less cost. The reason for this emphasis is rooted in history. Most countries of the Third World inherited systems of health care that were modelled upon those of the metropolitan countries. Priority was given to establishing curative facilities in the capital cities which would provide at least some solace and security for colonial civil servants. The curative emphasis was also a reflection of the skills, training, and professional background of doctors who were trained in and had come from European countries. The application of Western medical traditions resulted in an inappropriate attitude towards health care in countries where the conditions and resources were quite different from those in Europe and North America.

Botswana was no exception to this pattern, although more recently a determined bid to change the emphasis of health care towards benefiting the poorest people has been made. As with the introduction of schools, the missionaries were the first to establish modern medical facilities in Bechuanaland. By the late 1930s there were four mission hospitals at Maun, Molepolole, and Kanye, and three government hospitals at Lobatse, Serowe, and Francistown. Nine doctors and supporting staff ran these hospitals, and although health visits to the interior were beginning to be made, people in the smaller population centres generally had considerable distances to travel if they wished to see a western-trained doctor.

From the beginning, health facilities developed in a very centralized fashion. Although an early review of the services provided (BP, 1937) identified the need for village dispensaries staffed by Batswana who were trained in simple curative and preventive medicine, the concept of basic health care was slow to take root. Even by 1963 there were only 24 staffed health centres and 34 unstaffed dispensaries in the country. The majority of health expenditures, both by the Government and the missions were directed towards the seven hospitals that had been established by that date (BP, 1963a: 8).

During the first years after independence this policy was continued by the Botswana Government. Although government expenditure in the health sector remained modest—in most years accounting for 4 or 5 per cent of recurrent and capital budgets (Tables 4.2 and 4.3.)—much of this was absorbed by expensive curative facilities. For example, over the period 1968–73, hospitals, together with the Central Training

Institute for nurses in Gaborone, accounted for about 86 per cent of total capital expenditures, with health centres and clinics accounting for only 10 per cent (Gish and Walker, 1977). Although the number of hospital beds, at 1,900, had almost doubled since independence, half of the population still lived more than ten miles from any staffed health facility in 1973. Since hospitals and clinics tend to be used mainly by those living in the immediate vicinity,[23] a large part (in fact the poorest half) of the population remained relatively untouched by the hospitals' curative programme. Indeed, tuberculosis and venereal infections, which are, respectively, the biggest killer and most widespread disease in Botswana,[24] appeared to be increasing rapidly in the early 1970s. These were strong signs that the pattern of health expenditures appeared not to be improving the welfare of the community.

Since 1973, however, there has been a significant shift in strategy. That year marked a departure from the old policy of expanding the hospitals, and a major construction programme of rural health facilities was begun. The new service is based upon three different types of facility. The most basic is the health post, a one-roomed structure visited regularly by regional health personnel. Clinics, on the other hand, are permanently staffed, and include consultation rooms, a dispensary, and beds for observation or maternity cases. Slightly larger than the clinics are health centres which offer more ancillary services, a larger maternity ward, and a few in-patient beds.

Over the period 1973-6 over 60 per cent of government capital expenditure in the health sector was allocated to the construction of health centres, clinics, and health posts, and only one-quarter was taken up by hospital improvements. As a result a large network of health posts and clinics has been established (Table 8.5) and by 1975 about 80 per cent of the population lived less than 10 miles from a health facility. In view of the enormous size and low-population density of Botswana, this represents considerable progress. One indication of the success of the programme is that whereas the number of new out-patients at hospitals increased by about 5 per cent per year between 1973 and 1976, those at other facilities increased at an annual rate of over 30 per cent over the same period (CSO, 1976k).

This strategy has undoubtedly begun to redress the balance of medical care in favour of the rural areas. Significant problems remain, particularly as regards staffing the rural facilities. The quality of nurses in many of the clinics, for example, appears to be very poor—partly owing to the low level of basic education they possess. As in the education sector, the difficulty of tackling this lies primarily in the heavy salary costs of employing large numbers of people with higher levels of schooling, together with the fact that such persons are in any case

TABLE 8.5 *Government development expenditures and physical progress in the health sector, 1973-1976*

| Facility | Physical achievements | | Proportion of development expenditures |
	1973	1976	on Health 1973-6 (%)
Hospitals[1]	7	7	26
Health centres	5	7	
Clinics	45	64	63
Health posts	20	280[2]	
Training institute	1	1	11[3]

[1] Government facilities only.
[2] Includes mobile facilities.
[3] Includes other capital expenditures which cannot be directly related to one type of facility, e.g. central medical stores.

Sources: RB, 1973a: 286; CSO, 1976k: Table 2; Gish and Walker, 1977: Table 15.

unwilling to serve in the rural areas. Equally the very success of the rural policy has led to new pressures being created for the hospitals. The establishment of new health posts and clinics has led to a large increase in the number of referrals to hospitals, and there appears to be a need to introduce limited upgrading schemes for some hospital facilities if the referral system is to continue to work adequately and be improved. Nevertheless, a significant break with the past has been made, and provided that the new policy continues to be pursued, lasting benefits for the poorer rural people will have been achieved.

CONCLUSION

The colonial record in the education sector was a particularly bad one. Prior to independence there had been no public provision of facilities for post-primary education or technical training, and the country faced a dearth of local professional and technical skills. The new Government placed early priority upon rapid expansion of secondary and tertiary levels of education, largely because of urgent localization needs. But in spite of this, the long lead-time needed to produce highly schooled people together with the rapidly increasing employment needs of the formal sector caused the quantitative shortfalls to increase. Demand for skilled people remained high, and the rewards from skilled employment were great. These pressures consolidated the emphasis upon educational expansion rather than change, and upon the higher levels of the system rather than upon the primary schools. They also intensified the certification and selection syndrome, bringing a concomitant over-emphasis upon qualifications rather than understanding, upon examination rather than education in its wider sense, and upon an excessively formalistic approach to localization in both the public and private sectors. As a result, the emphasis within the school system became largely unrelated to the real educational needs of most Batswana.

Attempts to introduce more relevant and cheaper secondary schooling to Botswana failed as a result of unrest amongst the students, who resented the much more favourable conditions enjoyed by those at more conventional schools. The brigade experiment with cost-covering vocational training, however, has been more successful, in part, so far, because many brigade leavers have found jobs in the formal sector. Further expansion of the movement is likely to be conditional upon its receiving support from the Government. This could best be done not by increased subsidies for training costs, but through increasing the number of economic opportunities faced by the brigades. This includes not only increased access to public-contract work, but also the measures to stimulate basic rural production discussed elsewhere in this book.

More recently, comprehensive proposals for educational reform have been made. But there is a danger in the extent of confidence presently placed upon changes in educational policy alone being sufficient to have a major impact upon the wider availability of high quality schooling. Many of the distortions in education stem from the fact that access to secondary or higher education holds the promise of much higher standards of living—not only immediately after leaving school, but for life. If these income differences remain it is unlikely that the pressures to continue the expansion of the higher levels of education will be relaxed. The costs of education would thereby continue to increase, more education resources would be directed toward a small minority of children, and inequalities would not be reduced. The new strategy is likely to be threatened unless wider policies of economic reform are introduced.

Experiences in the health sector have been more promising. Following the construction of a large number of health posts and clinics, the poorer people have been given much greater and easier access to health services. These facilities are widely used, the referral system appears to be working reasonably well, and the benefits to rural people are clear.

These recent changes in education and health policies have demonstrated a clear commitment by the Government to redress earlier biases which favoured the richer groups. Success in this endeavour is within reach in the health sector. But in education it is likely to be more elusive until the diagnosis of educational problems is more firmly placed in the context of labour market structures, and of the important socio-economic functions performed by the schools.

CHAPTER 9
INSTITUTIONS
AND INFRASTRUCTURE

The building of infrastructure and the emergence of new institutions have been the most visible features of Botswana's development. Where there were no tarred roads at independence bitumen now stretches for several hundred kilometres across the country. Three major reservoirs have been built, at Gaborone in the early 1960s, and at Shashe and Mopipi a decade later. Gaborone itself has grown from a small government settlement to a thriving capital. Selebi-Phikwe and Orapa are completely new, and Francistown has had a face-lift. More than half a dozen new parastatal corporations have come into being. Ministries have grown and evolved, and local government expenditures have increased eightfold.

Most of these phenomena have been referred to in previous chapters, especially where they have related to particular economic sectors or issues. In this chapter a number of aspects of institutional growth and of the actual provision of infrastructure will be discussed. First, the rapid rate of urbanization, associated with growth of the modern sector, has required new infrastructure and new institutions. The central problem here is how to respond to the inevitable political and social pressure created by urban growth without pre-empting resources for rural development. Second, the building of rural infrastructure, which is a pre-requisite for rural development, involves a set of problems arising from remoteness, from the paucity of local institutions and enterprises, and the low density of population. In Botswana, the Accelerated Rural Development Programme was an ambitious attempt to overcome some of these difficulties. Third, there will be brief discussions of the road construction programme and of water availability in Botswana—two major aspects of infrastructure development. Finally, some of the legislation and institutions, which are directly concerned with stimulating and controlling economic growth and change, will be examined, together with the conflicts which can arise between promotion and control.

URBAN DEVELOPMENT AND INSTITUTIONS

A good indication of a developing country's commitment to rural development is its attitude to urban development. The urban areas, where local élites are to be found and where problems are visible, are more politically able to attract national resources than the rural areas, even though on objective criteria the latter's needs are greater.[1] Aware of this dilemma the Government in Botswana has attempted to place the provision of urban housing, infrastructure, and services on a financially cost-covering basis so as to avoid the urban areas becoming a constant and increasing drain on national resources. The execution and consequences of this policy are described in this section.

Although it now has a significant commercial and industrial sector, Gaborone has always been primarily a government town. Housing for civil servants was initially provided on the spacious scale of the colonial service. But, as the size of the Government itself grew rapidly in the early years after independence, much of the Government's investment resources, not to mention administrative capacity, was taken up with building new houses for civil servants. Thus in the first four years of independence more than half the capital budget of the Government was expended in the urban areas (Table 4.4), mainly in Gaborone. To cope with this situation the Botswana Housing Corporation, a government-owned parastatal, was established in 1971. In the following year nearly 1,600 government houses, the majority being in Gaborone, were transferred to the BHC, which was also expected to continue to build new houses to meet the needs of the civil service and of the private sector, and thereby relieve the Government of a considerable administrative burden.

The BHC operates on a cost-covering basis. By the end of 1975/6 it had borrowed about P17 million from the Government, at interest rates which vary from 7½ per cent for the initial transfer of houses to 10 per cent for some recent loans. It was hoped that it would also have been able to raise finance from other sources, but apart from some bridging loans it had raised less than two million Pula on its own account. The weakness of domestic financial institutions has made it impossible for the BHC to tap private domestic savings to any great extent.

The BHC's obligation to service its debt at commercial, or at least semi-commercial, rates of interest necessitated a general increase in rent levels in 1972 when it acquired its initial stock of houses. Typically the previous subsidized rents were about 40 per cent of the new, so-called economic, rents. The Government cushioned its employees against this increase by paying a housing allowance to those civil servants who were affected. The amount of the allowance was designed to cover the difference between the subsidized and economic rents of typical housing for each grade of government officer.

Since then the BHC has managed to remain viable, despite the considerable rise in building costs in the early 1970s. Rentals have been increased from time to time so that by the beginning of 1977, economic rents were generally 65 per cent higher than they were in 1972 (McCarthy, 1976). At the same time the proportion of civil servants who are obliged to pay economic rent has risen, and the policy now applies to the vast majority of the service and especially to those who are based in the towns. But the civil service is itself a strong political force, and it has only been possible to sustain the policy by raising the housing allowances commensurately and simultaneously with the rent increase.[2]

Nevertheless, the success in placing civil service housing on a more commercial basis than it was prior to independence is a major political achievement with important economic implications. Part of a civil servant's total emoluments, which was previously received in the form of a hidden housing subsidy, has been monetized. This gives him the discretion to reduce his housing standard and to use the corresponding monetary benefit for other purposes. There is little doubt that the expected reduction in urban standards is actually taking place. As a result public resources which would previously have been absorbed in unproductive urban investment are released and can, at least in principle, be reallocated to the rural areas. Moreover, as public housing becomes more commercialized the possibility of the private sector making a contribution to the housing problem is enhanced—though this has not yet happened to any significant extent in Botswana.

But one reason why governments in developing countries often find it impossible to avoid urban housing subsidies is that conventionally built modern housing is generally so expensive as to be beyond the reach of unskilled workers, let alone job seekers who may have virtually no income at all. Thus in Botswana because the BHC has had to cover its costs, it has made virtually no impact on this segment of the housing market. The only solution to this dilemma, if urban subsidies are to be minimized, is to tap the traditional skills in house building and to oranize urban self-help housing schemes. The Third and Fourth National Development Plans both recognized that up to 70 per cent of urban housing would have to be provided in this way, but implementation of that policy has been rather slow.

Gaborone had a self-help scheme in 1965, when about five hundred plots were demarcated in an area known as Bontleng, in order to provide accommodation for those who had come seeking construction jobs when the town was being built. The area is now a thriving and well-established community. But there has since been little new self-help housing in the capital, though the squatter community has steadily grown, and the other towns have led the way in this type of development.

One of the BDP Government's early objectives was to improve and re-develop Francistown which was a stronghold for the opposition BPP.[3] All the land on which the town is built was originally owned by the Tati Company, and although some had been sold off to settlers, the deeds of sale generally incorporated clauses which enabled the Tati Company to retain a restrictive control over trading within the town. The town was also racially divided. Africans squatting on company land had been moved to the south side of the river in 1958, which soon consisted of little more than irregularly scattered and largely unserviced traditional dwellings. Further, after the run-down of local mining activity the town had grown poor. In the late sixties its main economic activity was to act as a staging post in the recruitment of migrant mine labour for South Africa. The workers were flown into Francistown from as far afield as Angola and Malawi, and taken by rail from there to the Witwatersrand. On their return, it was often the first place where they could purchase beer and other services on the way home. In short, Francistown contained within itself elements of the racialism, repression, and unpleasantness which characterize South Africa and which the Botswana Government was determined to eradicate.

In 1969, the Government acquired some 1,400 hectares of land south of the river from the Tati Company.[4] Although this was negotiated acquisition, there is little doubt that the Government would have used its powers of compulsory purchase had that been necessary. The intention was to develop a major new town-extension on the land. But it soon became apparent that, as the existing settlers in the southern extension were predominantly poor and black, this strategy would reinforce the existing polarization of the town. In 1972 a new plan was divised. In August of that year, in a further agreement, virtually all the remaining undeveloped land in the town was surrendered by the Tati Company, and plans were drawn up to re-develop the town by infilling on the north side of the river, in order to form a racially and socially mixed community. The resulting project, which was partly financed by an IDA credit, incorporated the first comprehensive attempt in Botswana to mobilize self-help for urban development. Much of the institutional requirements for 'site and service' housing were pioneered in Francistown and later replicated in the other towns. A new simplified form of land tenure was devised, avoiding many of the technical complexities of Roman–Dutch law, which is the basis of freehold land ownership in Botswana and providing urban dwellers with the sort of tenure in the urban areas that they traditionally enjoyed in the tribal areas. By 1977, with the support of an efficient local administration, more than two thousand self-help houses had been developed or re-developed in the town, affecting perhaps a third of the town's population. If the same success can eventually be achieved in the other towns then it will be possible for Botswana to manage the physical problem of rapid urbanization and to avoid unplanned squatter settlements without having to commit vast resources to contractor-built, so-called low-cost, housing schemes.

As the rapid growth of Gaborone led to the creation of the BHC, so the building of Selebi-Phikwe in the early 1970s was the catalyst for the establishment of the Botswana Power Corporation (BPC) and Water Utilities Corporation (WUC). These statutory corporations came into being in 1971 to manage the new power station and dam which were being built for the Shashe Project. They also took over the operation of the existing supplies of power and water to Gaborone and Lobatse. The Government's objectives in setting up the BPC and WUC were broadly the same as in the case of the BHC. First, as the urban demand for both power and water grew there was a need for specialist institutions which would be better technically equipped to satisfy demand and plan future expansion. Second, it was necessary to establish cost-covering parastatals if subsidies for urban services were to be avoided. As with housing, power and water supplies had been subsidized in the past and both parastatals had to increase the tariffs charged in Gaborone and Lobatse as soon as they commenced operations. Since then there have been further substantial increases as costs have risen.

Avoiding urban subsidies has thus been one of the most persistent themes of the Government's attitude towards urban development. In the early years this policy was no doubt impelled by budgetary constraints, but there has always been a more fundamental justification. Urban subsidies not only pre-empt resources which might be better allocated to the rural areas, but also, by lowering the cost of urban services, make the towns more attractive to potential migrants. In practice the policy has implied first, that the three parastatals most concerned—the BHC, BPC, and WUC—have been expected to cover their costs, including the servicing of debt. This they have generally done. Second, the town councils themselves have not received recurrent grants from central government, except in recent years towards the costs of primary education (Table 2.1). Within this framework the policy has been a small successful measure in favour of better distribution of national income, despite mounting opposition to it from powerful urban interests, especially those within the civil service itself. But without the accompanying political will to allocate administrative and technical resources to the rural areas, and to search out and pursue rural rather than urban projects, such a narrowly conceived anti-subsidy policy could not be expected to have much effect in overcoming urban bias. In reality, as previous chapters have shown, the rate of urbanization has remained high and the allocation of public investment to the urban centres has been consistently greater than to the rural areas.

RURAL INFRASTRUCTURE: THE ARDP

The institutional problems of providing rural infrastructure are very different in character. The needs, although very real, do not press in so insistently on the urban-based decision-takers of central government. On the contrary, the difficulty is to overcome the centripetal tendencies of government departments in order to generate some activity in the rural areas, to delegate responsibility to local authorities and regional offices, and, in the case of Botswana, to nurture or unearth rural construction enterprises to carry out contracts. Local participation in the planning and management of rural projects is also necessary if these are effectively to meet local needs.

During the colonial period there had been a steady and unspectacular building of rural infrastructure by the administration. Much of this was provided for the administration's own requirements—offices, courts, police stations, and government houses—together with the necessary roads to get to and from the district headquarters (see Chapter 1). The tribal authorities made heroic efforts to build schools with their limited resources. Missionaries built small hospitals in most of the tribal capitals, and provided almost all the medical care available in the protectorate.

In the early years of independence this pattern did not change greatly. Government expenditure in the rural areas was still small and largely directed toward its own departmental needs. The tribal authorities were largely superseded by district councils, but they still had only limited resources. The missions continued to run district hospitals, though with increasing government support. Meanwhile, the Government promised that the savings which were eventually expected to accrue from mining would be invested in rural development.

The opportunity came in 1973. The recurrent budget had been balanced for the first time in 1972/3, and financial forecasts for the coming few years promised considerable surpluses. Against this background, and with the prospect of an election in the following year, about which the BDP was rather nervous, the President directed that an Accelerated Rural Development Programme should be mounted without delay. A number of existing and planned projects were selected, on the criteria of being located in the rural areas and capable of speedy implementation. They were grouped together into the ARDP. Inevitably the projects mostly concerned rural infrastructure, schools, clinics, water supplies, and so on, and tended to satisfy basic needs rather than directly to stimulate rural production.

The ARDP ran for three years from 1973/4 to 1975/6, though the first year was largely taken up with planning and there was little to show on the ground. About P31 million was spent under the programme, roughly two and a half times greater than all previous government

TABLE 9.1 *Government investment in the rural areas and the ARDP*
P million

	1966/7	1967/8	1968/9	1969/70	1970/1	1971/2	1972/3	1973/4	1974/5	1975/6	1976/7
								A R D P			ARDP totals
Rural and village roads								0.2	2.9	2.2	5.3
Primary schools								0.5	2.8	3.6	6.9
Village water supplies								0.4	2.2	2.0	4.6
Rural health posts and clinics								0.1	0.8	0.5	1.4
Rural administrative buildings								0.4	1.4	1.1	2.9
Other								0.1	0.1	0.1	0.3
ARDP totals								1.7	10.2	9.5	21.4
ARDP totals excluding roads								1.5	7.3	7.3	
Other rural investment								1.8	5.0	6.1	
Total rural investment (from Table 4.4)	1.4	1.5	0.9	1.0	1.4	1.0	1.6	3.3	12.3	13.4	11.4

Sources: Annual Statements of Accounts (RB, 1967–1977).

capital expenditure in the rural areas since independence. Table 9.1 shows the breakdown of ARDP expenditure by economic sector, and also demonstrates how the ARDP lifted the Government's rural expenditure from an annual level of rather less than two million Pula to rather more than ten million—although this is still less than the rate of urban investment. This new higher plateau of rural activity was sustained in 1976/7, after completion of the ARDP itself, and will probably continue in the future.

The Programme succeeded in its objective of providing rural infrastructure because a number of essential ingredients were brought together at the right time. A political decision had been taken a year or so earlier to strengthen the staff of the district councils, on whom much of the responsibility for the ARDP actually fell, by the recruitment of volunteers. Further, the councils had just undertaken a planning exercise as part of the preparation of the third National Development Plan. The Government itself had the financial resources available, and Norway and Sweden were just preparing to mount large rural aid programmes in Botswana. In consequence the ARDP was 55 per cent financed by Botswana and 44 per cent by these two Scandinavian donors (Chambers, 1977: 59), which are better adapted than most aid agencies to support rural development.

The very combination of these elements would probably have led to an increasing proportion of government capital expenditure being directed towards the rural areas without the creation of a formal programme. But the quintessential ingredient of the ARDP, as distinct from a mere set of rural projects, was the political impetus behind it. This had the effect of redirecting the attention of several government departments towards the needs of the rural areas, and of addressing attention to the actual implementation of rural projects, and particularly to the problem of construction capacity in the rural areas.

A number of criticisms have been levelled at the ARDP. First, the sudden imposition of additional demand caused some inflation in the construction sector. However, this has been estimated at as little as 8 per cent, which is not too high a price to pay for the social benefits and income redistribution effects which ensued (Chambers, 1977: XIII). Further, it has since emerged that the economy was taking a downturn at the time of the ARDP (Chapter 3), and consequently the programme was timely. A second criticism is that the staff were not available to run the new facilities built under the programme. This applies particularly to the sixty or so clinics and health posts which were constructed. But temporary difficulties in phasing are common in the process of development and should not be regarded as too serious. The building of the clinics almost certainly stimulated a more rapid expansion of the training programme for nurses and similar medical personnel. The most serious objection to the programme is that by concentrating on the provision of services it has not directly stimulated the capacity for rural production, either of food or of cash produce, even though better access to education, health, and water supply may ultimately work through into greater productivity. The ARDP was justified so far as it went but it should now be followed by a programme for the improvement of arable agriculture. This will be much more difficult to achieve, but is essential if the rural people are to realize their productive potential.

ROADS

A large sparsely populated country is inevitably obliged to devote a high proportion of its resources to communications, of which, in Botswana's case, road investment has constituted the major part. Government capital expenditure on communications constituted about 16 per cent of the total capital budget in the first six years of independence, or about two million Pula per year. But by the late 1970s this allocation had risen, both in real and percentage terms, so that in 1976/7 no less than 40 per cent of the capital budget (P17 million) was allocated to this sector (Table 4.4). There is every expectation that this pattern will continue until 1980 while present projects— especially the building of the north-south road to Zambia—are completed, and may continue beyond that date as the Government proceeds with its plans to take over the railway.

In fact, however, the problems of internal communication in Botswana are not very severe, and probably cause less of an impediment to development than in say a small, mountainous country such as Lesotho. The population is concentrated in the eastern side which is well served by the railway. It has been estimated that the railway accounts for more than half of goods transport in Botswana,[5] and it carries more than half a million passengers within the country each year. Access roads to and from the railway line, while not being good, are by no means impassable, even to ordinary vehicles.

Communication with the western side of the country is, however, difficult and one of the most important new roads is that running between Francistown in the east and Maun, five hundred kilometres away to the west. This project was initiated in 1963, financed by the IDA and, after some delays, finally completed in 1968. Since then, and especially since 1973, road construction has largely concentrated on building the north-south road. The strategic reasons for investing more than P50 million in a road which largely parallels the railway line were discussed in Chapter 6. But the choice and scale of this construction programme have also, very largely, been determined by the difficulty in using the growing available domestic and aid resources on other projects. The capacity to implement projects has become the major constraint to development expenditure. Road building, and to a lesser extent the ARDP, were both a response to this situation. The programmes were, broadly speaking, economically justified and, more importantly, easy to implement.

The dangers with this first-come-first-served approach to resource allocation are threefold. First, it is almost certainly sub-optimal. Projects which might show a higher return than road building tend to be postponed if their implementation seems too complex. Second, the maintenance of the roads which have been built will involve the Government in considerable recurrent expenditure in the future. Third, programmes such as road building can acquire a momentum of their own, whatever their merits may be. As a result an attempt to break through the constraints which prevent the implementation of other projects is constantly deferred. This issue will need to be addressed if a more production-oriented rural development strategy is to be pursued in the 1980s.

WATER

Fig. 9.1 shows schematically the main sources and uses of water in Botswana. The largest category of supply is surface water from small dams, rivers, or river beds. Most of this is drawn from the Limpopo river which runs along Botswana's eastern border, and is used for irrigated agriculture in the Tuli Block of huge freehold farms which border the river. In 1971, it was estimated that about 2,500 hectares were under irrigation there, producing potatoes, onions, and cotton, in addition to dryland crops (CSO, 1972b). The produce is generally sold in South Africa. The scale of this irrigated agriculture in such a dry climate comes as something of a surprise. It makes a major contribution to total agricultural output, and gives employment to several thousand people. Unfortunately, there is evidence that both arable and horticultural production on these farms has been declining and that they have been increasingly turned over to livestock in which sector, for the time being, a good return can be made for rather less effort.

Other surface water supplies—often no more than ponds, natural pans, or waterholes—are used to provide water for human and cattle consumption, especially during the wet season when much of the population lives at the lands. These sources tend to dry up quickly when the rains cease, partly explaining the traditional pattern of annual migration between the lands and villages, described in Chapter 7.

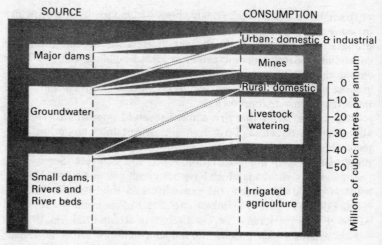

Fig. 9.1. Principal water sources and consumption
Source: Derived principally from National Development Plan 1973-78 (MFDP 1973a)

In terms of amount used, the next largest water source is ground water which is usually extracted from mechanically pumped boreholes, and is used throughout the country for cattle watering and for providing for domestic needs in the rural areas. Although reliable figures are not available, we believe that the total number of boreholes in Botswana has increased from about five thousand at independence to about eight thousand ten years later.[6] The additional three thousand boreholes, which in 1978 prices would cost between twenty and thirty million Pula, represent the single largest productive investment related to the agricultural sector during the period—apart from the natural growth of the cattle herd.

Ground water has long been used in the villages. But since 1971, partly as a consequence of the ARDP and partly as a result of Swedish aid becoming available, the improvement in village water supplies has been considerable. As Table 9.1 illustrates. nearly five million Pula was invested in this sector during the ARDP period, mostly using ground water and mostly for domestic use. This rate of investment is expected to continue.

However, boreholes in Botswana tend to be low yielding. This can be illustrated by means of a simple calculation. The total annual consumption of ground water is estimated at thirty million cubic metres (MFDP, 1977: 1). If there are approximately eight thousand boreholes then each borehole is producing on average rather less than five hundred litres per hour,[7] which by urban standards would be sufficient for less than a hundred people. The geological explanation for these low yields is that, in Botswana, underground water generally occurs in small faults and fissures in the strata rather than in extensive aquifers. Not only does this give rise to low yields, but it also makes it difficult, and in some parts of the Kgalagadi impossible, to predict the likelihood of extracting potable ground water at any particular place, without actually drilling a borehole.[8] For these and other reasons the unit cost of ground water tends to be high. On the other hand, ground water is generally clean and unpolluted, though it may be slightly brackish, and the supply itself is usually reliable.

Extracted, as it is, by widely dispersed boreholes for small localized requirements, the ground water resource seems to be in little danger of being depleted. Total extraction from any one borehole generally represents a minute percentage of rainfall in the corresponding area. But the high unit costs and low yields make groundwater unsuitable for satisfying the heavily concentrated water demands of towns or mines.[9] The final part of Fig. 9.1 shows that these requirements are generally met by a small number of large dams, all of which have been built since the early 1960s. Major dams supply Gaborone, Lobatse, Selebi-Phikwe, and Orapa, and the two associated mines. (Francistown presently uses ground water, but this supply is unlikely to be adequate for long.) The two mines themselves consume about twice as much as all other domestic and commercial users in the urban areas, and domestic per capita consumption in the towns is between ten and fifteen times higher than corresponding per capita consumption in the rural areas.

This fact—apart from being an illustration of the inequality in resource allocation between the urban and rural populations—also has implications for the future. If the towns continue to grow rapidly, and if a number of new mines are to be opened, there will be a considerable growth of heavily concentrated demands for water. Aware of this problem, the Government has attempted to discourage excessive water use by high income groups. For example, the WUC has, from its inception, charged a water tariff which rises with consumption and as a result per capita consumption in Gaborone has declined since the early seventies.[10] The use of water-borne sewerage in the towns has been limited wherever other acceptable systems are available. As a result of these measures both the Gaborone and Shashe dams have sufficient excess capacity to meet new demand through the 1980s but eventually new surface water sources will have to be found both for existing and new towns and mines.

Disregarding, for the moment, the Okavango delta and the three border rivers—the Limpopo, the Chobe, and Molopo—the mean annual surface run-off from Botswana's rivers, all of which are ephemeral, is believed to be 700 million cubic metres. Of this, we estimate that between ten and twenty per cent is currently impounded in dams or extracted from river beds, and, after evaporation and seepage losses, rather less than five per cent is actually consumed. There would thus appear to be ample reserves of surface water sources, were it not for two factors. First, the average run-off statistics hide considerable annual variation. In a low-rainfall year some rivers never flow at all. In consequence reliable yield from dams has to be computed with allowance for totally dry years. Typically, a dam might have to serve for three years without any inflow, and during that period evaporation loss could be as much as six metres depth of water. The second factor compounds the problems of the first. The general flatness of the terrain provides few good dam sites in the country and such as exist tend to be shallow.

However, it seems unlikely that there will be a major water shortage before the end of the century. In the meantime, the abundant water resources of the Okavango delta in the extreme north-west offer a tantalizing prospect. Annual inflow to the delta is about 1,200 million cubic metres, nearly double that of all the other rivers within the country. Most of this evaporates within the delta itself and the outflow into the Boteti river and into Lake Ngami is rather small and variable. Two major studies have investigated the possibility of increasing the outflow of the delta by reducing the evaporation area within. The increased outflow could then be channelled and pumped across the country to satisfy water demands in the east. The project seems technically feasible, and would not have a major detrimental impact on the ecology of the delta itself. But the projected costs are enormous and at the moment it is difficult to conceive of a sufficiently large demand in the east which could finance the conveyance of water five hundred kilometres or more across the country.

In the next few decades, the Limpopo would appear to offer greater promise as a new water source than the Okavango whether for irrigated agriculture or further mining projects. But since the Limpopo runs along the border between Botswana and South Africa, while the Okavango rises in Angola and crosses the Caprivi Strip, which is part of Namibia, before flowing into Botswana, use of either river would involve detailed international agreements. So in water supply, as in other aspects, a growing mineral sector in Botswana may entail increased economic co-operation with neighbouring countries at a time when political relations may become more difficult.

INSTITUTIONS AND LEGISLATION

So far this chapter has been mainly concerned with physical infrastructure, the foundation on which new productive enterprises and social services can be built. In recent years a number of institutions have been created which are directly concerned with promoting new production. The Ministry of Mineral Resources and Water Affairs, set up as an independent ministry in 1974, and the government planning machinery (which was outlined in Chapter 4) are the most important examples within the Government itself. The Ministry of Commerce and Industry, which might be expected to come in the same category, has in fact interpreted its role to be more regulatory than promotional. In addition, three parastatal corporations—the National Development Bank (which was discussed in Chapter 5), the Botswana Development Corporation, and more directly the Bank of Botswana—are active in this sphere.

The Botswana Development Corporation is a limited liability company wholly owned by the Government. It was incorporated under the Companies Act in 1970. Initially the BDC was expected to stimulate industrial development in Botswana, though its remit has never been limited to the manufacturing sector. In practice, because of the manifold problems of industrialization, its main efforts and successes have been in the commercial sector and in service industries. It has sponsored, either through full or partial equity ownership, or simply through institutional support, a range of enterprises which did not exist in Botswana in the 1960s—insurance companies, estate agents, industrial estates, commercial property, hotels, travel agents, car hire, equipment leasing, and wholesaling. One of its important successes has been a small national air service, a responsibility which it took over in 1972, after several previous attempts to run a viable airline had failed. Although the results of its efforts to promote manufacturing have been disappointing, the new service industries, which it has established, may be a prerequisite to greater future industrialization of the economy. In the meantime, they provide a range of services which previously had to be purchased in South Africa.

When in 1974 the Government decided to introduce a domestic currency and establish the Bank of Botswana it had two broad concerns. First, the use of Rand notes and coins in Botswana represented an interest free loan from Botswana to South Africa of about fifteen million Pula. Second, Botswana's monetary affairs were tied to the balance of payments position, interest-rate structure, and inflation rate of South Africa. As South Africa's economy deteriorated in the mid-1970s so its monetary and exchange-rate policies became increasingly inappropriate for Botswana. On the other hand, establishing an independent currency involved a heavy institutional and administrative burden and might have discouraged foreign investment. Indeed the decision might not have been taken if the negotiations with South Africa on formalizing the previously informal arrangements for the Rand Monetary Area had turned slightly more in Botswana's favour. In the event the Pula was introduced smoothly, and gained a sufficient measure of international confidence at an early stage. Although it is too early to judge the Bank of Botswana's impact on the economy, its determination to pursue an independent exchange-rate policy was made clear only nine months after the launching of the new currency, when the Pula was revalued by 5 per cent relative to the Rand.

The period since independence has also seen a spate of legislation regulating the development of various aspects of the economy—trading, industrial development, transport, town planning, and so on. Much of this legislation is described in terms which make it appear developmental such as promoting the orderly growth of one sector or another. But when examined in detail it turns out to be clearly restrictive. For example, under the Trading Act of 1967 anyone wishing to open a store or to trade has to apply for and be granted a licence, of which there are no less than seventeen different categories. Even hawkers have to be licenced.[11] It is difficult to see what benefit this legislation is meant to confer. If anything the commercial sector suffers from an excess of local monopolies rather than from an excess of competition. On the other hand the legislation makes illegal a great deal of trading, for which there is clear demand, in the peri-urban areas on the edge of the towns (CSO, 1974: 75). The net effect is that the poor pay more, and the entrepreneurs operating in the informal sector lose the opportunity to expand their business. Similarly, under the Road Transport (Permits) Act of 1973 licences have to be obtained for any use of a vehicle for hire or reward whether for passengers or goods, even though the commonest and probably the most economical way for people to travel in the rural areas has always been to hitch a lift on a passing vehicle in return for a small payment. The same legislation also requires that anyone wishing to convey his own goods on his own vehicle, if it has a carrying capacity of more than 3 tonnes, must obtain a licence. The legislation is intended to encourage the development of a transport industry, but because it goes beyond the minimum necessary for this obejctive and because the resources do not exist to administer it adequately, it has had a restrictive rather than promotional effect.

The problem of finding the right balance between freedom and legislative control is not peculiar to Botswana. It exists in all countries to a degree. But there may nevertheless be some local factors. Foreign experts have been numerous and influential in Botswana. Many of these experts have already toured the world with their own particular remedies and have long lost the ability to see the wider developmental implications of their proposals. It is always easy to argue to an uncertain Cabinet that a particular legislative proposal will protect the public by outlawing exploitation and at the same time make only a marginal increase in the restrictions and regulations in society. The Botswana leaders, having witnessed exploitation in South Africa, may be particularly receptive to this type of argument. But it is essential to perceive that the sum total of all this marginal legislation is the creation of an environment in which only those who have a good level of education or previous experience, often non-citizens, will be able to cope with the regulations and remain within the law.

CHAPTER 10

CONCLUSIONS

The problem of achieving rapid and widely distributed increases in incomes in a country which is extremely poor, highly dependent, and lacking infrastructure has been a major theme of this book. The Colonial Government which ruled Botswana for eighty years adopted a laissez-faire attitude towards its economic development. The territory's potential appeared so limited that very little investment was made and the British envisaged that its suzerainty would eventually be taken over by South Africa. But independence proved to be a turning-point, not only in political but also in economic terms. Since then very large increases in national output have been achieved. A run of good weather enabled the livestock sector to flourish. The fortunate discovery of minerals provided a new source of revenue and savings and—especially during the construction of the mines and their associated urban infra-structure—a stimulus to the rest of the economy.

The benefits of these developments would have been much less had it not been for the careful planning, economic management, and diplomacy which the country has enjoyed. The initiative in renegotiating the Customs Union was taken by Botswana; without this the impact of the mineral sector on government revenues would have been much smaller. If less care had been taken over the financial arrangements for the Selebi-Phikwe mine the burden of its failure would have fallen more heavily on the nation. Without intensive lobbying at Brussels, Botswana would probably have lost its most important market for beef. Thus, fortuitous circumstances, together with hard work by the country's elected representatives and officials, have combined to produce rapid economic development. Furthermore, over this period, freedom and democracy have been preserved and international dependence has been reduced.

These are notable achievements. However, one of the major lessons of this book is that aggregate increases in output *per se* are far less important than their structural composition. In Botswana, economic growth has so far been heavily concentrated in the livestock and mining sectors. This has had important consequences, which have been recurring themes of previous chapters. First, many people, having neither cattle nor wage employment, have been largely excluded from the effects of economic growth. Their productive potential has not been enhanced in any fundamental way and, although they have not been called upon to make sacrifices, they have enjoyed only a limited share of the benefits. Second, the growth is fragile: the livestock sector is vulnerable to changes in the weather cycle, and has caused major conservation problems; the mining sector is externally oriented, and the main factors which affect its sources of capital and technology, and its markets, are beyond Botswana's sphere of influence. Third, Botswana's position in southern Africa imposes political limitations which pose a considerable threat to future stability and prosperity. This chapter draws out the implications of these three major themes.

The questions of the distribution of capital and income were taken up particularly in Chapters 5 and 7. A significant minority of the rural population lacks adequate capital resources to engage usefully in productive agriculture. These people own neither cattle nor smallstock. Many of them are members of households in which the adult males are absent, and their economic position is deteriorating as a result of social change impelled by economic modernization. Income distribution as a whole has worsened—the rich have enjoyed proportionately more of the benefits of growth than have the poor. This tendency has been discernible since the end of the great drought of the 1960s, although it has been particularly marked in recent years.

Why has this happened? The simplest explanation would be that while the concentration of investment upon high-output, low-employment sectors in Botswana has increased the opportunities to alleviate poverty by maximizing the growth of the economic surplus, it has also generated pressures which now make this process more difficult. The rewards have initially been concentrated among a small section of the population. This has increased the power of this minority and its aspirations, changed its perceptions, and brought its own interests into conflict with those of the majority of the people. This partly accounts for the neglect of arable agriculture by the BDP Government—the leading members of which own large herds of cattle—for its lack of willingness to tax the livestock sector, and for its initiating a land reform which will tend to consolidate the position of a small group of affluent cattle farmers. But this view that the present generation of leaders in Botswana are merely pursuing their own narrow class interests is too simplistic: other political and economic forces are also at work, which have influenced policy in various important ways.

The most significant are perhaps those which stem from the democratic process itself. The BDP politicians, in contrast to many elsewhere in Africa, still depend on the rural population to be elected to power, and have their roots firmly in the rural areas. The increased attention which has been given to the provision of rural infrastructure since 1974 is a deliberate attempt to improve the distribution of national income.

Is this, then, the result of democratic forces working on politicians anxious to respond to the needs of their electorate on a continuing basis, or was it a mere palliative, a sop to the rural population introduced as a means of winning votes in the 1974 election? Although we would incline towards the former view, an adequate answer cannot yet be given to this question: the BDP have faced no serious opposition since the mid-1960s and democracy in Botswana has still to be really tested. The challenge will come as rural discontent emerges. If democracy is to survive, this discontent must find expression in an articulate mass party—whether or not emerging from the present BDP—which is strong and sophisticated enough to oppose the present pattern of ownership and the growing power of the unionized urban interest groups.

With or without democracy, however, the barriers to redistribution are much more formidable than a matter merely of political will. Our analysis has shown that there is also a range of technical factors which more cursory approaches often ignore or overlook. Administrative inertia, inappropriate professionalism, and a whole range of international, so-called 'modern', influences make it extremely difficult for political leaders to propose and effect major changes in policy even when they wish to do so.

Foremost amongst these in small countries like Botswana are the influences that come, in various ways, from abroad. Thus, while the impact of a democratic system of government on the shape of income distribution has been small but favourable, that of foreign influences has been much more ambiguous. It is true that many of the more clearly redistributive policies—the incomes policy, the attempt at progressive taxation, the avoidance of urban subsidies—have been advocated or encouraged by expatriate advisers working within the government service or by the aid agencies themselves. However, the extent to which these outside influences are an effective force for redistribution is probably small. Frequently lacking political impetus, expatriate or donor-inspired redistributive policies are often applied only half-heartedly and with limited effect. Moreover, aid agencies themselves, while preaching the needs of the poor, have continued to support projects which favour the wealthy, in part because they have been unwilling to simplify their own procedures and administrative requirements so as to enable their assistance to reach the most needy target groups. In addition, some of the expatriates whom they supply under technical co-operation arrangements are out of sympathy with this particular goal, and even when this is not the case such people often lack the local knowledge and cultural background to know how it might be achieved. Narrow professional specialisms learned abroad lead to the adoption of technologies and legislation which are often quite inappropriate to the skill availability and administrative resources in countries like Botswana, and which—albeit inadvertently—make living standards for the poorest groups yet worse. The additional influence of multinational companies attempting to introduce wage scales based upon foreign rather than local conditions makes the goal of an equitable distribution of income even more difficult to achieve.

As a result of this combination of political, technical, and international influences the enhanced government revenues have not as yet been used to pursue redistributive goals. Chapter 4 showed that although the budget grew sixfold in the first decade of independence, the pattern of government expenditure and its allocation between urban and rural areas was much the same at the end as it was at the beginning. More striking is that the proportion of the total budget assigned to agriculture was halved over the same period. Instead of expanding the productive base of the economy the new revenues have tended to be used in the expansion of a range of administrative and regulatory activities, which, while no doubt desirable, are not economically essential, and in the creation of 'strategic' but low-yielding infrastructure. The principal exceptions are the social services: the education and health sectors have fared well in budget allocations, although the present structure of expenditures on the former may well be subject to declining economic and social returns.

The Government has however been far more successful in reducing the nation's economic dependence upon other countries over this period. With the renegotiation of the Customs Union and the opening of the diamond mines, the Government became much less reliant on foreign aid than at independence, and its sources became much more diversified. Although donor agencies still provide significant amounts of capital and skilled manpower, in the short term the economy is now more dependent on the latter than on the former. During the 1980s, however, the expansion of higher education and training which has occurred will reduce this reliance upon foreign sources for skilled workers. It is much less likely that the country will be able to create sufficient opportunities for its unskilled workers to permit the early withdrawal of migrant labour from South Africa. Indeed there is a considerable risk that changes in South Africa itself will force the ending of the migrant labour system sooner than the Botswana Government would wish.

Dependence on foreign trade is always a feature of small economies. It tends to deepen as the economy modernizes and demands a greater range of more sophisticated goods, which the local manufacturing sector, even under the most favourable conditions, cannot be expected to supply. Botswana conforms to this general trend. Moreover, a very high proportion of its imports still originate in one country—South Africa—although the composition and destination of exports has been considerably broadened. The growth of minerals exports has been very rapid. Indeed, diamond sales are increasing in importance to such an extent that the country may become dangerously dependent on this commodity in the 1980s, although not as much as it was on beef a decade earlier.

On balance, government action since independence has promoted a healthy diversification in its sources of revenue, aid, and manpower, and in the range of export products sold. The economy itself now stands on two legs—livestock and minerals. In these respects an important transformation has occurred since the 1960s and overall economic dependence has been reduced. But the economy is still fragile and vulnerable, and the remaining heavy reliance on South Africa for the employment of many Batswana, for trade and transport, and for foreign investment, is a matter for continued concern.

While it has been possible to provide a firm analysis of Botswana's domestic political and economic structure, the analysis of its political status in southern Africa has had to be rather more tentative because of the rapidity of political change in the region. Hitherto Botswana has been relatively isolated from the struggle between the white and black races which has been waged further north in Angola, Mozambique, and Zimbabwe. Without being in the least cynical towards this conflict the nation's leaders were nevertheless able to turn its isolation to good advantage. A delicate but fruitful balance has been maintained between South Africa's desire to remain on good terms with its moderate black neighbour, and the wish on the part of some western nations to support Botswana as a democratic, and obviously successful, non-racial alternative in this troubled part of the world.

But from the mid-1970s the colours on the map of southern Africa have been changing. Black governments came to power in Angola and Mozambique, and the conflict in Zimbabwe and Namibia intensified. At the time of writing, the Smith regime in Southern Rhodesia was crumbling rapidly and a new Zimbabwe was about to emerge. What is clear is that the white minority government in South Africa itself will also come under increasing pressure—both internal and external, diplomatic and military—to give way to the black majority. Botswana cannot avoid being caught up in this forthcoming struggle, even if it wished to do so. At the very least this will imply a diminution of its economic links with South Africa, which in some ways—through the ready availability of imports and through the Customs Union—have proved beneficial. Foreign investors who might otherwise be interested in the country's mineral potential will be inclined to stay away so long as tension persists in the region. There may be economic disruption.

These three principal strands of argument—the uneven impact of past economic growth, the continued vulnerability of the mineral sector to events in southern Africa, and the probability that the country will become more drawn into the racial struggle of the region—lead to the conclusion that Botswana should follow a rather different development strategy in the 1980s than it pursued and largely achieved in the previous decade and a half.

The dominant theme of this strategy should be the creation of new productive opportunities for the mass of the ordinary people in such a way as to increase their own self-reliance and that of the nation as a whole. This would allow the benefits of growth to be more widely distributed, and the country's vulnerability to external events would be reduced. The mineral sector will not meet this requirement. For all the real and important benefits it has brought, mining will neither promote social equality nor will it bring any greater economic independence than has already been achieved. The same applies to manufacturing —at least the capital-intensive import-dependent type of manufacturing which is usually promoted. Moreover, Botswana has no significant comparative advantage in manufacturing, a handicap which would not be removed by leaving the Customs Union.

This book has shown that there is need for change and adjustment in a range of key policy areas and sectors. The agricultural sector, however, presents the major set of opportunities for the future: agricultural work is the activity in which the Batswana are most skilled; it can offer productive work for all; and it underpins the nation's self-reliance. Agriculture, especially livestock development, has been supporting Botswana's economic growth since independence, despite being accorded very low priority by the Government in the allocation of capital and administrative resources. This neglect originates in the harsh and bitter experience of the 1960s drought. The 1970s, however, have shown pessimism to be unjustified. This is not to say that drought will not return. But the very little local agricultural research that has been undertaken to date indicates that both arable and livestock farming could yield more in the good years and become more drought resistent in the bad. Moreover, the possibilities for irrigation have scarcely been examined. In short, if investments were to be made in the agricultural sector on the same scale as are happily contemplated for the mineral sector, the productive potential of the Batswana could be transformed without having to sacrifice economic growth.

But a renewed emphasis on agriculture, if it is to be equitable and efficient, must involve all the people of Botswana, including those currently excluded by poverty from useful agricultural production together with those now driven to work in South Africa. Capital, and especially cattle, must be provided to the many families whose agricultural efforts are at present frustrated by lack of access to draught power and implements for ploughing, and who lack the traditional security to survive a bad year that livestock ownership confers.

Such a strategy will need courage and determination. But it is the only way to increase the incomes of the poorer half of the population which has so far enjoyed few of the benefits of economic growth. That all the nation should and would share in these benefits has been a recurring theme of plans and policy statements since 1966. For economic, technical, and moral reasons the time is now ripe to give substance to this aspiration. But whether the forces of democracy in Botswana will be sufficiently powerful to effect this change remains a question for the 1980s and beyond.

APPENDIX 1

IMPORTANT DATES AND EVENTS

1882   Tati Concession granted by Lobengula.
1885   30 September, Protectorate declared.
1892   Montshiwa establishes the Rolong farms.
1895   Khama, Sebele, and Bathoen travel to London.
1896   Rinderpest catastrophe.
1909   South Africa Act.
1910   Customs Agreement signed between South Africa, Bechuana-
        land, Basutoland, and Swaziland.
1919   Native Advisory Council established.
1920   European Advisory Council established.
1923   Death of Khama.
1948   Marriage of Seretse Khama.
        Building of Moeng College begun.
1949   Exile of Seretse Khama to England.
1951   Joint Advisory Council established.
1954   Opening of CDC abattoir at Lobatse.
1956   Return of Seretse Khama to Bechuanaland.
1959   Prospecting Agreement signed with RST.
        Economic Survey Mission.
1961   Legislative Council established.
        Bechuanaland People's Party formed.
        Beginning of five years of drought.
        South Africa leaves the Commonwealth and becomes a republic.
1962   Bechuanaland Democratic Party (BDP) formed.
        August: disturbances in Francistown.
        Establishment of a Select Committee on Racial Discrimination.
1963   November: self-government constitution agreed.
        National Development Bank established.
1964   Census.
        University of Botswana, Lesotho, and Swaziland established.
1965   February: government departments begin to move to Gaborone.
        March: elections. Self-government constitution comes into
        effect.
        November: Economic Survey Mission.
        First Bridgades started at Swaneng.
        Botswana Meat Commission established.
        Local Government Act.
        Chieftainship Act.

Matimela Act.

Local Government Tax Act.

1966 February: Independence Constitution agreed in London.

July: District Councils come into being.

30 September: independence.

September: Transititional Plan published.

Rhodesia Railways takes over operation of railway.

BMC takes over operation of abattoir.

Drought breaks at the end of the year.

1967 February: BCL announces that 33 million tonnes of copper-nickel ore proved at Selebi-Phikwe and Matsitama.

April: AK1 diamond pipe at Orapa discovered.

September: Mineral Rights in Tribal Territories Act.

September: Ministry of Development Planning created.

1968 Tribal Land Act.

Completion of Francistown–Maun Road.

First National Development Plan published.

1969 June: new Customs Agreement signed.

September: Seretse Khama outlines Botswana's foreign policy in address to UN General Assembly.

Bathoen II resigns chieftainship and joins newly formed BNF.

October: general election, Bathoen defeats Vice-President Masire.

1969 Government acquires land from the Tati Company.

Trade Unions Act.

Trade Disputes Act.

Regulation of Wages and Conditions of Employment Act.

1970 Tribal Land Act brought into force.

March: decision taken to proceed with Shashe Project, and agreement reached on framework of fiscal regime.

March: agreement reached with De Beers for Orapa mine.

September: Okoh report on salaries and conditions of service for the civil service.

Water Utilities Corporation Act.

Botswana Power Corporation Act.

Botswana Development Corporation incorporated.

Second National Development Plan published.

District Development Committees formed.

1971 July: production commences at Orapa.

July: opening of Botswana campus of UBLS.

August: census.

Botswana Employers Federation formed.

Ministries of Finance and of Development Planning merged.

1972 Budgetary self-sufficiency achieved.

March: Shashe Project Agreements signed.

March: Government publishes: 'National Policy on Incomes, Employment, Prices and Profits'.

April: BHC takes over government houses and new civil service housing policy promulgated.

December: Botswana Housing Corporation (Amendment) Bill defeated in National Assembly.

1973   January: primary school fees halved.

July: new Income Tax Act comes into force.

Report on rural development published, and endorsed by Government.

Third National Development Plan published.

Accelerated Rural Development Programme initiated.

Construction of BotZam road commences.

Commissioning and failure of Selebi-Phikwe mine.

Arab oil producers impose embargo on sales to South Africa.

1974   Lifeline Programme launched.

April: Botswana Agricultural Marketing Board established.

May: salary increases awarded to civil service.

August: Central Government Wages Policy Committee formed.

September: President announces decision to take over railway.

September: election.

September: Rhodesia completes building of Beitbridge rail link with South Africa.

Decision announced to introduce Botswana currency.

Ministries of Mineral Resources and Water Affairs and of Health established.

National Centre for Vocational Training opened.

Botswana Enterprises Development Programme started.

European Community imposes levies on meat imports.

1975   February: Lome Convention signed.

June: new agreement reached with De Beers.

July: strike at BCL.

July: Government publishes: 'National Policy on Tribal Grazing Land'.

July: rebate of 90 per cent of meat levy agreed with the European Community.

Chinese embassy opens in Gaborone.

October: Lesotho breaks away from UBLS.

1976   March: Mozambique closes its border with Rhodesia.

June: National Radio Learning Campaign on new Tribal Grazing Land Policy.

23 August: Pula introduced.

August: University of Botswana and Swaziland created.

December: Completion of BotZam road.

President makes state visit to China.

Russia opens embassy in Gaborone.

Salaries Review Commission.

Fourth National Development Plan published.

Modification to Customs Union formula agreed with South Africa.

Soweto disturbances cause influx of refugees to Botswana.
1977   Refugees arrive from Rhodesia.
        Amendment to Income Tax Act.
        Border incidents with Rhodesian Army.
        April: Botswana Defence Force established.
        Outbreak of foot-and-mouth disease temporarily closes the
        abattoir.
1978   Raising of First Euro-dollar loan for Jwaneng mine.
        Third Salaries Review Commission.

APPENDIX 2

BATSWANA MIGRANT WORKERS IN SOUTH AFRICA: THE GROWTH IN LABOUR FLOWS, EARNINGS, AND CASH TRANSFERS

The number of workers involved

Discussions of the problem of migrant labour flows to the Republic of South Africa often do not take account of the facts that only about one half of such workers are recruited by approved recruitment organizations, and that of those workers who are recruited by such organizations, only about three-quarters of them are employed by companies included in the South African Chamber of Mines Organization. Thus it is a mistake to assume, as so often happens, that data issued by the Chamber of Mines provide a representative description of conditions affecting all, or even the majority, of migrant workers.

Official recruitment of workers for the farms and mines of South Africa is carried out by recruitment agencies that are registered with, and licensed by the Botswana Government's Labour Commissioner. Though all such recruiters are required to furnish the Labour Department with quarterly statistics on employment and recruitment of Batswana workers, these data, until recently, have been very incomplete and unreliable. However, an analysis of quarterly returns for the last three years suggests that the number of Batswana recruited by the Mine Labour Organization for Chamber of Mines employers has been typically between 65 and 80 per cent of the total number of Batswana officially recruited for mine work in South Africa. In addition, several thousand Batswana are recruited each year for farm work, mainly for fruit-picking in the Rustenburg area, at rates of pay which are much lower than those prevailing in the mines.

These 'official' flows, however, by no means describe the extent of labour migration from Botswana. A large number of people have always been able to find work in South Africa illegally, often with the help of close relatives living there. Many of these persons appear to migrate to South Africa on a permanent basis: this form of permanent emigration appears to have been running at between four and five thousand persons per year during the 1960s (CSO, 1972c: 191). Owing to the 'hidden' nature of part of this migration to South Africa, even population census estimates understate the true magnitude of migration: its illegal nature leads to under-reporting of absentees and in cases where no household members remain in Botswana, absentees cannot be identified by the census methodology.

For all these reasons, published figures have tended to underestimate the scale of migration from Botswana to South Africa. Our estimates,

TABLE A2.1   *Migrant Batswana Workers in South Africa, 1935-1977*

	Batswana workers in Chamber of mines organizations[1]	Total Batswana mine workers 'officially' recruited[2]	Census data on reported absentees working in South Africa[3]	Likely magnitude of total absentee workers in South Africa[4]
1935/6	7,000	n.a.	n.a.	10,300
1946	7,000	n.a.	14,250	20,000
1964	16,000	n.a.	35,000	52,000
1970/1	16,000	26,000	45,700	60,000
1974	20,000	n.a.	n.a.	60,000
1975	19,000	26,000	n.a.	60,000
1976	26,000	32,000	n.a.	70,000
1977	25,000	32,000	n.a.	70,000

[1] Data made available by Ministry of Finance and Development Planning, Gaborone. Compiled from MLO Annual Reports.
[2] 1970/1 figure from RB, 1970b:2. Later estimates based upon quarterly returns of licensed mine recruiters in Botswana, Ministry of Home Affairs. Data are for March of each year shown.
[3] BP, 1946; BP, 1964a; CSO, 1972c.
[4] 1935/6; 1946: Schapera, 1947. 1964: Leistner, 1967. 1970/1: Estimate given in CSO, 1972c: 111. 1974-7: Trend estimates.

presented in Table A2.1, suggest that those workers recruited by Chamber of Mines employers have comprised no more than one quarter to one-third of total labour flows, while the total number of Batswana officially recruited for mine work have been about half of all Batswana migrants. There are unfortunately no reliable data on the number of workers officially recruited for the farming sector, though it is known that the number are much less than those going to the mines. Nevertheless, this probably means that as many as one-third of Batswana migrants do not pass through registered recruiting organizations, and find work in the South African farms, mines, and industries unofficially. Nothing is at present known about the conditions of work, remittances, or length of absence of such workers.

Earnings and remittances

The average earnings of Africans in the South African mining sector increased more than sixfold between 1969 and 1977. Though there have been significant increases in earnings in most years since 1971, the inflation was particularly marked between 1973 and 1975. During this two-year period, the average earnings of Africans almost tripled (Table A2.2). The sharp increases at this time were the result of a number of national and international developments affecting the supply of labour to the mines. The most important factors were, first, that wages in other sectors of the South African economy had been rising faster than those in mining, which were kept down by the elastic supply of foreign labour. Over the years, this had caused a relative decrease in the number of black South Africans wishing to work in the mines. Second, following an air crash at Francistown, Botswana, in April 1974 which killed 74 miners returning to Malawi, the Malawian Government suspended all further recruitment for the mines from Malawi. Over the following twelve months the number of Malawian miners in South Africa dropped from over 100,000 to about 3,000 workers and by 1976 not more than a few hundred remained. Finally, with the imminent independence of Mozambique in 1974, the supplies of labour from that source—hitherto representing some 28 per cent of the total mining labour force in South Africa—became extremely uncertain. These circumstances, together with growing international disapprobation over the general level of wages paid to black South Africans, particularly by foreign and international companies in the Republic, generated a rapid escalation of wages between 1973 and 1976. The higher wages were not sufficient to prevent a dramatic fall in total mining employment from about 420,000 in 1973 to about 360,000 in 1974. Nevertheless, recruitment within South Africa increased, as did that from Rhodesia and the BLS countries, which to some extent counteracted the suspension of Malawian recruitment. It can be seen from Table A2.2. that this improvement in wages caused the number of Batswana officially recruited for Chamber of Mines employers in South Africa, after having remained relatively stable since 1960, to increase by more than one-third between 1975 and 1976.

These changes have, in turn, caused a significant shift in the pattern and levels of remittances of earnings from work in South Africa to Botswana—probably dramatically so since 1975. Such remittances are made in various ways. First, workers during their period of work abroad often send money through the post to relatives in Botswana. Second, returning workers bring with them goods that they have bought during their stay in South Africa, together with any cash savings they may have made. Third, the deferred-pay system, peculiar to minework, provides a means—through payroll deductions—of saving a proportion of earnings. These savings are collected by mineworkers from their local Mine Labour Organization recruitment office after their return home.

Transfers of cash earnings under the deferred pay system were probably in the region of one or two million Pula per year in the late 1960s.[1] More recently, transfers under deferred pay have increased considerably. However, the data appear to be unreliable, and estimates conflict in different sources.[2] Using the Mine Labour Returns sent to

[1] Conflicting estimates for this period have been published by the Botswana authorities from time to time, all of which are of these orders of magnitude.

[2] Compare for example, the estimates given in CSO, 1974a and CSO, 1975, with those in CSO, 1976j, which differ by a factor of 45 per cent for 1974.

TABLE A2.2 *Earnings, deferred pay, and remittances from mine work in South Africa, 1969–1977*
Pula

	Average African earnings for 9 month period[1]	Average deferred pay per returning mineworker[2]	Average value of remittance payments made[3]	Average value of remittances per employed worker[3]
1969	149	n.a.	n.a.	n.a.
1971	166	n.a.	n.a.	n.a.
1972	192	n.a.	n.a.	n.a.
1973	261	n.a.	n.a.	n.a.
1974	423	171	49	29
1975	711	252	71	43
1976	828	296	100	60
1977	918	n.a.	n.a.	n.a.

[1] Based upon monthly earnings data released by the South African Chamber of Mines, and reported in the *Rand Daily Mail* of 30 July 1977. Though some sources report that the average length contract is shortening, there is little evidence of this for Batswana workers at present. Nine months, for our purposes, can be taken as typical.
[2] Calculated from data held in Labour Department files, Gaborone. These data refer to payments made by MLO–WNLA only, and thus cover about 80 per cent of 'official' labour flows from Botswana to the South African Mining sector.
[3] As for fn. 2 above. The difference between these two columns arises from the fact that, according to data on the files, about 60 per cent of mineworkers typically send one remittance to Botswana during their absence. The average remittance per worker is therefore less than the average value of each remittance.

the Labour Department by the recruiting organizations, we have calculated average remittances from, and deferred payments to mineworkers returning to Botswana between 1974 and 1976. For earlier years, the data were too unreliable to use.

The following conclusions emerge from Table A2.2.

1. Assuming that Batswana work on average a nine-month contract in South Africa and that they receive earnings not dissimilar from those of other black workers on the mines, about 40 per cent of cash earnings have typically been remitted to Botswana in the form of deferred pay. Miners were on average receiving almost P300 each from this source on their return to Botswana in 1976.

2. According to the MLO information approximately 60 per cent of mineworkers send at least one remittance home to their families during their contract. The average value of all such remittances increased from about P50 in 1974 to P100 in 1976. Thus the average remittance per worker during one contract was about P60 in 1976.

3. It can be seen from Table A2.1, that MLO/Chamber of Mines recruits increased from about 20,000 to 26,000 between 1974 and 1976. The data in Table A.2.2 show that the average cash transfer from

deferred pay and remittances from these workers increased from P200 to about P360 per worker between these two years. Thus the estimated total cash transfers to Botswana from such workers increased from P4 million in 1974 to P9.36 million in 1976. These estimates exclude the value of goods or additional cash savings brought back by such workers from South Africa at the end of their contracts.

It should be remembered that MLO/Chamber of mines recruits comprise only about 80 per cent of total Batswana mineworkers in South Africa, and probably less than half of all absentee workers (Table A2.1). Though other employers do not generally have systems of deferred pay for their recruits, the savings made by such workers during their contracts may be considerable. Though such savings are likely to be less than those made by miners, it is possible that the total transfer of savings from South Africa to Botswana from all migrant labourers in cash and kind in 1976 was between P15 million and P20 million. It is clear, therefore, that the value of these transfers is now very much greater than it was before 1973.

NOTES

INTRODUCTION

1. The reasons for this should be easy to see. If income is initially unequally distributed, a strategy of growth based upon conventional investment criteria—such as the maximization of financial rates of return—implicitly gives more weight to the growth of the incomes of the rich than of the poor. For example, an increase of $100 to the income of a man earning $1,000 is given ten times more weight than a $10 increase for a man earning $100, even though, proportionately, each would be 10 per cent better off.
2. See Leys (1975a, 1975b) and Jolly (1975) for perhaps the best examples of these two positions.

CHAPTER 1

1. In fact the tribal capital of the Ngwato was moved from Shoshong to Palapye in the nineteenth century, and to Serowe in 1902 (where it has since remained) owing to failure of the water supply. Other tribes have shifted their capitals for the same reason (UK, 1933).
2. Sillery points out (1974: 29) that responsibility for the destruction of the mission is in doubt, and that it may lie with the Griqua, rather than the Boers.
3. Khama himself had requested British protection as early as 1876 (Sillery, 1974: 76).
4. *Blue Book*, C. 4588, p. 106, quoted in Stevens, 1967: 124.
5. See UK, 1952.
6. Excise duties on spirits and beer, however, were excluded, since trade in these items between the parties was restricted.
7. It was probably for the same reason that no provision was made in the agreement for reviewing the changing shares of imports which might go in future to each of the partners. See Ettinger, 1974: 60.
8. See RSA, 1961: Tables H-9 and H-23.
9. In fact, restrictions had already been enforced by South Africa, but these had been introduced for veterinary reasons following the persistence of lung-sickness in cattle from Bechuanaland between 1905 and 1923.
10. The minimum weights were further raised to 1100 lb. for oxen and 840 lb. for cows, measured at the point of entry to South Africa, to allow for weight loss during the journey to Johannesburg (UK, 1933: 15).
11. This is most clearly demonstrated in a letter from Hertzog to the High Commissioner, dated 23 October 1924, when he pointed out that the impending weight restrictions would be avoided if a decision to transfer the High Commission Territories to the Union were to be made. See UK, 1952: 15.
12. Smuts argued, in a memorandum to the Secretary of State for Dominion Affairs in 1933, that 'as they all have similar interests, it is essential that the native policy in the Union as well as in the territories be laid down and controlled by one Government'. See UK, 1952: 40.
13. As an additional incentive to collect the revenues early, the commission payable was reduced to 5 per cent on monies remitted after the end of October in each year.
14. There was a clause in the legislation which gave the District Commissioner power to exempt persons from payment of the tax if they were too poor to

pay 'without being deprived of the means of their subsistence'. The available evidence, however, suggests that such exemptions were unusual. Schapera, for example, reports that amongst the Kgatla in 1935, out of 3,645 registered taxpayers only 49 had been exempted from payment (Schapera, 1971: 111).

15. The proportion fell to less than fifteen per cent of total revenues during the 1950s, and to as little as five per cent by 1965.

16. For example, when introducing a Bill into the Cape Parliament in 1894 which incorporated a 10s. head tax on African males, Cecil Rhodes, who was then Prime Minister, stated: 'You will remove them [the Africans] from that life of sloth and laziness, you will teach them the dignity of labour and make them contribute to the prosperity of the State, and give them some return for our wise and good government.' Cape of Good Hope, *Hansard*, 1894, p. 352, cited by Wilson (1972: 2).

17. Letter from the Resident Commissioner to the High Commissioner, 7 Nov. 1933, Botswana National Archives 5 344/3, cited by Massey (1977: 3). Additional interesting evidence on the attitude of the colonial authorities to migrant labour is given in Massey's paper.

18. See Appendix 2.

19. An analysis of the problems posed by the migrant labour system is given in Chapter 7.

20. See UK, 1933: 25, UK, 1960: 182, and MFDP, 1977.

21. This system is discussed more fully in Chapter 5.

22. The significance of these more recent trends is discussed in Chapters 5 and 7.

23. For discussion of other early examples of the exercise of government power see Sillery 1952: 60-5, 124-7, 139-41, and Schapera, 1970: 5-6, 51-5.

24. Examples of legislation which was so affected during the 1920s and 1930s are given by Schapera, (1970: 58-9, 144).

25. Examples are given in UK, 1933: 104-7.

26. Kgamane was an uncle of Seretse, and third in line of succession to the chieftainship, after Seretse and Tshekedi.

27. As mentioned earlier in this chapter, domestic revenues were raised mainly from poll taxes on Africans and from customs revenues. Income taxation for Europeans (individuals and companies) was introduced in 1922, which by 1940 had become a very important domestic revenue source. However, in most years more revenue was raised from poll taxes than from income taxation on the European population. (See Hermans, 1974: Table 1.)

28. This year was not atypical, although grants had been made available for small amounts in earlier years, and in 1931/2 £100 was paid to the Tiger Kloof Institution in the Cape Province of South Africa, which was attended by African children from the Protectorate. (UK, 1933: 79.)

29. Census estimates for the population of Bechuanaland are as follows: 1911– 125, 350; 1921–152, 983; 1936–265, 756; 1946–296, 310; 1956–309, 175; 1964–543, 105. Those prior to 1964 are thought to be highly inaccurate and, generally, underestimates. The 1964 census suggested that the resident population had been growing at about 3 per cent per year, which would imply a population total of about 320,000 in 1946.

CHAPTER 2

1. There were in addition 7 nominated official members and 3 ex-officio members.

2. Much of the credit for the comparatively smooth transition to independence in Botswana should go to the initiative of Peter Fawcus (now Sir Peter Fawcus) who was Resident Commissioner during the critical years.

3. 'Responsible' seems to be one of the key adjectives describing the BDP's policies and image of itself in the early days.
4. There were similar sentiments among the settlers of the Tuli Block of farms, bordering South Africa along the Limpopo River.
5. For a fuller account of these events see Proctor, 1968.
6. For example, the local chief is an ex-officio member of all Tribal Land Boards and a nominated member of most District Councils.
7. Parson (1974) found that only 32 per cent and 39 per cent of rural households knew who was their local member of parliament and local councillor respectively. It seems highly probable that local headmen and chiefs are better known than this. The same survey discovered that 81 per cent of the sample knew the identity of the Botswana President, which suggests that some awareness at least of national government is widespread.
8. For instance in a Presidential Circular of 1970 when the DDC's were established (OP, 1970).
9. As evidence of this view: the formal grading of the post of DC is lower than most senior posts within central government departments; and there has been a recent tendency for the post of DC to be one for relatively inexperienced local graduate administrators prior to moving up the Gaborone hierarchy.
10. At the same time primary education was being given low priority by central government, see Chapter 8.
11. By comparison the current expenditure of central government over the same period grew fourfold, see Table 4.6.
12. So long as Botswana remains a multi-party democracy the BDP is unlikely to become a mass party. Unlike CCM its own structure and organization is quite separate from that of the government and local government, and the party does not have the resources of its own to strengthen its local organization.
13. Holm (1972) found that 62 per cent of councillors owned more than 25 head of cattle—see Chapter 5 for the significance of this finding—and 59 per cent claimed paternal kinship ties with the local chief or headman.
14. Two aspects of this provision of the Local Government Act are noteworthy. First, the act does not specify either the number of elected or nominated members in any local council, but simply gives the Minister power to settle these by regulation. Thus the governing party could always take control of any council whatever the local election result without reference to the National Assembly. Second, in most cases the local chief has been both nominated to the District Council and made ex-officio chairman, thereby limiting opposition of traditionalists to the existence and functioning of councils.
15. For a more detailed discussion of these questions see Wiseman, 1977, and Stevens and Speed, 1977.
16. One example was the defeat of the Botswana Housing Corporation (Amendment) Bill in December 1972 (Wiseman, 1977). Another example a few years later concerned a government proposal to lower the minimum retirement age for civil servants.
17. It will be recalled that the OAU had been regarding the BPP as the official liberation party.
18. This analysis and much of the supporting detail owes much to Ettinger (1974), a regrettably unpublished Ph.D thesis.
19. South Africa's attitude has not been entirely consistent even since 1961. For instance in 1963 Verwoerd proposed that Britain should let the residents of the three territories vote on whether they wanted Britain or South Africa to lead them to independence. This suggestion, which shows an incredible

misunderstanding of attitudes within the three countries towards South Africa, was simply ignored by the British Government. It is likely that these inconsistencies, as well as subsequent vacillation between threats and conciliatory gestures, simply reflects internal political disagreement within South Africa over its policy towards the BLS countries.

20. See Chapter 4.
21. So long as Namibia remained under South African control Botswana's relations with that country have been essentially identical to those with South Africa itself, and have therefore not been considered separately. For the time being, there are very few economic links between the two countries because of the intervening desert.
22. The Lusaka Manifesto was drawn up at a meeting of Presidents of East and Central African countries, not in fact including Botswana, in 1969. The most important feature of the manifesto, for the present discussion, is that it rejects dialogue with South Africa except on the basis of equal rights for all regardless of race.
23. In a constantly changing situation precise figures are elusive. But it seems likely that by the end of 1978 a hundred thousand refugees, very approximately, had arrived in Botswana of which a significant proportion has remained in the country.

CHAPTER 3

1. These included a World Bank Economic Mission (IBRD–IDA, 1964), a joint UN–British Economic and Aid Assessment team (UN, 1965), and an economic survey mission from the British Ministry of Overseas Development (RB, 1966b).
2. It is interesting, in the light of subsequent development, that the authors of the report devoted less than 20 lines, in a narrative of almost 150 pages, to a consideration of the possibilities in the mining sector. See RB, 1966b: 13, 104. By contrast, the Transitional Development Plan, prepared by the planning office in Botswana a few months after the British Mission left, identified the copper–nickel development known as the Shashi Complex as 'the one major development scheme at present envisaged capable of making a dramatic impact on the economy'. Even at this stage, minerals development was given a prominent place in the economic strategy of the new administration. See RB, 1966a: 8-9, 27, 70.
3. The anatomy of this transformation in the Government's finances is discussed in Chapter 4.
4. Comparison with Erasmus's estimate for geographical income of P19 million in 1955 suggests that production increased by about 5 per cent per year in current prices between 1955 and 1965. This would imply a real rate of growth of no more than one or two per cent per year throughout the last decade of the colonial period, and an annual fall in real per capita income of almost the same amount. These losses were concentrated in the years between 1961 and 1966 as a result of the onset of the drought. (See Erasmus, 1963, and Table 3.1.)
5. See Chapter 4.
6. Annual data on offtake and the size of the national cattle herd are shown in Table 5.3.
7. See RB, 1976b: Table 3.4.a.
8. This is an estimate, based upon information in RB, 1976b: Tables 1.4.4.a, 1.5.4.a.
9. A detailed discussion of these customs arrangements is given in Chapter 4.

10. The new customs arrangements partly account for the increase in trade sector output during this period. The reason for this is that all customs excise and sales duties, which are collected by the South African Government and transferred to Botswana as a lump sum, are allocated to the trade sector in the Botswana national accounts. In fact, some of these duties should properly be shown against other sector, to allow for items imported directly by establishments in those sectors. In addition, it seems that there was some underestimate of output figures for the retail sector in 1971/2. (See RB, 1976b: Chapter 6.)

11. See Chapter 7 below.

12. Rainfall for 1974/5 was 67 per cent above the long-term norm, as compared with 74 per cent higher in the previous year. See CSO, 1976d: Table 1.2.a.

13. See Chapter 7 and Appendix 2.

14. It should be remembered that the slaughter rates of the mid-1960s were artificially high because of the drought. Many of the cattle sent to the abattoir were in poor condition and the higher average weight of slaughtered beasts during the 1970s significantly increases the real output gains.

15. Chapters 5 and 7 below show that the benefits of the agricultural recovery have been very unequally distributed.

16. These criteria are suggested by Robert Mabro (1974: Chapter 8).

17. Apart from these direct effects, the mining developments also made Botswana more credit-worthy than would have been the case in their absence. The expectation of future prosperity made it easier for the Government to secure international loans, and a range of projects would probably not have been implemented if the prospects for growth had remained bleak. See Chapter 4.

18. This can be seen from Table 3.4, though it also follows from the national accounting identity $S - I = E - M$, where the symbols stand for national savings, investment, exports, and imports respectively.

19. It should be noted that in richer countries with a less dependent economic structure, the decision to stimulate consumption demand is an orthodox Keynesian remedy for avoiding recession. In Botswana, however, and in many other poor countries, a stimulus to consumption though salary increases for the employed labour force mainly leads to an increased demand for imports (and often to inflationary pressure on the exchange rate) rather than to enhanced levels of domestic production. In some circumstances a downturn in economic activity and the unequal distribution of income may both be aggravated as a result of such measures.

20. This includes the balances held in special funds for the purpose of servicing the future public debt and for revenue stabilization purposes.

CHAPTER 4

1. One of Botswana's chief negotiators of the revised 1969 agreement argues, admittedly on the basis of rather crude data, that the 1910 formula, as adjusted by the British Government, still gave Botswana about 10 per cent less revenue than the duty content of its imports in 1965/6. (Landell-Mills, 1971: 272-3.)

2. See Article 6 of the agreement.

3. The problems of promoting domestic industry in the context of the Customs Agreement are discussed in Chapter 6.

4. Many of the duties are set on a quantity rather than an ad valorem basis. These duties were not revised upwards as fast as the rate of inflation in the early 1970s; thus the average effective rate of duty declined.

5. See Chapter 6.
6. Table 6.3 provides more detailed data.
7. The tax is collected from the BMC which passes the costs on to the suppliers through reduced prices.
8. See RB 1976c: Paragraph 72.
9. These include Bamangwato Concessions (Pty) Ltd., De Beers Holdings (Pty) Ltd., and Holiday Inns (Pty) Ltd. Details of these taxation arrangements are described in Chapter 6.
10. Government accounts show higher expenditures than these owing to their convention of including the recurrent expenditures that specifically arose from development projects in the development fund accounts.
11. Calculated from Hermans, 1974: 115.
12. This ratio includes subventions to councils. In 1966/7 responsibility for primary education was transferred to local authorities. This caused a reduction in the central government education budget. To assist the councils in meeting the additional costs of primary schooling recurrent subventions from the Central Government to local authorities were introduced. This system of financing primary education continued until 1976/7.
13. In fact the total financial package was not finally agreed until March 1972. See Chapter 6 below.
14. See Table 3.5.
15. These were a Revenue Stabilization Fund to finance recurrent expenditures in future years of deficit, and a Public Debt Service Fund to meet the growing repayment instalments of existing and future loans. See RB, 1972a: paras. 53–62.
16. Analysis which suggests that the 1973 Act did not, in fact, achieve these aims is given in Chapter 7 below.
17. See Chapter 1.
18. The much less generous approach taken by ODM in its negotiations with Lesotho is described by David Jones (1977: 190–203).
19. Data are from Wood and Morton, 1977: 62, and from UN, 1977a: 823.
20. See Ohlin, 1973.

CHAPTER 5

1. Direct evidence that this group does not benefit greatly from the 'mafisa' system for ploughing can be found in MOA, 1973: Table 8.8 where it can be shown that only 9 per cent of the draught power used by this group consists of 'mafisa' cattle. See also Curtis, 1972.
2. The Rural Income Distribution Survey estimated a total cattle population in 1974/5 of about 1.5 million. On the other hand, more reliable sources give an estimate of about 2.6 million in 1975 and approximately 3.0 million at the end of 1976 (MFDP, 1977: 138). The survey itself attempts to reconcile the two estimates in a way which would make the actual ownership of cattle even more skewed than the raw data. For the purposes of this chapter, all the cattle numbers in the survey have been doubled, thus the apparent shape of the distribution of cattle ownership revealed by the survey has not been changed.
3. Another plausible explanation of this trend is that those without cattle are less likely even to attempt to produce a crop in a poor rainfall year. Thus in the poorer years the group of non-cattle owners who did not attempt to plough falls out of the survey population. On the other hand, all the years shown in Table 5.1 received relatively good rainfall.

4. Authors' estimate.
5. It is true that under the Agricultural Resources Conservation Act of 1974 the Government has powers to require destocking in the event of overgrazing, but the traditional resistance to compulsory destocking is so great that it is unlikely that the powers will be used in the foreseeable future. The purpose of the act appears to be more educative than restrictive.
6. See, for example, the *Preliminary Report on the Public Consultation on the National Policy on Tribal Grazing Land* (MLGL, 1976) which demonstrates widespread popular suspicion of group management. Nevertheless, it is to the credit to the Government that an effort was made to explain the policy to the people and to ascertain popular views.
7. Such an economic rent might prove to be very low. Hitherto land has been a free good in the cattle economy of Botswana which might cease to be viable if the price on land was too high. Remarkably, little economic study has been done of the proposed changes in land tenure or indeed of modern ranching methods in Botswana's circumstances.
8. It should be stressed that the Table refers exclusively to those engaged in farming. Thus the data for non-cattle owning households is not distorted by the inclusion of those with other rural employment or by the old or infirm.
9. The high proportion of woman-headed households among non-cattle owning households may arise because women do not usually control or inherit cattle. According to an FAO report (1974) 70 per cent of households headed by males hold cattle, compared with 27 per cent of households headed by females.
10. Bond (1974: 42) found that 64 per cent of farmers did not even know what the job of an agricultural demonstrator was.
11. Apparently the new farming system is only new to Botswana; the most important elements are well established in parts of the United States and other work has been done in Senegal, India, and other countries.
12. Very preliminary results available at the time of writing indicated that farmers who adopted the new system were getting a fourfold increase over the yield they had achieved in the previous year using traditional methods (personal communication: Archie McLaren).
13. For example Lever (1970: 13) and the Ministry of Agriculture (RB, 1967b: 10) both indicate that in 1967 sorghum producers were receiving about P17 a tonne from traders. The Maize Board of South Africa's floor price for that year was P31 a tonne.
14. In addition, since the mid-1960s, WFP has provided one meal a day for all primary school children, and food for more than a hundred thousand people in 'vulnerable groups', nursing mothers, pre-school children, and TB patients. There seems little doubt that these programmes have played an important part in maintaining a relatively high nutritional standard in Botswana, where serious nutritional diseases are comparatively rare. Up to the end of 1975, WFP had committed $26 million for food aid to Botswana, which at $40 per capita is more WFP assistance per head of the population than any other country (Stevens, 1978).

CHAPTER 6

1. Manganese has again been mined since independence but only on a small scale.
2. RST stood originally for Rhodesian Selection Trust but the name was changed to Roan Selection Trust following the break up of the Central African Federation of the Rhodesias and Nyasaland. In the late 1960s RST was 43 per cent owned by Amax.

3. BCL finally abandoned prospecting at Matsitama during 1976. The expenditure incurred was written off (BCL, 1977: 21).

4. The original proposal was that the access road to Selebi-Phikwe should be built from Shashe. This was later changed to Serule.

5. The economic multiplier effects of choosing the first scheme were negligible. Most of the additional investment would be on capital imports. The additional employment of Batswana as a result of choosing the first scheme is probably less than a thousand including both direct and indirect employment. The balance of payments have almost certainly been adversely affected by the decision to adopt the first scheme, as the additional interest on loans and purchase of recurrent services is probably much greater than would have been the cost of imported power. But the balance of payments was not an issue in 1968. Adoption of the first scheme has, however, had an important multiplier effect on government revenues because, in terms of the 1969 customs agreement, the Botswana Government received from the revenue pool an element, probably around 18 per cent, of the capital imports for the project as recurrent revenue in later years. However, it is doubtful that this factor came into consideration at the time, as the negotiations on the new customs agreement were only completed towards the end of 1969.

6. In the case of the Canadian-built power station it is commonly believed that the cost was up to 50 per cent higher than it would have been if the contract had gone to international tender. The Canadian loan, however, was interest free, repayable over fifty years, which implies a grant element of between 70 and 80 per cent.

7. In Zambia, for example, the mines had been in existence for twenty years or more before significant economic linkages were established. Unfortunately for Botswana, Selebi-Phikwe is just one small mine which will be exhausted in a little over twenty years.

8. Some of the major problems were (i) it was found that the ore should be washed before going to the crusher. No washer had been installed either for the opencast or for the underground workings. The former was built by January 1975, the latter rather later; (ii) the magnetic separators in the concentrating section failed to work and had to be bypassed. As a result occasional pieces of iron and steel reached the crushers and damaged them; (iii) the silos which stored the concentrate were subject to spontaneous fires and explosions as a result of the pyrophoric nature of the ore; (iv) there was little surge capacity between sections of the plant. Thus if one part of the plant went down other parts of the plant also had to be halted; (v) the flash smelter furnace could not run on coal as originally intended. For a while it had to be run on oil. In addition there was considerable loss of material from the furnace in the form of dust going up the chimney. In consequence metal recovery from the ore was very low; (vi) one of the electric furnaces ran for a few months only before it required relining which put it out of action for half a year; (vii) the sulphur recovery process did not work. (BCL, 1975: 12-14.) Many of these difficulties arose out of a decision, late in the planning phase, to change the mining plan and introduce some opencast working.

9. Based on the initial output of 2.4 million carats.

10. In mid-1973, six months before the plant was due to be commissioned, the Government estimated that it would receive 50 per cent of the pre tax profits of BCL, or up to P5 million a year in the first eight years rising to P12 million during the last ten years of the project's life (MFDP, 1973b). We have estimated that if the plant had been successfully commissioned on time the accumulated

net profit at the end of 1976 would have been at least P50 million, a reasonable return on an equity of P39 million. However, this type of calculation is extremely speculative.

11. The Botswana Meat Commission provides a good illustration of this. Although it is entirely owned by the Government, and although many ministers and civil servants have a personal interest in its success, the Government has frequently had difficulty in controlling it, in acquiring information from it, or, in some matters such as wage policy, in ensuring that it complied with government policy.

12. This difficulty has often been overcome in Botswana by appointing expatriate civil servants or advisers to the mining company boards. However loyal these expatriates may be, their appointment somewhat frustrates the objective of local representation.

13. There are six principal mechanisms for providing this downside protection: (1) the P750,000 minimum royalty which had to be paid under any circumstances should be sufficient to meet the additional recurrent costs incurred by the Government as a result of the project; (2) under the Power and Water Agreements the tariffs payable by BCL are formulated in such a way that the company has to pay the fixed costs of operating the utilities concerned however much power or water is consumed by the mine; (3) a similar arrangement applies to the railway branch lines which are owned by the Government though operated by Rhodesia Railways; (4) all the sales proceeds from the mine have to be paid into a London-based trust which then services BCL's various obligations to the Government, the parastatals, and the lenders, before remitting the balance to the company; (5) the World Bank, together with BCL's own lenders, share in a hypothec over BCL's mining lease and a mortgage over BCL housing in Selebi-Phikwe; (6) the two major shareholders, together with Metallgesellschaft, were obliged to guarantee the loan from IBRD and to repay it in the event of the project being terminated early (MFDP, 1973b).

14. For example A.M. Macgregor discussed the possibility of this link in a report dated 1929 (Macgregor, 1929).

15. Two stretches in the southern half are being financed by the World Bank and by the German Kreditanstalt für Wiederaufbau, two agencies which are notoriously slow in their appraisal procedures.

16. The long-standing trade between Zambia and South Africa used to travel by rail through Zimbabwe and across the Zambezi at Victoria Falls. When the border between these two countries was closed in January 1973, rail communication was curtailed. Much of the trade was then diverted through Botswana and across to Zambia at Kazungula.

17. Selwyn (1975: 119) and Jones (1977: 31) cite a number of cases in which South Africa appears to have blocked the establishment of an industry in Lesotho or Swaziland.

CHAPTER 7

1. Some of these settlements have populations in excess of 30,000 people, and, on this criterion, could be described as towns. We shall refer to them as villages, as is commonly done elsewhere, to distinguish them from the modern urban centres that have developed particularly since the early 1960s.

2. Schapera, for example, gives the following monthly wage rates as typical in the early 1930s. *Botswana*: domestic servants £1 to £3, plus housing and food; 'yard boys' £1.10s.; cattle herders, 10s. to £1. *South Africa*: (Johannesburg),

unskilled labourers, £3 to £4; average African wages in the gold mines, £2.17s.6d., plus food, housing, and medical services. (Schapera, 1971: 128-33.)

3. These estimates are based upon a male *de facto* population between the ages of 15 and 64 years of about 99,000 persons, and an absentee male population of about 48,000 persons in 1971. The calculation assumes that absentees not counted in the census of that year can be attributed in the same ratios between mining and other work, and between males and females, as those that were counted. See Appendix 2 and CSO, 1972c: 111.

4. Additional data, together with the reasons for these increases, are given in Appendix 2.

5. See Appendix 2, Table A2.1. Though most of the increased flow of migrant labour appears to be to the South African mining sector, it is likely that labour flows to other sectors have also increased—though less strongly—since independence. Wage movements may have had some influence here also, but since little is known about the sectoral activities of the remainder of the Batswana migrants, one cannot be sure.

6. The above calculations are based only upon data for mineworkers. Wages earned by migrants working in other sectors are often lower than those paid by the mines. However, the practice of providing board and lodging, and the consequent possibility of workers saving a high proportion of their earnings, is common in other sectors employing migrant workers.

7. See Appendix 2.

8. Of the 189 households in the village with absentee workers, only 124 had received money from such workers during the preceding six-month period. Half of the households in the latter group had received P10 or less. Only eleven households had received P40 or more during the period. See Eding *et al.*, 1972: 145, 257.

9. CSO 1976f: 72. These savings from deferred pay do not include cash or kind savings from other sources remitted to Botswana during or at the end of workers' contracts.

10. The RIDS reports that the pay points in Botswana 'are surrounded by brewers of traditional beer, retailers of modern beer, and prostitutes,' and that miners spend a significant part of their 'deferred pay' in these ways before returning to their village. (CSO, 1976f: 70).

11. Average earnings for blacks in the South African mining sector in 1974 were reported to be P46 per month, or P423 for a nine-month contract. See Appendix 2, Table A.2.2.

12. See Chapter 3.

13. See for example, Kerven's work in Tsamaya (MOA, 1976d). Tsamaya is a small village particularly subject to absenteeism in which, in 1976, 74 per cent of the adult population were women. Over half of the households headed by women owned no cattle, compared with 10 per cent of those headed by men. Many of the former group had absentee males working in town or abroad. Ownership of cattle was reported to be strongly correlated with having been a migrant worker in South Africa. Similarly, a recent study in Kanye found that 54 per cent of a sample of 147 migrant mineworkers owned no cattle at all, and a further 32 per cent owned less than 5 head. Over 80 per cent of those who did own cattle had bought some or all of them with money earned in the mines. See Lyby, 1977: 5-6. Further evidence of the high absolute and relative importance of remittance income to some of the poorest groups with few or no cattle is given in FAO, 1972b: Tables 16-20 and in CSO, 1976f: 97-8.

14. The effects are clearly negative only in the short run. To the extent that the savings of migrant labourers help to increase the capital stock in the agricultural sector, including holdings of cattle, the effects on output over the long run may be positive.

15. In 1971, about 40 per cent of the men aged between 15 and 54 years were absent from the Kgatleng, Kweneng, and Ngwaketse Districts. Allowing for under-reporting, it is likely that from these districts—which include about one-third of the population of Botswana—over half of the males in the working age-group were absent at that time (CSO, 1972c: 113).

16. Schapera, for example, found that the occurrence of adultery increased considerably as labour migration became more widespread: 'the number of women unfaithful to their absentee husbands is very great indeed. Many a man has come back to find that his wife has during his absence given birth to one or more children of whom he is not the father . . . In the few cases where he has brought a charge of adultery against the wife's lover, the court has generally found him in the wrong for having stayed away until she could no longer resist temptation.' (Schapera, 1971: 87.) These circumstances are no less unusual today.

17. The sample size was 1,340 households. See FAO, 1972d: 32–3 and Appendix Table IIB. Additional data relating to the south-eastern part of the country, which paints a similar picture, can be found in Bond, 1974.

18. The conceptual distinction between the formal and informal sectors was first generalized by ILO (1972: 6ff. and Ch. 3). That report pointed out that informal-sector establishments tend to be small, in terms of capital employed, turnover, and number of employees; they are often unlicensed and use less sophisticated technology than those in the formal sector; the markets they face are often more competitive and their products less protected by subsidies and other government policies. But the reality is one of a continuum in which firms in different markets and economic sectors have 'formal' characteristics to a greater or less degree. In Botswana, as in other countries, published employment series are based upon surveys of all licensed establishments. Here the convention is adopted of referring to all of these licensed enterprises as formal, and all others as informal. Though this can serve as a proxy for some important differences, the reality is less distinct. At the margin, the division tells us more about the ways in which government statistics are collected than about differences in the circumstances of individual workers.

19. The labour-force projections for the period since 1971 are based upon calculations in MFDP, 1973c: 105–6.

20. In so far as the mining towns of Selebi-Phikwe and Orapa did not exist before independence, it could be argued that the charge of urban bias is unjustified, in that the Botswana Government was opening up new growth centres in rural areas which previously had neither population nor infrastructure. Though this is true, the significant observation is that the investment pattern has been highly concentrated in a few different locations—the fact that this involved the growth of new towns rather than of existing ones is less important.

21. Slightly more than one thousand people who were living in Mafeking, which at that time served as Bechuanaland's administrative capital, are included in this statistic.

22. By 1975 the population of Orapa was estimated to be 2,000 persons, about 1,200 of whom had jobs in the mine or its urban services. The enclave nature of this urban development, together with the limited benefits it has had for the few rural settlements close by, has been a source of criticism of the Government.

Because of this a decision was taken in 1977 to open up the town, and an increased rate of population growth in this area can be expected for the future.

23. See BP, 1964a and RB, 1977a: 86.

24. Employment in domestic service has been excluded from the above discussion, though in numerical terms this is a very important informal economic activity. Census evidence suggests that the total number of such workers doubled from about 4,000 to 8,000 between 1964 and 1971. This is the same rate of growth as that of formal employment. Although there are no data on the rural–urban breakdown of domestic service employment, this implies still higher activity rates throughout the period. A rough estimate of these rates for all cash earners in the towns, including informal-sector workers and domestic servants, would be about 45 per cent in 1964, declining slightly to about 42 per cent in 1975, in the light of the above trends (see Table 7.3).

25. There is evidence from Botswana's peri-urban areas, where most recent urban migrants live, that income transfers *from* the rural areas are as significant as income flows in the opposite direction (CSO, 1974: 75). Such rural–urban income transfers, which are needed particularly by recent migrants during their period of job-search, are common in many other poor countries. See Connell *et al.*, 1976: 101–2.

26. Fitzgerald had recommended that the ratio should be three-fifths (BP, 1948: 16), but this was changed to three-quarters by the High Commissioner.

27. Perhaps the argument that such officers needed supplementary payments as an inducement to serve in the protectorate itself was a stronger one. But this was already catered for by the payment of a Bechuanaland allowance, of £60 per year.

28. See BP, 1959a, published with BP, 1959.

29. According to the commissioner's report, the allegations of racial discrimination in Swaziland and in Botswana were mainly a civil-service matter. But in Lesotho the salary policy was also having 'most unfavourable reactions on relations between Africans and Europeans generally'. See BP, 1961.

30. The salaries commission of that year introduced a unified administrative cadre which incorporated the earlier clerical, executive, and administrative grades (RB, 1978a).

31. There was one further set of adjustments to the scales prior to independence. This commission left the structure created by Ramage unchanged, and granted cost-of-living increases of about 5 per cent of all grades. See BP, 1964c.

32. See Bennell, 1978 and UN, 1978: Table II.15.

33. See Chapter 9.

34. Evidence that, in terms of pre-tax salaries, Botswana made faster progress over the period than many other African countries in narrowing differentials is given in UN, 1978: Table II.15.

35. The World Bank estimated that the opportunity cost of increases of 100 per cent in minimum government wages, as compared with 50 per cent, amounted to about 1,700 jobs over a five-year period.

36. This is mainly because of the lead-time required to produce skilled or educated workers. The shortage of skilled Batswana was not caused by inadequate incentives for people to undertake courses of education or training. Indeed the private rate of return remained very high. The problem lay in a shortage of educational opportunities for Batswana, which could not be affected by changes in wage rates, but only by increasing the amount and quality of investment in education by the Government. See Chapter 8.

37. There is a parallel here with the British experience of incomes policy in 1977/8.
38. The increases were 43 per cent in the construction, manufacturing, and transport sectors, and 100 per cent in the trade and catering sectors. By comparison, the urban cost-of-living index had increased by about 40 per cent since 1974. See BGG, 1977a.
39. This is really the problem of making sure that incomes and costs are measured in exactly the same way. The calculation of a PDL for a particular household on the basis of agreed minimum standards for nutrition, clothing, shelter, education, etc., is complex enough using market prices. It is much more difficult to ensure that the house improvements, dressmaking, manufacture of utensils, and own consumption of crops and livestock of rural (and urban) families are reflected in the income comparison on the the same basis. There was almost certainly some underestimation of incomes in the rural-incomes survey as a result of these factors.
40. An urban couple with a small child were estimated to require an income equivalent of P947 per annum in 1976, whereas the same couple in the rural areas would have required the equivalent of about P500 at that time. This differential, however, is an overestimate, owing to the inclusion of some luxury items in the urban PDL which are excluded from the estimates for rural families. (See CSO, 1976i: Table 2 and CSO, 1976f: 213. Estimates from the latter source are inflated to allow for cost-of-living increases between 1974 and 1976.)
41. CSO, 1976f: 84–8. Recent analyses for other countries suggest that in Africa, Kenya, Senegal, and Ivory Coast have a more unequal distribution, with the poorest 40 per cent of their populations receiving around 10 per cent of total income. On the other hand, Benin, Tanzania, Madagascar, Zambia, Chad, and Niger are more equal, with the poorest 40 per cent receiving between 13 and 18 per cent of income. It should be noted, however, that these data refer to the national picture rather than just to the rural areas, as in the case of Botswana, and that international evidence suggests that rural income distribution tends to be more, rather than less, equal than that for the country as a whole. See Chenery *et al.*, 1974: Tables 1.1 and 1.4.
42. Some direct evidence for this comes from agricultural surveys conducted in 1974. The authors found that 'only 74 per cent of households which at one time held trek oxen presently have them, and 26 per cent do not, 19 per cent once held six or more oxen'. These ratios are broadly comparable with those given in the text. See MOA, 1974a: 43.
43. Table 7.3.
44. Median household income in 1974 for residents of small villages was P610 p.a., compared to P887 for residents of the eight large villages. CSO, 1976f: 88.
45. They are also more likely to have had favoured access to educational opportunities than residents of small villages, and their preferential access to the formal labour market, to that extent, will have been further strengthened. See Chapter 8.
46. For those households with employment income, average real earnings per household in 1974 were P258 p.a. in the small villages, and P739 p.a. in the larger villages. These are not wage rates, since some households may have had more than one employed member. CSO, 1976f: 41.
47. In fact, remittances from minework in South Africa appeared to decline from about 47 per cent to about 42 per cent of earnings between 1974 and 1976. See Appendix 2, Table A2.2.

48. Based upon data in Table 3.1.
49. The peri-urban areas included in the survey were the 'traditional' housing areas around the towns of Francistown, Selebi-Phikwe, and Gaborone. These are the parts of town to which rural–urban migrants first move (elsewhere often called 'squatter' areas), and they include those parts of town where most informal economic activities take place.
50. Although unemployment rates are in some ways the obverse of activity rates, the latter could decline with a shift in household structure towards younger people or the aged, or with a shift in leisure/work preferences of household members. There is no evidence that either of these things have happened, and the real increases in minimum wages since 1974 will, if anything, have tended at the margin to shift preferences in favour of seeking work, rather than in the opposite direction.
51. There are no time-series data on the changes in average earnings from employment in the informal sector or in domestic service, although there is some evidence to suggest that earnings from domestic service have been increasing less quickly than earnings from unskilled employment in the formal sector. Average earnings for urban domestic servants were put at P15 per month in 1972, and median earnings were estimated to be P22 per month in 1976. Although median 1972 earnings were probably less than P15, this implied increase of 47 per cent is very much less than the increase of about 200 per cent in minimum government wages over the same period. See MFDP, 1973c: Table 4.1; Macliver, 1977: 102.
52. See BPSL, 1963.
53. Rates as specified in RSA, 1962 were adopted in Botswana.
54. See BPSL, 1962: 171 and RBSL, 1967e: B235.
55. African Tax had previously been payable by all African male residents over 21 years, and was fixed–as was Personal Tax–at a flat rate. Though the African Graded Tax had increased with the income of the payee, poorer people paid a much higher proportion of their income in tax than the richer people.
56. The case of married persons only is shown in Fig. 7.1. Our conclusions are based upon a detailed analysis of the effects of changes in tax legislation since the late 1950s, and, except where indicated, are true for all categories of tax payers, including single persons.
57. This was also true for single persons earning up to P500 per year.
58. For single persons the rates were increased for those earning more than P5,000 per year.

CHAPTER 8

1. Livingston's mission station at Kolobeng was established in 1847. It is possible that one or two schools had been built in the far south of the country a few years earlier, as offshoots of the mission station at Kuruman, which had been established in 1824 by Robert Moffat (BP, 1958: 6).
2. These colleges were opened in 1956 and 1963 respectively.
3. This school, Swaneng Hill, at Serowe (q.v.) was established with rather different aims and purposes in view than was the case with the other schools.
4. Dale, 1974: 122 and BP, 1958: 12. These institutions have had an important, and as yet untold impact upon politics in southern Africa, including Botswana.
5. This point is acknowledged by the Director of Education in his report for 1957 (BP, 1958: 9).
6. This, after the independence of the three countries, was to become the University

of Botswana, Lesotho, and Swaziland, having, in 1965, 23 students from Botswana. In 1976, following extended disagreements between the three governments over the issue of the devolution of teaching facilities from Lesotho to Botswana and Swaziland, the university split into two separate institutions: The National University of Lesotho, and The University of Botswana and Swaziland.

7. See Chapter 7.

8. Finance for the Botswana Training Centre, as it was subsequently called, was provided by the British Government in 1964.

9. The planned enrolments in the first form of secondary schools for 1975 were increased from 775 in 1966 to 1,700 in 1968, 2,760 in 1970, and 2,765 in 1973. In fact, actual enrolments in 1975 were higher still, at more than 2,800 pupils. See Colclough, 1976b.

10. A discussion of this plan (MFDP, 1973) and of its impact upon policy is given in Colclough, 1976b.

11. Calculated from IBRD, 1974, Table 2.

12. Table 4.3. This calculation includes subventions from central government to local councils for primary education expenditures.

13. Comparative cost data for 1972–1975 are given in RB, 1977b: 276.

14. These were at the rate of P6 per child per year until 1974, in which year they were decreased to P3, then equivalent to about one-tenth of the annual costs per pupil. The fall in local revenue was balanced by increased education grants from central to local government authorities.

15. This is the 'adjusted' ratio for the 7 to 13 years age group.

16. Data supporting these conclusions are given in Campbell and Abbott, 1976.

17. There are few studies that satisfactorily demonstrate that additional years spent at primary school have beneficial effects upon productivity in agriculture in the Third World (Colclough and Hallack, 1976). Most would agree that literacy and numeracy are ends in themselves, yet the evidence suggests that Botswana's primary schools are very inefficient in achieving even these minimum social goals. (RB, 1976b: 53–83).

18. In a recent monograph (Van Rensburg, 1974) the founder gives a fascinating personal account of this attempt to pioneer a different approach to secondary education.

19. For an earlier account of the Botswana Brigades, which comes to similar conclusions as our own, see Sheffield and Diejomaoh, 1972: 65–74.

20. The recommendations made in the report of the commissioners (RB, 1977b) which have been accepted by the Government are indicated in the white paper on educational policy (RB, 1977c).

21. This dynamic interaction—rising levels of educated unemployment, leading to a need for higher qualifications in order to get a job, in turn fuelling the popular demands for faster expansion of higher education—has been called an 'explosive model' (Rado, 1973). For an application of this thinking to Sri Lanka, see ILO, 1971.

22. A more general analysis of these themes and conclusions, which draws upon evidence from other African countries, is given in Colclough, 1977.

23. Survey work conducted in 1974 revealed that almost three-quarters of all out-patients and two-thirds of in-patients had travelled less than five miles to a health facility. People living less than five miles from a staffed health facility utilized out-patient services at a rate that was more than five times greater than did people living more than ten miles away. Those persons living within a ten mile radius had a ten times greater chance of being admitted

to hospital than those living further than 25 miles away. (CSO 1975a; Gish and Walker, 1977.)

24. It is estimated that over one-quarter of the population over 14 years of age suffers from venereal disease (RB, 1973a: 293).

CHAPTER 9

1. See Lipton (1977) where the concept of 'urban bias' is developed as a major explanatory theory of patterns of development.
2. Local civil servants were also able to purchase BHC houses at historical cost between 1972 and 1976, a considerable concession in view of the steep rise in building costs and house values at the time. Ironically, this concession has probably reduced civil service pressure to stabilize BHC rentals, as the most influential of them made a purchase under the scheme.
3. Chapter 2. There is little doubt that the BPP hold on the Francistown electorate stirred the Government to initiate the Francistown Urban Development Project.
4. In the same deal the Government acquired more than a thousand square kilometres of freehold farming land in the north-east from the Tati Company for the settlement of farming families which had no land of their own. The shortage of land for traditional farmers remains a serious problem in that part of the country. It is noteworthy that in these and other negotiations with the Tati Company the Government has always remained within the law, though it has been willing to use its legal powers to the full. Some observers feel that in the circumstances the Government would have been morally justified in disregarding the law.
5. Jennings (1973: 10) estimated that the railway accounted for about half of all tonnage and 86 per cent of the total ton-kilometres of goods with origin or destination in Botswana. These proportions have probably increased since the Selebi-Phikwe mine and Morupule colliery commenced operation.
6. This estimate is based on a personal communication from the Geological Survey Department and should be regarded as an informed guess on the best available information in 1977. A 1972 study was aware of 3,000 boreholes but acknowledged that there were probably more (FAO, 1972a: 70). Some more came to light subsequently as a result of the land-use planning exercise conducted in connection with the Tribal Grazing Land Programme.
7. This assumes continuous pumping. In practice many boreholes are pumped for only a few hours each day, so average yields may be somewhat higher than estimated here.
8. This predictive uncertainty is one of the planning problems for the Tribal Grazing Land Programme. See Chapter 5.
9. Nevertheless a number of very high yielding boreholes have been sunk, notably around Orapa.
10. Daily per capita consumption in Gaborone fell from about 280 litres in 1970/1 to about 170 litres in 1975/6.
11. The seventeen categories are: Agent, Auctioneer, Chemist, Driller, External Representative, Fresh Produce, General Trading, Hairdresser, Hide and Skin Buyer, Insurance Agent, Petrol Filling Station, Produce Buyer, Restaurant, Small General Trading, Speciality, Travel Agent, and Wholesaler.

REFERENCES

OFFICIAL BOTSWANA DOCUMENTS

Bechuanaland Protectorate

BP, 1898–1965. *Annual Reports*. Issued first by the Colonial Office, and then by the Commonwealth Relations Office.

—,1937. *The Report of the Commission of Enquiry into Medical Matters in the Bechuanaland Protectorate*, by Sir Walter Johnson.

—,1946–1967. *Annual Report of the Education Department*. Issues in most years.

—,1946. *Census, 1946.*

—,1948. *Report on the Salaries and Conditions of Service in the Public Services of the South African High Commission Territories 1947–48*, T. Fitzgerald. Mazenod Institute, Basutoland.

—,1958. *Education Department Triennial Survey 1955–57.*

—,1959. *Report of the Commissioner Appointed to Examine the Salary Structure and conditions of service of the Civil Service of Basutoland, Bechuanaland, and Swaziland 1958–59.* Parrow, Cape.

—,1959a. *Memorandum from the Office of the High Commissioner for Basutoland, the Bechuanaland Protectorate and Swaziland.* Pretoria.

—,1961. *Report on the Structure of the Public Services in Basutoland, Bechuanaland and Swaziland, 1961*, by Sir Richard Ramage, Cape Town.

—,1963. *Annual Report of the Department of Agriculture for the Year Ended 30th September 1963.*

—,1963a. *Medical and Sanitary Report for the year 1963.*

—,1964a. *Report on the Census of the Bechuanaland Protectorate, 1964.*

—,1964b. *Annual Report of the Department of Agriculture for the Year Ended 30th September 1964.*

—,1964c. *Review of Emoluments in the Public Service*, by T.M. Skinner. Mafeking.

—,1964d. *Legislative Council Paper No. 10 of 1964.*

—,1966. *Report on Localisation and Training*, by T.C. Luke.

Bechuanaland Protectorate Statute Law

BPSL, 1962. Volume XLV. *Income Tax (Rates) Law No. 24 of 1962.*

—,1963. Volume XLVI. *The Income Tax (Consolidation) Proclamation, 1959.*

—,1965. Volume XLIX. *The Local Government (District Councils) Law, 1965.*

Botswana Government Gazette

BGG, 1965. 24 December, Supplement. *Local Government Tax Law, 1965. Law No. 20 of 1965.*

—,1974. 4th September, Supplement C. *Statutory Instrument No. 118 of 1974. Establishment of Selebi-Phikwe Township Order, 1974.*

—,1974a. 15 July. Supplements. *Statutory Instruments Nos: 102, 105, 107, 108 and 109 of 1974. Wages Regulation Orders.*

—,1975a. 2nd May. Supplement A. *Financial Institutions Act, 1975.*

—,1975b. 2nd May. *Tribal Land Amendment Act, 1975.*

—,1975c. 2nd May. Supplement A. *Bank of Botswana Act, 1974.*

—,1975d. 15th August. *De Beers Botswana Mining Company (Proprietary) Limited Agreement (Amendment) (Ratification) Act of 1975.*

—,1976. 31st December. Supplement A. *Local Government Tax (Amendment) Act, 1976.*

—,1977. 15th April. Supplement A. *Botswana Defence Force Act, 1977.*

—,1977a. 24 June. Supplements. *Statutory Instruments 79, 80, 81, 82, and 83 of 1977. Wages Regulation Orders.*

Central Statistics Office

CSO, 1967. *Statistical Abstract 1967.*

—,1968. *Labour Force Survey 1967/68.*

—,1968-1977. *Education Statistics.* Annual editions.

—,1970. *National Accounts 1967-68.*

—,1970a. *Statistical Abstract 1970.*

—,1972a. *National Accounts 1968-69.*

—,1972b. *Freehold Farm Survey 1970-71.*

—,1972c. *Report on the Population Census 1971.*

—,1973. *National Accounts of Botswana 1971-72.*

—,1973a. *Statistical Abstract 1973.*

—,1974. *A Social and Economic Survey in Three Peri-Urban Areas in Botswana, 1974.*

—,1974a. *Statistical Abstract 1974.*

—,1975. *Statistical Abstract 1975.*

—,1975a. *Medical Statistics 1975.* Medical Statistics Unit, Ministry of Health.

—,1976a. *Employment Survey (August 1975).*

—,1976b. *Statistical Bulletin,* Vol. 1, No. 2.

—,1976c. *External Trade Statistics 1975.*

—,1976d. *National Accounts of Botswana 1974-75.*

—,1976e. *Botswana National Accounts and Selected Indicators, 1966-1976.*

—,1976f. *The Rural Income Distribution Survey in Botswana 1974/75.*

—,1976g. *Statistical Bulletin,* Vol. 1, No. 3.

—,1976h. *Employment Survey, August 1975.*

—,1976i. *Poverty Datum Line for Urban Areas of Botswana.*
—,1976j. *Statistical Bulletin,* Vol. 1, No. 3.
—,1976k. *Medical Statistics 1976.* Medical Statistics Unit, Ministry of Health.
—,1977. *Statistical Bulletin,* Vol. 2, No. 1.
—,1978. *National Accounts of Botswana 1976/77.* (Preliminary Figures.)
—,1978a. Employment Survey (August 1977) (draft).

Directorate of Personnel

DP, 1974. *Personnel Directive No. 26 of 1974.*
—,1974a. *Personnel Directive No. 12 of 1974.*
—,1976. *Personnel Directive No. 26 of 1976.*

Laws of Botswana

LB,1974. Cap. 74: 04.

Law Revision Order

LRO, 1974. *Constitution of Botswana.*

Ministry of Agriculture

MOA, 1968. *The 1967/68 Agricultural Survey.*
—,1970a. *The 1968/69 Agricultural Survey.*
—,1970b. *The 1969/70 Agricultural Survey.*
—,1971. *Agricultural Survey 1970/71.*
—,1973. *Agricultural Survey 1971/72.*
—,1974. *Dryland Crop Production in Botswana, A Review of Research 1969-74.*
—,1974a. *A Study of Constraints on Agricultural Development in the Republic of Botswana.*
—,1975a. *A Report on Livestock Marketing,* by G.C. Bond.
—,1975b. *A Five Year Programme of Integrated Beef Cattle and Range Research in Botswana 1970-75,* Part 2.
—,1975c. *Division of Co-operative Development (including the Co-operative Development Centre) Annual Report 1974.*
—,1976a. *Division of Co-operative Development (including the Co-operative Development Centre) Annual Report 1975.*
—,1976b. *An Application by the Government of Botswana for a Loan to Finance a Second Livestock Development Project.*
—,1976c. *Farm Recording Scheme 1972/73 and 1973/74 seasons.*
—,1976d. *Report on Tsamaya Village North-East District,* by Carol Kerven.
—,1978. *Agricultural Statistics 1977.*

Ministry of Finance and Development Planning

MFDP, 1973a. *National Development Plan 1973-78.*
—,1973b. *The Shashe Project in North-East Botswana.*

—,1973c. *Manpower and Employment in Botswana,* by Colclough, C.
—,1974. Department of Taxes: *Annual Report for the Year 1973/74.*
—,1977. *National Development Plan 1976–81.*
—,1978. *Impact of minimum wage rise in July 1977 on employment,* by Lipton, M.

Ministry of Local Government and Lands.

MLGL, 1966. *Three Town Councils, Nine District Councils, Estimates of Expenditure and Income for 1966–67.*
—,1969. *Three Town Councils, Nine District Councils, Estimates of Expenditure and Income for 1969–70.*
—,1975a. *Town Councils Estimates of Revenue and Expenditure, Recurrent Budget 1975/76.*
—,1975b. *District Councils Estimates of Revenue and Expenditure, Recurrent Budget 1975/76.*
—,1976. *Preliminary Report on the Public Consultation on the National Policy on Tribal Grazing Land.*

Ministry of Works and Communications

MWC, 1974. *Rural Roads Project Annual Report,* 1st April 1973–31st March 1974.

Office of the President

OP, 1970. *Presidential Circular 1970: District Commissioners, District Councils and Ministerial Staff at District Level, Co-ordination of Work.*
—,1972. *Permanent Secretary to the President Circular, No. 2 of 1972, Government Housing Policy after 31st March 1972.*

Republic of Botswana

RB, 1966a. *Transitional Plan for Social and Economic Development.*
—,1966b. *The Development of the Bechuanaland Economy, Report of the Ministry of Overseas Development Economic Survey Mission* (November 1965).
—,1966c. *Report of the Education Department for the Years 1965 and 1966.*
—,1967a. *Annual Statements of Accounts 1966/67.*
—,1967b. *Annual Report of the Department of Agriculture for the year 1966/67.*
—,1967c. *National Assembly Paper No. 8 of 1966/67.*
—,1968a. *Annual Statements of Accounts 1967/68.*
—,1968b. *National Development Plan 1968–73.*
—,1969. *Annual Statements of Accounts 1968/69.*
—,1970a. *Annual Statements of Accounts 1969/70.*
—,1970b. *National Development Plan 1970–75.*
—,1970c. *Report on the General Elections 1969.*
—,1970d. *Report of the Commission on the Salaries and Conditions*

of Service of the Public Service and the Teaching Service.
—,1971. *Annual Statements of Accounts 1970/71.*
—,1972. *Annual Statements of Accounts 1971/72.*
—,1972a. *Budget Speech 1972.*
—,1972b. *National Policy on Incomes, Employment Prices and Profits,* Government Paper No. 2 of 1972.
—,1973. *Annual Statements of Accounts 1972/73.*
—,1973a. *National Development Plan 1973-78,* Part 1.
—,1973b. *Budget Speech 1973.*
—,1973c. *Income Taxation in Botswana with Special Reference to the Income Tax Bill, 1973,* Government Paper No. 1 of 1973.
—,1974a. *Annual Statements of Accounts 1973/74.*
—,1974b. *Report to the Minister of State on the General Elections 1974.*
—,1975a. *Annual Statements of Accounts 1974/75.*
—,1975b. *National Policy on Tribal Grazing Land,* Government Paper No. 2 of 1975.
—,1975c. *Daily News,* Friday, 25th July.
—,1976a. *Annual Statements of Accounts 1975/76.*
—,1976b. *National Accounts of Botswana 1973-74.*
—,1976c. *Budget Speech 1976.*
—,1977. *Annual Statements of Accounts 1976/77.*
—,1977a. *National Development Plan 1976-81.*
—,1977b. *Education for Kagisano,* Report of the National Commission on Education.
—,1977c. *National Policy on Education,* Government Paper No. 1 of 1977, July.
—,1978. *Financial Statements, Tables and Estimates of Consolidated and Development Fund Revenues 1978/79.*
—,1978a. *Report of the Third Salaries Review Commission.*
—,1978b. *Speech by His Honour The Vice President, Dr. Q.K.J. Masire, on introducing Jwaneng Diamond Loan Authorisation Bill, 1978.*

Republic of Botswana Statute Law

RBSL, 1966a. Volume L, *The Trading Act, 1966.*
—,1966b. Volume L, *Legal Notices Nos.: 38-46, 48-50.* Establishment of District Councils.
—,1967a. Volume LI, *The Water Act, 1967.*
—,1967b. Volume LI, *The Mines and Minerals Act, 1967.*
—,1967c. Volume LI, *The Agricultural Charges Act, 1967.*
—,1967d. Volume LI, *Mineral Rights in Tribal Territories Act.*
—,1967e. Volume LI, *Income Tax (Rates) Law, No. 46 of 1967.*
—,1968a. Volume LII, *The Industrial Development Act, 1968.*
—,1968b. Volume LII, *Tribal Land Act, 1968.*
—,1969a. Volume LIII, *Trade Unions Act, 1969.*
—,1969b. Volume LIII, *Regulation of Wages and Conditions of*

Employment Act, 1969.

—,1969c. Volume LIII, *Trade Disputes Act, 1969.*

—,1970a. Volume LIV Part I, *Selebi-Phikwe Tax Agreement Ratification Act, 1970.*

—,1970b. Volume LIV, *Botswana Housing Corporation Act, 1970.*

—,1970c. Volume LIV, *Water Utilities Corporation Act, 1970.*

—,1970d. Volume LIV, *Botswana Power Corporation Act, 1970.*

—,1970e. Volume LIV, *De Beers Botswana Mining Company (Proprietary) Limited Agreement Act, 1970.*

—,1973. Volume LVIII, *Road Transport (Permits) Act, 1973.*

—,1977. Volume LXII, Income Tax (Amendment) Act, 1977.

BOTSWANA PARASTATALS

Bank of Botswana

BB, 1977. *Annual Report 1976.*
—,1978. *Annual Report 1977.*

Botswana Agricultural Marketing Board

BAMB, 1975. *First Annual Report, 1975.*
—,1976. *Second Annual Report, 1976.*
—,1977. *Third Annual Report, 1977.*

Botswana Development Corporation

BDC, 1976. *Sixth Annual Report for the Year ended 30th June 1976.*

Botswana Housing Corporation

BHC, 1971–1976. *Report and Accounts at 31st March 1971–1976* (annual editions).

Botswana Livestock Development Corporation (Pty) Ltd.

BLDC, 1975. *Second Annual Report 1975.*

Botswana Meat Commission

BMC, 1967–1977. *Report and Accounts for the Years Ended 31st December 1966–1976* (annual editions).

Botswana Power Corporation

BPC, 1972–1976. *Annual Report and Statement of Accounts* (annual editions).

National Development Bank

NDB, 1967–1977. *Annual Reports 1966–1976* (annual editions).

Water Utilities Corporation

WUC, 1971–1976. *Annual Reports and Accounts for the years ended 31st March 1971–1976* (annual editions).

OTHER OFFICIAL DOCUMENTS

Food and Agriculture Organization

FAO, 1972a. *Surveys and Training for the Development of Water Resources and Agricultural Production, Botswana,* 'The Water Resources of Eastern and Northern Botswana and their Development'. Rome, (mimeo).

—,1972b. *Surveys and Training for the Development of Water Resources and Agricultural Production, Botswana,* 'Technical Note No. 31. Income Expenditure and Wealth in the Shoshong Area', by Lucy Syson. Gaborone (mimeo).

—,1972c. Proposals for the Improvement of Crop Marketing, by P.S. Calkin. Rome (mimeo).

—,1972d. *Surveys and Training for the Development of Water Resources and Agricultural Production, Botswana.* 'Technical Note No. 27: The Population of the Shoshong Area', by Lucy Syson, Gaborone (mimeo).

—,1973. *Surveys and Training for the Development of Water Resources and Agricultural Production, Botswana.* 'Technical Note No. 2: Absentees' Remittances as an Item of Household Income', by Lucy Syson. Gaborone (mimeo).

—,1974. A Study of Constraints on Agricultural Development in the Republic of Botswana (including an assessment of the role of food aid). Rome (mimeo).

International Bank for Reconstruction and Development/International Development Association

IBRD, 1964. *The Economy of Bechuanaland.* Washington.

—,1974. *Education Sector Working Paper.* Washington.

—,1977. World Bank Atlas. Washington.

International Labour Organization

ILO, 1971. *Matching Employment Opportunities and Expectations. A Programme of Action for Ceylon.* Geneva.

—,1972. *Employment Incomes and Equality: A Strategy for Increasing Productive Employment in Kenya.* Geneva.

—,1973. *Employment in Africa: Some Critical Issues.* Geneva.

International Monetary Fund

IMF, 1970. *IMF Staff Papers,* March. Washington.

Republic of South Africa

RSA, 1961. *Union Statistics for Fifty Years,* Department of Statistics, Pretoria.

—,1962. South African Income Tax Amendment Act, No. 90 of 1962.

United Kingdom

UK, 1933. *Financial and Economic Position of the Bechuanaland Protectorate,* Dominions Office, Cmnd. 4363, London.
—,1950. *Bechuanaland Protectorate: Succession to the Chieftainship of the Bamangwato Tribe,* Commonwealth Relations Office, Cmnd. 7913, London.
—,1952. *Basutoland, the Bechuanaland Protectorate and Swaziland: History of Discussions with the Union of South Africa, 1909-1939.* Commonwealth Relations Office, Cmnd. 8707, London.
—,1960. *Basutoland, Bechuanaland Protectorate and Swaziland: Report of an Economic Survey Mission.* Commonwealth Relations Office, London.

United Nations

UN, 1965. Basutoland, Bechuanaland Protectorate and Swaziland: Report of an Economic and Technical Assistance Mission. New York (mimeo).
—,1977. Assistance to Botswana. United Nations Security Council S/12307, 28th March 1977. New York (mimeo).
—,1977a. *Statistical Yearbook 1976.* New York.
—,1978. *Survey of Economic and Social Conditions in Africa, Part I.* UNECA. New York.

OTHER DOCUMENTS AND PUBLICATIONS

BCL, 1967. Annual Report, 1967. Francistown.
—,1970-1976. Annual Reports 1969-1976 (annual editions), Gaborone.
Bennel, P., 1978. 'The Historical Legacy of Colonial Civil Service Salary Structures in Anglophone Africa: A Case Study', IDS Working Paper, Brighton (mimeo).
Biggs, H., 1966. Report on the Marketing of Agricultural Produce and some Aspects of the Marketing of Livestock in Bechuanaland. Ministry of Overseas Development, London (mimeo).
Bond, Carol, 1974. Women's Involvement in Agriculture. Gaborone (mimeo).
Boserup, Ester, 1970. *Women's Role in Economic Development.* London.
Bostock, M., and Harvey, C. (eds.) 1972. *Economic Independence and Zambian Copper, A Case Study of Foreign Investment.* New York.
Botswana Democratic Party, BDP, 1969. Election Manifesto. Gaborone.
Botswana National Front, BNF, 1974(?). Manifesto. Gaborone (?).
Botswana Notes and Records, BNR, 1971. *Special Edition No. 1*; Proceedings of the Conference on Sustained Production from Semi-Arid Areas with Particular Reference to Botswana. Botswana Soceity. Gaborone.
BRST, 1968. Prospectus. Johannesburg.
—,1969. Annual Report 1968. Gaborone.

—,1970. Annual Report 1969. Gaborone.
—,1971. Annual Report 1970. Gaborone.
—,1972a. Annual Report 1971. Gaborone.
—,1972b. Issue of 8,972,725 Ordinary Shares. Gaborone.
—,1973. Annual Report 1972. Gaborone.
—,1975. Annual Report 1974. Gaborone.
—,1977. Annual Report 1976. Gaborone.
Campbell, N., and Abbott, J., 1976. 'Botswana's Primary School System: A Spatial Analysis'. *Institute of Development Management, Research Paper No. 1*. Gaborone.
Chambers, R., and Feldman, D., 1973. Report on Rural Development. Ministry of Finance and Development Planning, Gaborone.
Chambers, R., 1977. Botswana's Accelerated Rural Development Programme, 1973–6, Experience and Lessons. (Draft.) Gaborone (mimeo).
Chenery, H., Ahluwalia, M., Bell, C., Duloy, J., and Jolly, R., 1974. *Redistribution with Growth*. Oxford.
Colclough, C., 1974. 'Educational Expansion or Change? Some Choices for Central and Southern Africa', *Journal of Modern African Studies Vol. 12, No. 3*. Cambridge.
—,1976a. 'Basic Education: Samson or Delilah?' *Convergence, Vol. IX, No. 2*. Toronto.
—,1976b. 'Some Lessons from Botswana's Experience with Manpower Planning', *Botswana Notes and Records, Vol. 8*, Gaborone.
—,1977. 'Formal Education Systems and Poverty-Focused Planning'. *Journal of Modern African Studies, Vol. 15, No. 4*. Cambridge.
—, and Hallak, J., 1976. 'Some Issues in Rural Education: Equity, Efficiency and Employment', *IDS Discussion Paper No. 89*. Brighton.
—, and Chambers, R., 1977. Evaluation of British Technical Co-operation. Botswana: A Case Study. Ministry of Overseas Development, London (mimeo).
—, and Fallon, P., 1979. 'Rural Poverty in Botswana', in Ghai and Radwan (eds.), forthcoming.
Comaroff, J., 1977. The Structure of Agricultural Transformation in Barolong. Gaborone (mimeo).
Connell, J., Dasgupta, B., Laishley, R., and Lipton, M., 1976. *Migration from Rural Areas: The Evidence from Village Studies*. Delhi.
Curtis, D., 1972. 'The Social Organisation of Ploughing', *Botswana Notes and Records, Vol. 4*. Gaborone.
Dale, R., 1974. 'The Functional Web of Inter-dependence between Pre-Independent Botswana and South Africa: a Preliminary Study', *Botswana Notes and Records, Vol. 6*. Gaborone.
De Beers Botswana Mining Company (Proprietary) Limited DEBSWANA (undated). Debswana Diamonds. Gaborone.
—,1972–1977. Annual Reports 1971–1976 (annual editions). Gaborone.
Dini, L., Quinn, B., and Wohlgemuth, L., 1970. 'The Economy of Botswana', in IMF, 1970.

Eding, D., Udo, A., and Sekgoma, M., 1972. Report on Village Studies: Moshupa, Manyana, Molepolole. Gaborone.

Erasmus, E., 1963. 'The National Income of Bechuanaland Protectorate, 1955', in Samuels, 1963.

Ettinger, S., 1971. 'Economic Relations Between Botswana, Lesotho and Swaziland and South Africa', *Botswana Notes and Records, Vol. 3.* Gaborone.

—,1972. 'South Africa's Weight Restrictions on Cattle Exports from Bechuanaland 1924–41', *Botswana Notes and Records, Vol. 4.* Gaborone.

—,1974. 'The Economics of the Customs Union between Botswana, Lesotho, Swaziland and South Africa', Ph.D. thesis, University of Michigan.

—,1975. 'The Bechuanaland Protectorate's Participation in Pre-1910 Customs Unions', *Botswana Notes and Records, Vol. 7.* Gaborone.

Experience Incorporated, 1973. The Technical/Economic Feasibility of Establishing Additional Meat Processing Facilities in Botswana. Minneapolis (mimeo).

Faber, M., and Potter, J., 1971. Towards Economic Independence, Papers on the Nationalization of the Copper Industry in Zambia, *University of Cambridge, Department of Applied Economics, Occasional Papers: 23.* Cambridge.

Gabatshwane, S., 1966. *Seretse Khama and Botswana.* Mafeking.

Ghai, D., and Radwan, S. (eds.) (forthcoming). *Rural Poverty and Agrarian Policies in Africa.* ILO. Geneva.

Gibb, Sir Alexander, and Partners, 1968a. Botswana Shashe River Feasibility Studies, Final Feasibility Report. London.

—; 1968b. Shashe Complex, Town Planning Report for Phikwe Township. London.

—,1970. Lobatse Water Supply, Feasibility Study. London.

Gillett, S., 1973. 'The Survival of Chieftaincy in Botswana', *African Affairs, Vol. 72, No. 287.* London.

Gish, O., and Walker, G., 1977. *Mobile Health Services.* London.

Grundy, K., 1973. *Confrontation and Accommodation in Southern Africa, The Limits of Independence.* California.

Hailey, Lord, 1953. *Native Administration in the British African Territories, Part V: The High Commission Territories.* London.

Helleiner, G. (ed.), 1976. *A World Divided, the Less Developed Countries in the International Economy.* Cambridge.

Hermans, Q., 1973. *'Botswana's options for independent existence',* in Cervenka, Z. (ed.), *Landlocked Countries of Africa.* Uppsala.

—,1974. 'A Review of Botswana's Financial History, 1900 to 1973', *Botswana Notes and Records, Vol. 6.* Gaborone.

Holm, J., 1972. 'Rural Development in Botswana: three basic political trends', *Rural Africana.* East Lansing.

Institute of Development Studies, 1975. *IDS Bulletin, Vol. 7, No. 2.* Brighton.

Jennings, A., 1973. Aspects of Road Transport Organisation in Botswana. Gaborone.

Jolly, R., 1975. 'Redistribution with Growth–a Reply', in Institute of Development Studies, 1975.

Jones, D., 1977. *Aid and Development in Southern Africa.* London.

Khama, Sir S., 1969a. Dissolution Speech. The Fourth Meeting of the Third Session of the First National Assembly. Government Printer. Gaborone.

—,1969b. Address to the General Assembly of the United Nations, Government Printer. Gaborone.

—,1971a. A Decade of Achievement–Decade of Challenge, Speech at the Botswana Democratic Party Anniversary Conference at Maun on 10th April 1971. Government Printer. Gaborone.

—,1971b. A People's Progress. Speech opening the Third Session of the Second Parliament of Botswana on 3rd December 1971. Government Printer. Gaborone.

—,1975. Speech addressing workers at Selebi-Phikwe, 19th December 1975, Government Printer. Gaborone.

Kuper, A., 1970. *Kalahari Village Politics: An African Democracy.* London.

—,1975. 'The Social Structure of the Sotho-speaking Peoples of Southern Africa', *Africa, Vol. 45, Nos. 1-2, 1975.* London.

Landell-Mills, P., 1970. 'Rural Income and Urban Wage Rates', *Botswana Notes and Records, Vol. 2.* Gaborone.

—,1971. 'The 1969 Southern African Customs Union Agreement', in *Journal of Modern African Studies, Vol. 9, No. 2.* Cambridge.

Langdon, S., 1977. 'Multinational Firms and the State in Kenya', *Institute of Development Studies Bulletin, Vol. 9, No. 1.* Brighton.

Legum, C., Collings, R., 1974. *Africa Contemporary Record, Annual Survey and Documents, 1973-74.* London.

—,1976. *Africa Contemporary Record, Annual Survey and Documents 1975-76.* London.

Leistner, G., 1967. 'Foreign Bantu Workers in South Africa', in *South African Journal of Economics, Vol. 35, No. 1, 1967.* Cape Town.

Lever, B., 1970. 'Agricultural Extension in Botswana', *University of Reading, Development Study No. 7.* Reading.

Lewis, D., 1975. 'Direct Foreign Investment and Linkages in a Less Developed Country', *Botswana Notes and Records, Vol. 7.* Gaborone.

Leys, C., 1975a. *Underdevelopment in Kenya, The Political Economy of Neo-Colonialism.* London.

—,1975b. 'The Politics of Redistribution with Growth', in Institute of Development Studies, 1975.

Lipton, M., 1977. *Why Poor People Stay Poor. A Study of Urban Bias in World Development.* London.

Lyby, E., 1977. 'A preliminary report on the effects of mine migration in Botswana'. National Migration Study Workshop. Gaborone (mimeo).

Mabro, R., 1974. *The Egyptian Economy, 1952-1972.* Oxford.

Macartney, W., 1974. 'Local Government and Development in Botswana', *Botswana Notes and Records Vol. 6,* Gaborone.

Macgregor, A., 1929. Report on the Makarikari Reconnaissance Geological Survey of Southern Rhodesia. Botswana National Archives (mimeo).

Macliver, S., 1977. 'Gaborone Migration Survey Follow-up June 1976', *National Institute for Research in Development and African Studies, Documentation Unit, Working Paper No. 4.* Gaborone (mimeo).

Masire, Q., 1970. Speech to 9th Annual BDP Conference at Molepolole 29th May 1970, quoted in *Surveys and Training for the Development of Water Resources and Agricultural Production, Botswana,* 'Technical Note No. 26: Narrowing the gap—some guidelines to the social problems of agricultural production in Botswana'. Gaborone (mimeo).

—,1971. Community Relations in Botswana, with special reference to Francistown; Statement delivered to the National Assembly on 13th September 1971, Government Printer. Gaborone.

Massey, D., 1977. 'The Hut Tax and Migrant Labour in Botswana', paper presented to the National Migration Study Workshop. Gaborone (mimeo).

McCarthy, S., 1970. Achievement of Development Plan 1970-72. Gaborone (mimeo).

—,1976. 'Progress through Self-Help: Urban Housing in Botswana', Institute of Development Management. Gaborone (mimeo).

Merz and McLellan, 1969. Report on the Water and Electricity Unit for Gaborones—Part I Electricity. Johannesburg (mimeo).

—,1971. Report on Power Supplies to the Botswana Meat Commission. Johannesburg (mimeo).

—,1974. Interim Report on Power Supplies in Botswana. Johannesburg (mimeo).

—,1975a. Report on Rural Electricity Supplies in Southern Botswana. Johannesburg (mimeo).

—,1975b. Report on Rural Electricity Supplies in Central and Northern Botswana. Johannesburg (mimeo).

Mosley, P., 1978. 'The Southern African Customs Union: A Reappraisal', *World Development, Vol. 6, No. 1.* London.

Muzorewa, B., 1974. 'Botswana's Share of Revenue from the Use of the Rand Currency', *Botswana Notes and Records, Vol. 6.* Gaborone.

Ohlin, G., 1973. 'Swedish Aid Performance and Development Policy', *ODI Review, No. 6, 1973.* London.

Parson, J., 1976. Aspects of Political Culture in Botswana: Results of an Exploratory Survey. Gaborone (mimeo).

—,1977. 'Political Culture in Rural Botswana: a Survey Result', in *Journal of Modern African Studies, Vol. 15, No. 4.* Cambridge.

Penrose, Edith, 1976. 'Ownership and Control: multinational firms in less developed countries', in Helleiner, G., 1976.

Picard, L., 1977. Rural Development in Botswana: The District Administration and the Creation of District Development Committees, 1966–1973. Lincoln, Nebraska (mimeo).

Proctor, J., 1968. 'The House of Chiefs and the Political Development of Botswana', in *Journal of Modern African Studies, Vol. 6, No. 1*. Cambridge.

Rado, E., 1973. 'The Explosive Model', *Manpower and Unemployment Research in Africa Vol. 6, No. 2*. Montreal.

Reynolds, N., 1977. 'Rural Development in Botswana', *University of Cape Town, Southern Africa Labour and Development Research Unit, Working Paper No. 13*. Cape Town.

Rhodesia Railways, 1968. Historic Milestones. Bulawayo.

Samuels, L. (ed.), 1963. *African Studies in Income and Wealth*. London.

Sandford, S., 1976. Dealing with Drought and Livestock in Botswana. London (mimeo).

Schaffer, B., 1975. 'The Politics of Dependence', in Selwyn, P., 1975a.

Schapera, I., 1947. *Migrant Labour and Tribal Life: A Study of Conditions in the Bechuanaland Protectorate*. London.

—,1970. *Tribal Innovators: Tswana Chiefs and Social Change, 1795–1940* (1st ed. 1943). London.

—,1971. *Married Life in an African Tribe* (1st ed. 1940). London.

Seers, D., 1972. 'What are we trying to measure?' in *Journal of Development Studies, Vol. 8, No. 3*. London.

Selwyn, P., 1975. *Industries in the Southern African Periphery*. London.

— (ed.), 1975a. *Development Policy in Small Countries*. London.

Sheffield, J., and Diejomaoh, V., 1972. *Non-Formal Education in African Development*, African-American Institute. New York.

Sillery, A., 1952. *The Bechuanaland Protectorate*. Cape Town.

—,1965. *Founding a Protectorate: History of Bechuanaland 1885–1895*. The Hague.

—,1974. *Botswana: A Short Political History*. London.

Smit, P., 1970. *Botswana Resources and Development*. Pretoria.

Stahl, C., 1975. 'A Commerical Strategy in the Labour Export Market with Reference to Botswana, Lesotho and Swaziland' *Botswana Notes and Records, Vol. 7*. Gaborone.

Stephens, Betsy, 1976. 'Gaborone Migration Survey—December 1975' *National Institute for Research in Development and African Studies, Documentation Unit. Working Paper No. 6*. Gaborone (mimeo).

Stevens, C., 1978. 'Food aid and nutrition: The Case of Botswana' *Food Policy, February 1978*. London.

Stevens, C., and Speed, J., 1977. 'Multipartyism in Africa: the Case of Botswana Revisited' in *African Affairs, Vol. 76, No. 304*. London.

Stevens, R., 1967. *Lesotho, Botswana and Swaziland*. London.

Stevenson, A., 1977. 'Agriculture Water and Environment in Botswana: A problem of policy' *Natural Resources Forum 2*. New York.

Tlou, T., 1974. 'The Nature of Batswana States: Towards a Theory of Batswana Traditional Government—The Batswana Case' *Botswana Notes and Records, Vol. 6*. Gaborone.

Todaro, M., 1973. 'Income Expectations, Rural-Urban Migration and Employment in Africa', in ILO, 1973.

Tordoff, W., 1973. 'Local Administration in Botswana—Part I and II' in *Journal of Administration Overseas, Vol. XII, No. 4 and Vol. XIII No. 1.* London.

URS Research Company, 1970. Botswana Zambia Transportation Survey. San Mateo, California (mimeo).

Van Rensburg, P., 1974. *Report from Swaneng Hill.* Uppsala.

Vengroff, R., 1977. *Botswana, Rural Development in the Shadow of Apartheid.* London.

Wilson, F., 1972. *Labour in South African Gold Mines 1911-1969.* Cambridge.

Wilson, H., and Wormesley, L., Scott Wilson Kirkpatrick and Partners, 1970. Francistown Planning Proposals. Gaborone.

—,1971. Gaborone Planning Proposals. Gaborone (mimeo).

Winstanley, G., 1965. The Bechuanaland General Election 1965, Ballot Envelopes and Voting Counters. Botswana National Archives (mimeo).

INDEX